WE ARE WISCONSIN

WE ARE WISCONSIN

EDITED BY
ERICA SAGRANS

THE WISCONSIN UPRISING IN THE WORDS OF THE ACTIVISTS, WRITERS, AND EVERYDAY WISCONSINITES WHO MADE IT HAPPEN

Tasora

Editor: Erica Sagrans
Cover and Interior Design: Christopher Hass
Copy Editor: Joel Handley

Printed in the United States of America

Tasora Books
5120 Cedar Lake Road S
Minneapolis, MN 55416
(952) 345-4488
Distributed by Itasca Books

10 9 8 7 6 5 4 3 2

TABLE OF CONTENTS:

@MelissaRyan
Scott Walker just declared war on Government workers.

FOREWORD

John Nichols
JULY, 2011

IT BEGAN OUTSIDE THE UNIVERSITY OF WISCONSIN
Memorial Union. A few dozen members of the Teaching Assistants' Association (TAA), the oldest graduate employee union in the world, rallied on a frigid February morning to object to Republican Governor Scott Walker's plan to strip public-employee unions of collective bargaining rights. The message from TAA organizers to union members was blunt: "All public-sector workers are under attack. Faculty and staff are under attack. The UW as a whole is under attack. ... You need to get active now!"

It worked.

Two weeks after that first protest, upwards of 125,000 Wisconsinites rallied at the Capitol in Madison as tens of thousands more gathered in communities across the state. And while the crowds outside the Capitol were massive, inside were thousands more—students, teachers, and snow-plow drivers who had occupied the building around-the-clock for more than a week.

Yet the demonstration on that third Saturday was not the largest to occur during the month of protests at the Capitol. Two weeks later, a significantly larger crowd would fill the downtown of the city and hail the return of Democratic state senators who had decamped to Illinois for the better part of a month in order to deny the governor and his Republican allies a legislative quorum.

But the Wisconsin uprising was not just about crowds, protests, or occupations. Like all epic struggles, what happened in Wisconsin in the first months of 2011, and what continues to this day, cannot be reduced to simple story lines. The full picture is always a nuanced one—complete with a history, economic demands, social complexities, and prospects that are only beginning to be realized. All of the vibrant colors, the black-and-white contrasts, and the shades of gray that make the picture of what has happened in Wisconsin, or what is still happening in Wisconsin, are reflected in this fine collection of writing.

If there was a day when it seemed absolutely clear to me that what was happening in Wisconsin would shape the lives not just of Wisconsinites but of Americans for years to come, it was that third Saturday, Feb. 26. And it was not just because of what I saw in Madison—although what I saw in Madison was awesome.

Snow fell throughout the day, and temperatures were brutal. The day-long demonstration surrounded the Capitol, spilled down the streets of the city, and filled every floor of the statehouse for what local historian Stuart Levitan described as "the largest political event ever in Madison."

The people-power surge came in response to what the senior member of the Wisconsin Legislature, state Sen. Fred Risser (D-Madison) described as Walker's "dictatorial" actions, and to what state Rep. Cory Mason (D-Racine) leveled "tyranny." Those are charged words, but Wisconsinites recognized them as appropriate to the moment.

In interviews with national networks, Walker had tried to spin the fantasy that the crowds that had surrounded the Capitol for almost two weeks weren't made up of real Wisconsinites. That was a lie, coming from a politician who was spinning a web of deception.

The people were offended by their governor's false premises—not just with regard to the makeup of the protests but with the trumped-up "budget crisis" Walker was using to bust unions, attack local democracy, and slash funding for schools and public services. Wisconsinites do not take offense in the ordinary way, however. They do not get all huffy. They get all creative. And their handmade signs put the liar in his place:

"Walker: Governor of Wall Street, Not Wisconsin"

"I'm From Wisconsin, What Planet Is Walker From?"

Hundreds of signs recalled the governor's 20-minute conversation—revealed days earlier—with a prank caller who had gotten past Walker's receptionists and staffers by identifying himself as conservative billionaire David Koch:

"Walker Has One Constituent: David Koch"

"Governor Walker, Your Koch Dealer Is On Line Two"

That Saturday's rally in Madison was the largest gathering of activists to that point in what had already become an unprecedented state-based movement for economic and social justice. But what made the day a turning point was the fact that the movement was no longer playing out in a single state. The Wisconsin protesters were joined that day by supporters in every one of the nation's state capitals, as well as Washington, D.C.

Energized by the images of Wisconsinites rallying night after winter night—and filling the state Capitol with chants of "What's disgusting? Union-busting!"—the nation's savviest unions were coming to recognize that they were in a fight for survival. And they had to take that fight to the streets—not just on behalf of labor rights but for basic premises of a just and equitable society.

The National Nurses United union took the lead in organizing national solidarity marches and rallies that Saturday, with executive director Rose Ann DeMoro declaring that the first lesson to be taken from Wisconsin is "Working people—with our many allies, students, seniors, women's organizations, and more—are inspired and ready to fight."

That became clear as the day unfolded.

MoveOn.org and other progressive groups, along with unions across the country, celebrated the success of "Rallies to Save the American Dream," explaining that, "In Wisconsin and around our country, the American Dream is under fierce attack. Instead of creating jobs, Republicans are giving tax breaks to corporations and the very rich—and then cutting funding for education, police, emergency response, and vital human services."

Standing in solidarity with the people of Wisconsin on Feb. 26, those who rallied in all the nation's capitals announced that: "We demand an end to the attacks on workers' rights and public services across the country. We demand investment to create decent jobs for the millions of people who desperately want to work. And we demand that the rich and powerful pay their fair share."

"We are all Wisconsin. We are all Americans," they declared.

They stood in Atlanta and Boston, in Columbus and Denver, in Juneau and Jefferson City, Santa Fe and Sacramento, in Tucson and Tallahassee.

And they stood in Madison.

In solidarity.

This book tells the story of that solidarity, and of the radical possibility it has given Wisconsin and America.

JOHN NICHOLLS
July, 2011

#SOLIDARITYWI

INTRODUCTION:

WE WILL FIGHT WE WILL WIN

Erica Sagrans
JULY, 2011

I WAS IN LONDON WHEN THE WISCONSIN PROTESTS BEGAN.
I had immersed myself among British activists as they prepared for one
of the biggest demonstrations in London's history—where half a million
people took to the streets to protest the deep and painful cuts to basic government services that were about to take place. The protests had grown out
of Britain's student uprising that began earlier that winter, when high school
and university students stormed the Conservative Party's headquarters to
protest tuition hikes and were met with violent police confrontations.

After several years working in national Democratic politics, I had fled
Washington, D.C. earlier that winter. Like many progressives, I was dispir-
ited by large losses in the midterm elections, frustrated with some Democrats' inability to stand up for progressive values, and wondering when the
left would find a way to match the Tea Party's grassroots energy bubbling
up on the other side. I knew there was energy on our side too; it just wasn't
being channeled or organized as effectively—and much of it took the form
of frustration directed at the Democratic Party. As a staffer at the Democratic National Committee, each week I read survey responses from some-
times-supporters who admonished Democrats to "toughen up" or "show
some spine"—and those were among the gentler words they had for us. Like
many of the young people who had started working in D.C. politics after
Obama's 2008 victory, I often agreed with them. So we shook our heads

and did what we could to steer the huge ship we were on a few feet to the left whenever possible.

But something changed while I was away. In Wisconsin, teachers and students and police officers and farmers gathered at their Capitol and refused to leave, for days and then weeks—and Democratic state senators stood with them. The people of Wisconsin were no longer waiting for politicians to lead—they were finding their own voice, and their own power. Their actions helped inspire similar protests at capitols around the country, breathing some new life into both the labor movement and the progressive left overall.

In London, as we prepared for the March 26 demonstration it was impossible to stop thinking about the Wisconsin protests, as well as the awe-inspiring Egyptian revolution that had just unfolded. At an East London gathering a few weeks before the big march, a thousand people cheered Egyptian activist Gigi Ibrahim, who had been part of the revolution that had toppled her country's dictator after a brutal 30-year rule. During a teach-in at a London university, hundreds of us spoke with activists in Madison through Skype video, and watched a YouTube clip of farmer Tony Schultz firing up crowds in front of the snowy Wisconsin Capitol. A British activist told me how he had been riveted by the live video stream my American friend had broadcast from his iPhone during the Madison Capitol occupation—video that was seen over a hundred thousand times by people who were fascinated by what was going on, but unable to watch it elsewhere. It was a strange but beautiful confluence of earth-shaking change. From Madison to Cairo to London, it felt like we were all connected, all part of something incredibly unlikely and incredibly powerful.

After returning to the U.S., I went to Wisconsin to see what it was like there during the weeks following the protests that shook the Capitol and the state. There were no more 100,000-person rallies, but it was impossible to miss that something incredible had just happened. In the neighborhood where I stayed, handmade signs remained in nearly every window or yard: "Governor Walker, the whole world is watching," "Walker gives welfare to the rich," and "Care about educators like they care for your child" were just a few. Stores along State Street were filled with posters and pins and bumper stickers that combined Wisconsin pride with support for unions and state workers ("We have 'State workers are sexy' pins," one chalkboard sign on the sidewalk proclaimed). Chalk messages were scrawled on the sidewalk outside the Capitol; inside, large letters spelling out the word "Solidarity" hung facing outward in legislators' office windows.

I was also struck by how good life seemed to be in Madison. People biked along the tree-lined streets and on paths next to the shimmering lakes; tasty, local food was plentiful; strangers were friendly (one greeted me with an energetic "Hello citizen!" and a salute from across the street). Madison seemed like a place where you could live well, regardless of whether you had a job with a fancy title or a big salary. I could see why, when these folks' way of life was attacked by Governor Scott Walker's efforts, they stood up to fiercely defend it.

This collection is a first draft of the story of the Wisconsin uprising. No doubt it is a story that will be told and retold for years to come, in formats more nuanced and more in-depth than this one. But this anthology attempts to bridge the gap between the immediacy of Twitter and the permanence of academic study. The story told here is by no means complete, because the story is far from over. Battles continue in Wisconsin each day, from the elections to recall Wisconsin's state senators to the (likely) eventual push to recall Governor Scott Walker himself. For now, Walker's attack on collective bargaining has become law. It's a huge loss, to be sure. Yet regardless of the fate of this particular piece of legislation, the impact of what happened during those unlikely months in Wisconsin will be felt for a long time to come.

Though the organizing in Wisconsin continues, there is also a palpable sense of fatigue, along with a desire to recharge and figure out what comes next. In this, there is now an opportunity to begin to take stock of the events that have taken place. Many of the Wisconsinites I spoke with had not yet sat down and truly reflected on what they had been part of—they were too busy getting back to some semblance of normal life after weeks spent completely consumed by the demonstrations.

That isn't to say there is not a strong desire to tell the Wisconsin story to a larger audience. After all, it was the protesters—almost every one of them—who told the story of the uprising using their phones, laptops, and cameras, through Twitter and Facebook and email and blogs. Telling individual stories was a way of sharing and documenting the protests, but storytelling also played a central role in the Madison Capitol occupation itself. The statehouse takeover began when protesters packed a hearing room to give their personal testimonies in opposition to Walker's "budget-repair" bill, keeping the proceedings going all night long and into the next day. From that impromptu occupation grew an incredible new community unlike anything protesters had experienced before. As more and more people flocked to Madison to show their support, those inside the Capitol found what had been lacking for too long—a sense of power and a true feeling of solidarity.

While this is not my own story in any significant way, I wanted to help tell the story of the Wisconsin protests as a way of documenting what happened and inspiring others to continue the fight that began in Madison—in whatever form that may take. While the protests eventually captured the attention of the mainstream media, this collection focuses on telling the story of the people directly involved: the Wisconsinites who spoke out in hours of testimony and speeches at the Capitol; those who blogged, tweeted, and reported updates from the protests day and night. This collection pulls together many of the blog posts and links you may have stumbled upon while the action was at its height, but that have already begun to fade away into the ether of the internet. It also includes a glimpse of the parallel story that was told in real-time through Twitter updates from those at the scene of the protests. These short messages came together to form a fascinating narrative that was captured daily through the liveblogging done by web editors at the Madison *Isthmus*, which served as an invaluable resource when putting together the posts included in this book.

We Are Wisconsin highlights a range of voices from the left, broadly-defined: Democratic elected officials, progressive journalists, radical grassroots activists, union members, and those who did not previously consider themselves at all political. While there are certainly real disagreements that these writers don't shy away from, the aim is to push each of us to look beyond our narrower labels and consider where we—as progressives, the left, or people with certain shared values—can come together around common goals.

This book is for people who were not there to hear the stories told in the Capitol rotunda. It is for those who merely caught glimpses of the Wisconsin protests through the mainstream media, as well as those who spent days scrolling the #WIunion hashtag on Twitter for the latest update.

It is for progressives who don't think that the idea of unions or collective organizing matters for them.

It is for union members, organizers, and leaders, and anyone who wants to build a stronger labor movement, but wonders how they can appeal to a broader audience.

It is for anyone who believes in the tenets of basic fairness and economic justice, but wants to know what regular people can really do to stand up for these values.

This story is much bigger than just Wisconsin. It is about people around the world who are standing up and saying "no" to the budget cuts and austerity measures that use real or perceived crises to pull the rug out from under working people. It is about the global connections that are starting to be built between movements, from the places that have already begun rising up to the places that are next.

In the streets of London, as I walked with demonstrators on March 26, I saw a sign that read: "London, Cairo, Wisconsin, we will fight, we will win." What's become clear to me over these past few months is that when we do choose to fight, we can win. But no matter whether we win each particular battle, by fighting we inspire others to do so—and onward it goes.

ERICA SAGRANS
July 2011

For a detailed overview of the events surrounding the Wisconsin protests, see the timeline beginning on page 281.

ON AN EX-GIRLFRIEND, A 96-YEAR-OLD LABOR JOURNALIST, AND BURNING DOWN THE FOREST

Mike Elk
JULY, 2011

GROWING UP THE AWKWARD SON OF A UNION ORGANIZER, the one thing I learned about myself at a young age was that whenever I joined my father at picket lines and union meetings, my uncomfortable sense of insecurity vanished in the face of all that brave determination. Spending time with workers who stood up for themselves and organized against powerful corporations, even at the risk of losing their jobs, inspired me to fight back against the bullies who teased me heavily as a child. What workers taught me was that while someone may be more powerful than you and make your life miserable, they could never truly beat you down as long as you stood up for yourself. These experiences had a profound effect on me, and that is why I've dedicated my career as a labor journalist to giving a voice to the workers who helped me grow so confident and happy in my own voice.

At times though, it's been tougher than I expected for both the labor movement and myself. This past winter I found myself sinking into a dark lull, as it appeared that the labor movement was going to be wiped out for good, just as my girlfriend left me shortly before the Christmas holidays. To make matters worse, I was still reeling from a bout of chronic pneumonia, and most days I was so tired that I could barely crawl out of bed. And as a freelance labor journalist, I was broke and with bleak prospects, since few publications were interested or had the funding to print stories about organized labor.

At the time, most of the media conversation about labor was focused on the themes of the documentary film *Waiting for Superman*—which argued that overpaid public employees and teachers were to blame for the decline of American society. It was hard to find anyone who disagreed, even among middle-class liberals and Democrats in Washington, D.C., where I live. They all seemed to agree that organized labor was a part of the problem, rather than the solution, to the current economic recession. And it went right up to the top: Democrats like President Barack Obama even seemed to endorse the attack on public-sector unions by calling for a wage freeze on federal workers in January.

As that dark winter stumbled slowly into February, newly elected Republican governors in Wisconsin, Ohio, and Florida were racing at breakneck speed to see who could take away public employees' collective bargaining rights first. It was so over-the-top and aggressive that it almost didn't seem real; and yet, nobody except a small handful of reporters seemed to be writing about these new attacks on organized labor. It was unclear if labor would even stand up for itself anymore—was this still the same gutsy labor movement whose stories inspired me in my childhood?

In February I went to New York to take a break from the problems haunting me in D.C., and in part to understand why New York City's Building and Constructions Trades Council President Gary LaBarbera had turned on public-employee unions. LaBarbera had endorsed a controversial group that called for policies curtailing New York's public-employee unions. The leadership of the trades council, whose members were facing 40 percent unemployment, were convinced that they could find political support and additional revenue to fund construction projects by advocating for the cutting of benefits and wages of public employees. It seemed as if labor was doomed, and that some union leaders might try to make separate deals to save their own individual unions at the expense of others.

I was also going to New York City to see the legendary 96-year-old labor journalist Harry Kelber.

Kelber had covered the labor movement's birth in the 1930s, when Kelber himself was still in his twenties, and he continues to write three columns a week for his website, the Labor Educator.

The year before, my activist grandparents had passed away within months of each other; both were 92 when they died. They had always helped me get through my occasional bouts of depression by sharing their wisdom about the many twists and turns in life. I missed them dearly, and as I headed to New York I hoped Harry Kelber could provide me with the same kind of insights that my grandparents used to share.

Kelber lived in a beautiful apartment in Brooklyn Heights, with a jaw-dropping view overlooking the harbor. His apartment was littered with books and sheet music that he was using for his own original compositions; the walls were adorned with gorgeous paintings and posters depicting labor's great struggles of the past; and there were so many plants it seemed they were sprouting out of every corner. The mood inside the apartment was bright and cheerful, contrasting sharply with my own darkness. Kelber seemed upbeat, inspired by the recent revolution in Egypt, whose dictator looked like he would be stepping down any day now after weeks of popular protests.

"I can just feel it," Kelber told me, "people will see what is happening in Egypt and all of a sudden they will realize they have a voice. Once people see they have a voice, it's tough to put that away. It will spread like wildfire. I saw it happen in the 1930s, and it will happen here again with the great attack labor is under." I left Brooklyn Heights that day desperately clinging to Kelber's dream of a working-class uprising, but it was hard not to be skeptical; it was hard to think that the American working class would march together in strength ever again.

On Friday Feb. 11, three days after I visited Kelber, Wisconsin Governor Scott Walker upped his war against public-employee unions by threatening to call out the National Guard to prevent state workers from striking. I received a phone call from a friend, American Federation of Teachers organizer Jan Van Tol, who told me that people were outraged by Walker's actions and that they expected protests the following week that could possibly number in the thousands.

By Monday they had already exceeded that expectation, when 10,000 people showed up at the Wisconsin state Capitol. The following night, the Teaching Assistants' Association made a daring but key decision to step up the protests and occupy the Capitol, and they began sleeping there overnight. One of the union's leaders was Alex Hanna, a graduate student who had just returned from Cairo a few days before. After seeing the events in Egypt firsthand, Hanna was confident that students and workers would have their voices heard by turning the Wisconsin Capitol into their own Tahrir Square.

And it spread: On Tuesday, hundreds of students from high schools around Madison, who, of course, had never been union members, started walking out of class. Madison's teachers union voted to go on a "sickout" strike, and teachers around the state of Wisconsin began to join students in walking out of school. Crowds swelled by the tens of thousands nearly every day.

I couldn't believe what was happening. I sat glued to my computer in D.C. for upwards of 20 hours a day, trying to get a sense of what was unfolding while frantically making phone calls to any labor organizer I could find in Wisconsin.

Even though I wasn't in Wisconsin during that first week of protest, thanks to Twitter I felt like I was there. Stories like the woman who, during a rally, scattered the ashes of her union member father on the Capitol grounds, and the images of the Capitol covered in a sea of red T-shirts, painted a picture so rich in my mind that I often forgot I was in D.C., looking at a Twitter stream.

Thursday Feb. 17, when the Wisconsin state Senate was scheduled to vote on the "budget-repair" bill to restrict public employees' collective bargaining rights, I was getting antsy; I wanted to be inside the Capitol rotunda, not in D.C. I watched as 75,000 people jammed the Capitol grounds, hoping somehow to present a show of force that would cause the Republicans to back down from passing the anti-labor bill.

I thought it was only a symbolic gesture when Wisconsin Democratic state senators left the chamber together, holding up solidarity fists and disappearing into the crowd outside. I realized I was witnessing a flickering of the old Democratic Party, fighting for labor—nothing like the Democratic Party hacks in Washington constantly attacking teachers' unions. An hour later news broke that Wisconsin's 14 Democratic state senators had not only left the Capitol chambers, but had fled the state in order to deny Republican members the quorum needed to vote on Walker's bill. Senators that day were inspired to literally shut down the Wisconsin Senate.

I started seeing reports on Twitter that groups of 30-40 union activists had barricaded each of the doors to the Senate to prevent Republican senators from re-entering the chamber. Activists held tight that day, and Republicans left the building unable to pass the bill. Tweets of rejoice began streaming out as it became clear that the people's stand in the Capitol had won that day's battle.

And then, all of a sudden, a photo of the sea of Wisconsin's Badger-red T-shirts covering the marble floor of the Capitol emerged on my Twitter feed and captured the collective nature of what we as the labor movement are able to achieve.

I began to cry—we had saved the labor movement. We workers, through our mere voices, had saved the labor movement, my God, we did it.

Over the following days, occasionally I found myself home alone singing "Solidarity Forever" as I frantically typed updates from Twitter sources on what was happening in Wisconsin, but I couldn't shake the disappointment of being stuck in D.C. Wisconsin was where the big fight was, and I knew I had to be there.

I made phone calls to different editors, asking them to send me to Wisconsin. Finally, filmmaker Michael Moore agreed to sponsor me to go to Madison under an arrangement where I would write for a variety of publications.

Within hours, I had a ticket to Wisconsin. I couldn't contain my joy and my pacing: This was the most exciting thing that had ever happened to me. When I arrived at the airport, all flights were delayed due to an ice storm, but things in Wisconsin were moving so rapidly that I couldn't wait another a day to get there. With most of Madison's teachers out on sickout strike, it seemed like anything could happen, perhaps even a general strike. I had to get to Wisconsin right away.

I quickly rebooked a flight to Chicago and found a bus from the Windy City that took me straight to Madison. The bus was so full that two-dozen people were forced to stand in the aisles. I spent the trip anxiously flipping my iPhone in and out of my hands, fidgeting impatiently.

I felt like a nervous combat correspondent touching down in a hot LZ–in my case, ground zero of the class war.

Almost immediately upon arriving in Madison, I went straight to the Capitol. The first sight that struck me was of people mopping up the floor with gentle strokes, bent down on hands and knees. This was their house. The people had reclaimed it, and they were taking care of it as they would their own house—they aimed to protect and preserve what had become a symbol to the nation of the power of workers' voices.

No sooner had I arrived than I ran into my friend Brett Banditelli, a labor journalist who runs a small radio show in Central Pennsylvania. "Look who finally decided to show up to the class war, Mr. Elk," was how he greeted me.

Brett was representative of the small network of labor reporters and citizen journalists who provided the bulk of the coverage of the Wisconsin protests. Labor had largely been ignored by all but a few reporters from mainly smaller publications and those who worked for labor-funded pro- grams like Banditelli's. Previously our audiences had been quite small, but we now found ourselves trying to explain what was happening in Wiscon- sin to the larger world, to whoever was following us through Twitter.

But first, we had to make sense of the situation for ourselves. It wasn't easy, to be honest: Just a few weeks earlier, absolutely nobody in the labor movement—outside of the old optimists like Harry Kelber—thought this was even possible. For the moment, Banditelli and I were bewildered by the campsite of protesters sleeping out on the floor of the Capitol, with old- time potbelly union activists in sleeping bags camped next to college hip- pies cuddling in a corner. The Capitol had turned into some strange version of Paris Commune meets old-school Midwestern union hall, complete with bratwursts and drum circles.

I went a second night without sleep due to the excitement. I made my way to the headquarters of the occupation, a command center set up by the University of Wisconsin-Madison Teaching Assistants' Association. It was a crazy, chaotic, caffeine-soaked scene, now in its ninth day, fueled by cold pizza and high fives. Students were running around like headless chickens, setting up phone banks to get more graduate students to come out for protests, arranging for more food deliveries to the Capitol, and coordinating volunteer protest marshals who had been self-policing the protesters.

As I looked around the room I noticed several laptops with "Obama/Biden" stickers. These were kids who had worked for Obama in 2008 and despite the disappointment that many had felt about the President's administration, they had not given in to despair. They had learned valuable lessons about how to organize, only this time they were organizing for themselves, not for Obama. Holy crap, I thought, hope and change are still alive, but in the occupation of a state Capitol.

While most reporters focused on covering the legislative and political action playing out, I tried to cover something different. Something much deeper was happening among the activists. There was a growing sense of confidence that was emerging that turned ordinary students and workers into gung-ho union organizers.

Most of the media narratives coming out of Wisconsin were about how this had changed the politics of union-busting and shifted public opinion in the unions' favor. I would argue that it went even deeper than that: Wisconsin changed the way people do politics, period.

Madison revived the concept of street protests, strikes, and solidarity actions that had seemed to be all but extinct, replaced by the passive point and click activism of the internet age and cautious top-down, D.C.-centric labor leadership. As labor fought for its life in Madison, I worked feverishly to document the revival of the in-your-face direct action, civil disobedience, and organizing that had built the labor movement in the 1930s.

I worked around the clock interviewing people, and filed three to four stories a day from the front lines. I was so caught up in it that I even managed to forget about the girlfriend who left me. Hell, I forgot about everything: I forgot about sleeping; I even forget to eat most of the time. I don't know exactly how, but suddenly all those months of lethargy after coming down with pneumonia just disappeared and I was full of energy again. The adrenaline of the protests kept me working 20 hours a day covering the new dynamic emerging on Wisconsin's streets.

Then one morning, my body crashed. I woke up and was nearly unable to move my legs. My immune system, weakened from pneumonia and lack of sleep and food, had caught up with me. My doctor ordered me to go back home to D.C. to rest. I returned home physically exhausted, but mentally energized and full of hope for the future—going over the possibilities of rebuilding the labor movement that Wisconsin had unleashed.

A week later, in violation of the state open-meetings laws, the Wisconsin Legislature was able to illegally, as pro-union activists argue, push through the bill stripping public employees of their right to collectively bargain. Protesters stormed the Capitol, busting down barricades and reoccupying the building in disgust, but there was nothing they could do.

It was a body blow. It seemed like for the time being we had lost in Wisconsin. Corporate America, like always, had figured out a way to strong arm the labor movement. It seemed like things were getting back to usual, with the boss always winning out over workers.

But then I started noticing a new optimism about the labor movement that hadn't been there before. Everywhere I went, workers seemed inspired by Wisconsin. General Electric workers in Erie, Pennsylvania adopted the Wisconsin Badger as their mascot as they threatened strikes against GE, which was pushing for workers to make concessions. Now, at every union rally I go to across the nation, I see people wearing shirts of the state of Wisconsin shaped like a solidarity fist. Wisconsin has become a rallying cry that gave activists a sense that they could win. As United Steelworkers Local USW 7-699 President Darrell Lillie told me when I visited him during a bitter year-long lockout at a Honeywell uranium facility in Southern Illinois: "You have to understand Wisconsin to understand that we can win here and win as a labor movement."

Wisconsin lit a spark in me; it lit a spark in all of us. A spark that union organizer August Spies, one of the Haymarket martyrs, talked about shortly before he was put to death in 1887 for a crime he did not commit: "If you think that by hanging us you can stamp out the labor movement, then hang us. Here you will tread upon a spark, but here, and there, and behind you, and in front of you, the flames will blaze up. It is a subterranean fire. You cannot put it out. The ground is on fire upon which you stand."

Wisconsin was a new spark of that subterranean fire of justice that burns deep in all of us. A spark that the 96-year-old labor journalist Harry Kelber had witnessed with his own eyes when labor first came alive in the 1930s. As Kelber predicted, once people found their voices, as they did in Wisconsin, it started to spread like "a wildfire."

Let's burn down the whole goddamn forest.

MIKE ELK
July 2011

@daveweigel
Not sure what democracy looks like. Could somebody point it out, preferably by chanting? **#wiunion**

WHAT DEMOCRACY LOOKS LIKE: A CAPITOL CITY EMERGES

FOR SIXTEEN DAYS AND NIGHTS, protesters occupied the Wisconsin Capitol in an attempt to stop Governor Scott Walker's attack on unions and state workers. What began as a spontaneous sleep-in of people waiting their turn to testify against Walker's "budget-repair" bill soon evolved into a highly-organized, diverse community determined to stand its ground for as long as necessary.

Side-by-side they slept on the hard marble floors of Madison's Capitol—farmers next to student activists, teachers beside firefighters, those who would be directly affected by the bill and those who saw it as an assault on all workers' rights. It was part protest, part sleepover, part new city sprung up to meet the unique needs of its residents.

Volunteers set up an information station, first-aid facilities, and a "People's Mic" for anyone who wanted to speak to the crowds gathered at all hours. They coordinated food donations from local businesses and around the world, created a charging station to plug in electronics, and designated a children's area where families could go to get away from the crowds. Protesters cooperated with Capitol cleaning crews, and stood in solidarity with the police officers that patrolled the grounds.

As the physical center of the resistance, the Capitol became the place where protesters negotiated tactics and discussed strategies. Even amid intense disagreements, they showed what a real, developing democratic process looked like. There were moments of anger and frustration, but many more of joy and connection, from the daily drum circles to nightly gatherings for old labor films and protest music.

The remarkable occupation lasted for more than two weeks, despite attempts throughout by Walker and his allies to tighten building access and push protesters out of the Capitol. People who took part in the occupation describe it as an almost sacred community that kept them camped there for days or continuing to return for more. In a rare instance, they had claimed the Capitol back from the usual lobbyists and legislators and turned it into a true people's house.

@ttagaris Tim Tagaris
No idea if it will materialize, but it really feels like Scott Walker's actions could inspire something special in Wisconsin
5:19pm Feb 13

@millbot Emily Mills
Est. 3-400 ppl at rally, went right to gov's office with big pile of v-day cards protesting budget bill. **#wiunions**
12:52pm Feb 14

@DefendWisconsin Defend Wisconsin
Tomorrow is going to be huge, follow this account for any necessary updates during the protest, today was for love! **#handsoffourteachers**
2:33pm Feb 14

@JamesEBriggs James Briggs
People waiting in line to get into the public hearing.
9:56am Feb 15

@weeks89 Lin Weeks
Weirdly high number of signs ref'ing egypt. And now chanting: "From Egypt/ to wisconsin/ power to the people."
11:20am Feb 15

@ACLUMadison ACLU Madison
RT @WORTnews: East High School staff member calls in to say that 700 students walked out of school to join the labor rallies at the Capitol.
12:30pm Feb 15

@millbot Emily Mills
Contingent of firefighters showing support for unions tho Walker exempted them from bill. **#wiunion**
12:37pm Feb 15

@bluecheddar1 blue cheddar
We belong. This is our Capitol today **#solidarityWI** **#wiunions**
12:57pm Feb 15

THE INCREDIBLE ECOSYSTEM OF THE WISCONSIN STATE CAPITOL

David Dayen

FIREDOGLAKE, FEBRUARY 24, 2011

The Wisconsin labor fight has no shortage of compelling storylines. When I got to Madison, I expected to talk to the lawmakers who were holding back an assault on workers' rights and the union leaders fighting for their continued existence. I expected to break down vote counts to determine whether the "budget-repair" bill had the numbers to pass, or look up arcane Wisconsin law to see if Republicans could engineer a workaround to get their anti-union measures passed into law. And I expected to check in with Wisconsin's 14 Democratic senators, safely ensconced out of state, to see if they would hold out, or if they would crack and return to Madison.

But I was drawn to something quite different. And that's the story of the state Capitol, under a virtual occupation for the tenth straight day. What started as a protest has taken on the quality of a virtual city on the square. It's very hard to explain unless you see it for yourself, but I'll try. The Capitol has become a site for dissent, an information center, an organizing hub, a pizzeria, a display of wit and the site of a new progressive movement. That's really not overstating the case.

As you walk into the Capitol, the walls are basically covered, and not just with protest slogans and witticisms, though they are there as well ("Hey Stewart/Colbert, we came to your rally, now come to ours"; "The Curdish rebels of Wisconsin"; "Thank God for CNN or I'd never know what's on

Twitter"). Governor Scott Walker is getting a lot of mockery as well; my favorite banner reads, "Hey Scott Walker, this is David Koch, will you talk to me?" Madison is the birthplace of *The Onion*, after all. But the walls are also festooned with a surprising amount of graphs and charts depicting inequality in America, the percentage cuts to BadgerCare[1] in the budget-repair bill, or how much of the federal budget is spent on war and the military. There are even historical treatises about how Abraham Lincoln once jumped out of a window to avoid a quorum call in the Illinois Senate. This is a wonk rebellion too, furthered by the internet and the easy accessibility of data.

And then there's the organizing. While protesters rally and wave signs and give public testimony on the legislation (a process that has been going on for days), others are harnessing the frustration and passion. Phone banks have been set up. Other flyers announce self-organized protests, including one today in front of the new lobbying offices for Koch Industries, which popped up just a couple weeks after Walker's election. There's a sign-up sheet that reads, "I would strike to kill the bill," with a pretty long list of names. (The idea of a general strike has been discussed and even endorsed by a local labor council. Private unions wouldn't be able to go out because of the Taft-Hartley Act, but by mid-March most public unions would not be operating under a contract with the state, so you could absolutely see something like this happen, depending on what legislation goes forward.) At another station on the ground floor is the pizza distribution; Ian's Pizza on State has basically become the official supplier of the protests, paid for by donations coming in from around the country and the world. There's coffee as well, and periodically calls for supplies go out and get fulfilled. There are websites up devoted to the protest, like DefendWisconsin.org. Other fliers announce Twitter feeds to follow for information or sites collecting YouTube videos of the event.

There's a lot of earnestness, knowledge and even humor throughout the Capitol. You know what there's not a lot of? Lobbyists. I've been to a few state capitols in my day, and the suits are invariably flitting about, pushing their little riders to help out their clients. You're seeing none of that in Madison; it's really a takeover. And the unity in the rotunda is remarkable.

[1] State-run government program that provides health coverage to low-income Wisconsinites

Some of the most visible union members in there are police and firefighters, who are exempted from the collective bargaining restrictions under the bill. I saw a guy walking around with a sign reading, "Private Sector Nonunion Employee – I Stand with Labor." High school and college students are extremely active as well.

One person said to me that the outpouring here is paradoxically similar to the outpouring that ended up sweeping Walker into office. People are tired of losing good jobs, of seeing wealth float to the top, of being part of a generation falling behind that of its parents. They want something different, but they don't know what that is. Now they see the true agenda of these Republicans who got elected, and the same energy has gone into fighting that. It's an interesting theory, and I think there's a bit more nuance than that; Madison is a liberal town, and this isn't Walker country no matter what. But in the bars and on the streets, people who I would characterize as townies, people who weren't all that political to begin with, are incessantly talking about this issue. It has consumed the town and, in many ways, has consumed Wisconsin and the nation. We're finally talking about things that matter to the mass of people.

@DefendWisconsin Defend Wisconsin
Sen. Taylor just entered the overflow room to a standing ovation! She's telling people to stay, they'll get a chance to speak **#killthisbill**
2:29pm Feb 15

@DefendWisconsin Defend Wisconsin
Get your pillows and pull an all-nighter at the Capitol! Sign up to speak and keep this hearing going till the morning! **#killthisbill**
5:16pm Feb 15

@millbot Emily Mills
Um, we elected you? Don't get to ignore us. RT @jef4wi Gov Walker's budget head said that no amount of testimony will change this bill.
6:03pm Feb 15

@JacquelynGill Jacquelyn Gill
@GBsOwnMrsDiSH It was so clear today that folks aren't just stereotypical Madison liberals. Lots of working class folks from all over WI.
7:24pm Feb 15

@DefendWisconsin Defend Wisconsin
Come sign up to speak IMMEDIATELY. They may cut off the number of speakers they are accepting. NOW NOW NOW. **#killthisbill**
8:45pm Feb 15

@eigenjo Jo Nelson
My thumbs hurt but i will persevere
9:52pm Feb 15

@bluecheddar1 blue cheddar
#Madison is no Cairo. But I for one felt inspired by Egypt's strong desire 4 a say in governance. Rights. Democracy **#solidarityWI #wiunion**
11:57pm Feb 15

@DefendWisconsin Defend Wisconsin
We're hearing Republicans are going to leave and Democrats are going to keep hearing testimony through the night.
12:07am Feb 16

DAS CAPITOL

How a bunch of pro-union, anti-Republican protesters turned the hallways of the Wisconsin state house into a commune

David Weigel

SLATE, FEBRUARY 25, 2011

They call themselves the Cuddle Puddle. They did not come up with the name. There are 10 of them, and they were among the first people to start camping out in the Capitol.

"We were all lying down in the sleeping bags," says CJ Terrell, an unofficial spokesman for the cuddlers, "and somebody said, 'They've got a cuddle puddle going on.' And we liked it."

"We didn't know each other before this happened," says Tom Bird, a University of Wisconsin-Madison grad student.

"Most of us met between 10 and two days ago," says Terrell. He and Bird became Facebook friends only this week.

You can walk the halls 100 times and not lose your sense of wonder and amazement at the occupation. It's hard to admit this without it sounding like an endorsement of the pro-labor, anti-Republican stance of the protesters. It's not. It's just that things like this don't ever happen in state capitols.

Sure, there have been temporary sit-ins at statehouses. There were scattered one-day sit-ins to protest the Iraq war. The graybeard liberals of Madison—this city does not lack for them—remember sit-ins to build pressure for a nuclear weapons ban and against the Vietnam War. But those aren't the same thing as a 10-day sit-in of a public building, fueled by donations from thankful liberals in other states, peopled by union workers and college students who have built a little commune on marble. They film themselves and upload the videos to YouTube, and they are constantly in front of cameras gathering footage for news or for exposés by the conservative MacIver Institute.

How'd it happen? Because it's legal to sleep in the Capitol if hearings are going on, and because the minority Democrats started hearings last week. Since Monday, police have tightened up access to the Capitol. Instead of every door to the building being open, only two are. All four wings had unrestricted access; two do now. Starting on Saturday, Senate offices—some of which had been used to house protesters for sleeping or strategizing— will be closed to anyone who's not a senator.

Thus the little village protesters have built will be disrupted, perhaps even disbanded. It's got to happen sometime. Before it does, I decided to spend a night with the micro-commune. My night happened to coincide with the night that Republicans pushed the budget-repair bill through the Assembly, and the striking thing was how little changed after that happened.

6:28 p.m.: Governor Scott Walker's press conference ends with no real news. The hallway outside his office is lined with letters collected by MoveOn.org from Wisconsinites, pleading with Walker to cave. A sign says the group has 10,000 or so letters.

Down the stairwell, on the second-floor atrium, a crowd has parted for a nine-piece funk fusion group called VO5, which is performing an original song tentatively called "Wisconsin (Cheddar Revolution)." Bandleader Andrew Rohn is still thinking about where to put the parentheses. It's an old song he has repurposed with new protest-specific lyrics:

You think you'll beat us, we're gonna lay down and die?
Screw us and we multiply!

6:55 p.m.: Parts of the second floor have been closed off, but protesters have complete control of the area around Office 116N. On the left: a table for medical supplies, crowded with aspirin, Band-Aids, feminine hygiene products, and so on. There are no photos allowed, and volunteers are told to give a "press release," handwritten on notebook paper, to anyone who asks questions; it just confirms that the supplies are dropped off by Samaritans who ask what's needed.

On the right: two tables of foodstuffs, with supplies that dwindle and change quickly. At the moment, they include a Tupperware container of chocolate chip cookies, a tub of peanut butter that a volunteer describes as "various peanut butters working together in solidarity for the cause of deliciousness," regular bread and gluten-free bread, tart candies, and piles of bagels. The food is paid for by donations; volunteers buy it and serve it, as well as remind people to use the hand sanitizer nearby liberally.

In the center: a "family area." It's a safe space with no cameras allowed, where children frolic, play with communal toys, or rest on yoga mats. I'm bonked in the head painlessly by a ball tossed by a child being watched by Trina Clemente. "I'm a student right now," she says, "because there are no jobs."

7:23 p.m.: Ryan Henry, a construction worker from Baltimore, stands in a first-floor hallway singing original songs with a kind of Bob Dylan or Fred Neil lilt:

Tea Party on the Capitol lawn
And Sarah Palin, singing along
Laughing all the way to the Pentagon.

The song is drowned out at times by the sound of a whistle being blown by Drake Singleton, who's drawing attention to his silk-screened T-shirts commemorating the sit-in.

7:44 p.m.: Dane Spudnik, who works at the Willy Street Co-op in town, is manning the anarchist lending library set up next to a stairwell. He doesn't mind if people make off with the "Capitalism is Doomed" posters or "Organizing in the Workplace" guides, but he wants to make sure "nobody sees this copy of *The Shock Doctrine* and says, oh, I can sell that for $5."

8:27 p.m.: The "War Room" of the Teaching Assistants' Association (TAA) is tucked away on the third floor. The walls are lined with donated coffee, takeout containers, cereal, and charts—lots and lots of charts—to sign up for cleaning duties, or to pick up a bright-green vest and act as a marshal. The room itself is about to be closed down on Saturday, a casualty of the Senate's tightened security.

"That's been our Situation Room," says one graduate student, Ben Stein, a little glumly. "We organized everything from there, and I don't think we could have put together any of this without that room. Now that we have, I think we can keep it going, but—that was a nice room!"

Rep. Tammy Baldwin, who represents Madison, is in the Situation Room talking to some students. Other students are grading papers or calling people in for shifts. "I asked them what they needed," says Baldwin, "and they said they needed air mattresses." She points to the inflatable mattresses she just delivered, which will be deployed within hours.

8:43 p.m.: The TAA offers to let me do a round of trash cleanup. After a moment's hesitation, my journalistic instinct takes over: Collecting trash would give me exclusive access to a whole new part of the commune. I grab plastic gloves and a bag, and start downstairs. My ethical qualms vanish when Diane Blum, a secretary at a nearby school, demands to carry the trash bag.

So: The trash pickup, which has kept the Capitol remarkably clean, has two components. The usual Capitol custodians do cleanup on regular hours; the TAA does regular runs around the building, putting their trash bags next to trash cans, per an agreement with the custodial staff. There has been very little damage to the building. Once protesters were warned that taping signs everywhere might damage the property, they switched to blue electrical tape. Once protesters realized that some people were writing unkind things on the Scott-brand toilet paper containers in bathrooms, signs went up warning against this. The scribbling stopped.

9:14 p.m.: Protesters who'll sleep in the Capitol are starting to settle in. The protesters who can't are heading out. George Boulamatis, a corrections officer in Racine, has to leave for a 10:30-6:30 shift, but he listens to an ad hoc string band play folk songs before he goes.

9:50 p.m.: The debate in the Assembly is dragging on. Republicans sit as still and look as alert as they can. Rep. Dave Cullen is on the floor, and he sounds like a tape slowed down on the reel as he hammers Walker over his conversation with a phony "David Koch."

"That's one of our quietest members on the floor right now," says Rep. Chris Danou. "We can keep going for a long time. One of my fellow representatives was telling me he has three hours of labor history to talk about."

A lot of Democratic members are talking about the Kochs; when they do, they often get boisterous cheers from the second floor of the Capitol, where the proceedings are audible.

10:31 p.m.: League of Conservation Voters organizer Matt Dannenberg was listening to the speakers playing the Assembly debate. He's one of the first people to notice that Republicans have made an end-run around the Democratic filibuster and are about to force a vote.

"Get people over here!" he says, swinging his arm toward the Assembly. "This is not democracy! This is not democracy! Come on, we need more people!"

Protesters jump off of their mats and bedrolls and run toward the police tape blocking them from the Assembly. A heavyset trumpet player is allowed to the very front of the crowd; screams and chants get intermingled with smooth jazz. A Democratic staffer emerges from the chamber and waves his arms in a "raise the roof"-type gesture.

11:20 p.m.: The protesters calm down a bit. One sign around the Capitol says, explicitly, "The Assembly Will Pass The Bill, We Need to Focus on the Senate." So there's a sense of resignation at a vote that was always going to go against them. Kristina Nielsen, a UW student wearing her mother's American Federation of Teachers (AFT) shirt, knits a solidarity bracelet and talks about staying even after the bill passes.

"We've been here 10 days and I'm starting to get used to the marble floor," she says. "It actually helps that we're more exhausted." What about the constant noise? "It's fine. It's like living in a dorm."

1:01 a.m.: The Assembly debate dragged on for hours after Republicans started to force the vote—by now, it's been going on for more than 60 hours, and Republicans are fed up.

"Everything that's being said has been said three or four times already," said Speaker Pro Tempore Bill Kramer. "Until seven minutes ago, no one was listening. Except me."

Minutes later, Kramer gavels in a quick vote. Democrats explode, furious not just at the result but at the fact that the vote lasted fewer than 15 seconds.

They start to file out of the chamber, and one by one they go to a railing and wave to the hundreds of people crammed onto the floor below. Rep. Leon Young tosses his orange T-shirt into the crowd; a protester grabs it as if Eddie Van Halen has tossed a guitar pick.

"This is a travesty!" says Rep. Bill Hulsey, who'd yelled, "Shame" at Republicans louder than almost anyone. "What do I want to do next? I don't even want to say." He joins his colleagues in a caucus meeting.

1:20 a.m.: In the first-floor atrium, Rep. Cory Mason joins the Cuddle Puddle, who have a megaphone at the ready, and thanks the protesters. "I've never been so glad that we have two chambers," he says. In the other chamber, of course, striking Senate Democrats are not present for a vote, so the bill is stuck.

The megaphone is passed to Damon Terrell, CJ's brother. He's wearing a cutoff shirt that displays a fresh tattoo, a fist in the shape of Wisconsin with "SOLIDARITY" written alongside. "For the first time in my life," he says, "I know I am doing what I was born to do."

Reporters try to talk to Terrell, but he gives them little information before holding up. "I really want to be in the moment now," he says. He returns to the circle for hugs.

2:14 a.m.: Every night there's a rumor that the Capitol will be cleared. It's not being cleared tonight. Some protesters are sitting up straight; some seem to have slept through the apocalypse.

"How can you sleep?" says Mary McDonald, a representative of AFT Healthcare in Washington. "It's so dramatic! It's so upsetting! How can these people possibly work together now, you know? There have been so many double-crosses."

7:45 a.m.: The doors to the Capitol are about to open again, and before they do I take a quick survey of the feeding/sleeping areas. Some of the sleepers, roused, are doing TV interviews through heavy eyelids. The food has been replenished, with stacks of bagels and cream cheese in the breakfast nook. (There's no fresh coffee just yet.) There are rumors, as there are every day, that the Capitol will be closed to protesters, but there's a massive rally planned for Saturday. Tom Bird, the first of the Cuddle Puddle to wake up, stops me and speaks happily about the sleep he managed to get, after Democratic staffers left and handed him and other protesters the cold remainders of their Ian's Pizza.

"I had to sleep," he says, "because this is going to be a big weekend."

@bluecheddar1 blue cheddar
Another person testifying at the J.F.C. hearing is talking/crying. A teacher.
A man. This is LIVE here http://www.wiseye.org/
#solidarityWI
1:24am Feb 16

@TAA_Madison TAA Madison
Sen. Lena Taylor "I'm staying until everyone has testified." **#killthisbill**
2:31am Feb 16

@eigenjo Jo Nelson
do not be discouraged - we have demonstrated an unfathomable
opposition to the bill, and we must continue to do so. we are
making history!
2:56am Feb 16

@ryan_rainey Ryan Rainey
I estimate at least 300 here right now. Jauch: "at 3am, this state is alive,
this is the rebirth of the progressive movement here."
3:20am Feb 16

@DefendWisconsin Defend Wisconsin
Dems are addressing crowd now, getting resounding applause
#killthisbill
3:22am Feb 16

@DefendWisconsin Defend Wisconsin
Sen. Taylor announcing that hearing will continue in 411S. And Ian's Pizza
has donated pizza?! **#killthisbill**
3:25am Feb 16

@JamesEBriggs James Briggs
Rep. Mark Pocan, D-Madison, is looking a bit disheveled, with a tieless,
untucked shirt. **#capitolfashion #wiunion #latenight**
10:34am Feb 16

@JacquelynGill Jacquelyn Gill
We're calling it a work stoppage, includes fac/staff @DanMotor
RT @eigenjo: rumored uw ta teach out tomorrow. Spread the word
11:56am Feb 16

THE UNBREAKABLE CULTURE OF THE OCCUPIED CAPITOL

Ben Brandzel
THE HUFFINGTON POST, MARCH 1, 2011

As Wisconsin Governor Scott Walker bolts the windows and bars the doors of the Capitol to scare, shrink and starve the ongoing protest within, it's important for everyone outside to understand just what he's so afraid of, and why.

I write this after completing a once-in-a-lifetime week in Madison as one of the many camped out in the occupied Capitol. And now I know why Walker is so frightened.

Imagine a group of several hundred sleep-deprived, hungry people crammed into a confined, noisy, bright, uncomfortable space for weeks on end. There are no showers, no reliable food supply and no proper beds. They're surrounded by police day and night. And they're mere inches away from the chambers where the devastating legislation they're gathered to protest is being rammed through right in front of their faces. Surely, a recipe for total meltdown.

And yet there hasn't been a single episode of serious conflict between protesters or with the police. And there's no sign of any such confrontation to come. How is this possible? It's not an accident, and it's not a miracle. It's the product of a sophisticated, unbreakable culture that has evolved in the hallways of the occupied Capitol. And that's exactly why Walker is so desperately tightening the screws.

If you were to walk through the halls of the Capitol, you would see the bedrocks of this incredible culture all around you:

Responsibility. Volunteer marshals of every age and background, wearing now-iconic reflective vests, distribute information, convey instructions from the legal authorities and gently keep the peace. The marshals are all fellow protesters. There's no hierarchy to it; you just sign up with the Teaching Assistants' Association and get a brief training on that night's priorities. The system ensures the protest remains a largely self-regulating phenomenon. This limits tension with the police and inculcates a spirit of responsibility and good stewardship among every participant.

Respect. Handmade signs everywhere urge respect for the premises. The bathroom door sign reminds you "Tagging the wall is hurting the movement." On the second floor a large poster reads, "Remember, this is OUR house—so let's keep it clean!" When the cleaning crew takes its floor-sweeping Zamboni out onto the rotunda floor, it is greeted with thunderous applause and chants of "Thank you!" All the thousands of posters are hung with special blue tape that will leave no trace. In my entire time there, I didn't see a single example of permanent damage or the slightest desecration of the building.

Health. A dedicated volunteer medical team operates a well-stocked first-aid clinic (with all-donated supplies). Medics patrol the building wearing handmade badges or red-tape crosses, looking out for injury or signs of illness. Hand sanitizer dispensers are taped to the walls. Piles of Emergen-C line the hallways. Before you can touch the megaphone in the rotunda, you're asked to use Purell. I can speak to the effectiveness of this system firsthand: While distributing flyers one evening, I tumbled down a flight of stairs and badly sprained my ankle. Immediately, a man I'd never met half-carried me to the medical station, where medics who would never think of payment administered top quality care, cold packs, ace bandages and lots of attentive follow up. The occupied Capitol has become a far safer, healthier place than, say, your average major city.

Generosity. Everything is donated. The community survives because people from Madison to Cairo have chipped in for Ian's Pizza, endless bagels, or breakfast burritos from an organic cafe. Fabulous homemade stews and soups appeared daily for lunch until the police were ordered to ban Crock-Pots. I saw masseuses drive for hours and haul their chairs up three flights of stairs just to give free massages (before, of course, the massage chairs were banned). I saw people who had slept on cold marble for weeks gladly share or give away camping mats and pillows. This weekend, when food supplies were blocked and reserves ran dangerously low, locals started smuggling pizzas in through the windows from the snowy ground (prompting Walker's unspeakably cruel order on Monday to bolt the windows closed). And when the pizza supply was cut off, I saw people who hadn't eaten all day gladly share their only slice.

Nonviolence. Hand-drawn signs on every floor declare, "Remember, this is a peaceful protest." Every speech from the rotunda, no matter how thunderous, declares a firm commitment to avoid violence at any cost. When AFL-CIO union officials announced their commitment to provide legal and logistical support, they made it extremely clear all offers would evaporate for anyone committing a violent act. Every night, several trainings are held throughout the building on how to remain "peaceful and prepared." The volunteer facilitators help protesters understand their rights, but are equally focused on teaching breathing techniques and planning skills to avoid even an unintentional flash of violence during a tense moment. For nonviolence to solidify as an unshakable collective commitment, it cannot come from above. It requires a thousand individual efforts to build resolve from the bottom up. In the occupied Capitol, that resolve is everywhere.

Solidarity. Last Wednesday evening the entire crowd erupted in uproarious cheers as a line of Wisconsin firefighters in full uniform streamed into the building to spend the night on the floor with us. As one of the few public-sector unions not to oppose Walker's election, the firefighters are exempted from the devastating restrictions in the "budget-repair" bill. But what Walker didn't realize is that these guys risk their lives every day to save others from burning homes—and for people like that, solidarity is a way of life. One of the firefighters held up a hand-drawn sign of "Divide and conquer" written in a circle with line through it. That pretty much says it all. The spirit of solidarity drives everything in the occupied Capitol. It's why managers and students and private-sector workers are sleeping in hallways to protest an attack on public school teachers and civil servants. It's the word two brothers from Madison camping with us had tattooed on their arms. And it's what defines perhaps the most remarkable feature of life there: the strongly positive relationship with the police.

The culture of respect for the police in the Capitol runs very deep. We all knew they might at any moment be ordered to remove us. But we also knew they were never our enemy. As a giant poster on the first floor declared, "Officers stand with activists, activists stand for officers." For their part, the Capitol Police, Madison Police, as well as State Troopers and officers brought in from other municipalities were consistently friendly, helpful and polite—even when forced to take all-night shifts sandwiched between two consecutive day shifts, as was frequently the case. The officers knew their duty and executed it well, but they knew we would be here camping out to defend their rights if they were on the chopping block (police unions, many of which also endorsed Walker, were also exempted from the bill). On Friday afternoon I saw an elderly member of the pipefitters union going up to each uniformed police officer, extending his hand, and saying, "Thank you for being here." One of them smiled back and said, "Thank you! We know if this goes through, we're next!" Many of the same officers who guarded us during the day would take their uniforms off at night and join us in protest, often bringing large "Cops for Labor" signs with them.

The occupied Capitol has become so much more than a protest. Bound by these principles, it has become a tightly woven community that now stands together at a crossroads in history.

And these principles—responsibility, respect, health, generosity, nonviolence and solidarity—are more than just the defining qualities of the protest camp in the Capitol. They are the values of the society we are protesting for, that Walker is trying to tear down. They are who we want be and how we want to live.

That's why Walker is so scared of this community. Because he knows he's not up against a fleeting burst of anger. He's up against human nature at its best—and its strongest.

No matter what happens next at the standoff at the Wisconsin Capitol, the occupation has given rise to a new and powerful culture. It's a culture that wins more allies and draws more strength every day.

And it is unbreakable.

@millbot Emily Mills
Firefighters have entered main throng of rally with bagpipes! Style.
11:58am Feb 16

@MelissaRyan Melissa Ryan
This crowd is made up of families, students, teachers, people who love their state. Will all stay as long as it takes. **#notmyWI**
12:05pm Feb 16

@eigenjo Jo Nelson
Unions do good for the people. Let this be heard in the corridors of the capitol. And they can hear. I hope they pause and listen.
12:08pm Feb 16

@bluecheddar1 blue cheddar
If you didn't know, you do now: Wisconsin is ground zero. Holding the line against the onslaught against Progressive values
12:10pm Feb 16

@bluecheddar1 blue cheddar
Lemme lay it out: #Madison AND #WI has a literal shit-storm of protest rt. now. We have Dems who R conducting a 24hr+ hearing
12:35pm Feb 16

@eigenjo Jo Nelson
It is amazing to be a part of history today
12:41pm Feb 16

WALKER IS WAKING UP WISCONSIN'S ORGANIZED LABOR MOVEMENT

Emily Mills

ISTHMUS, FEBRUARY 16, 2011

I've spent the last few days almost entirely immersed in the ever-growing protest on behalf of workers' rights and against Governor Scott Walker's attempt to take them away. Tuesday I found myself in the middle of a 10,000-plus crowd of students and workers, union and non-union alike, as they stormed the Capitol and filled its halls with the almost overwhelming echoes of their chants and cheers.

It's been intense, but incredibly inspiring.

I don't know what the outcome will be—whether Walker and his cronies will simply ignore the deafening will of the people of their state and push the "budget-repair" bill through as is—or if reason and compassion will actually win the day, and force them to at least delay and reconsider.

What I do know is that there are tens, if not hundreds of thousands of people in Wisconsin who are out there walking the line, showing support for their friends and families, and doing so peacefully but passionately.

I walked with over 700 students from East High School as they marched up East Washington Avenue to the Capitol to join the protesters there. While I'm sure there were some in the crowd who simply found themselves swept up in the moment and the opportunity to miss class, the vast majority knew what the issue was and what was at stake. I spoke with several who expressed a desire to fight for the rights of their teachers and family members who worked for the state. There will always be those cynics who dismiss the activism of youth as naive and pointless, but this is our future, folks. As far as I could see yesterday (and again today, as yet more students joined the throngs), the future's looking pretty damn good.

Today I stood on a stone pillar on the King Street side of the Capitol, craned my neck in every direction and couldn't see a single patch of ground unoccupied by someone. I saw union workers, both public- and private-sector, from every occupation—nurses, steelworkers, teachers, sanitation workers, law enforcement, social workers, prison guards, civil servants. A group of firefighters, though exempted from Walker's scheme, came out in force, bagpipers and all, to show support for fellow union members. Children stood with their parents or schoolmates and waved handmade signs in support. Music blasted, people danced, and all around there was an all-encompassing sense of determination.

If Walker's goal was to galvanize the organized labor movement in this state, he's succeeded admirably. But that's about all I'd be willing to give him credit for.

Talking with a couple of local teachers who turned out to the rally, it became all the more clear the damage this bill will do on the ground—not just for the teachers themselves, but for children across the state who rely on them for education, for a second home, for security even.

Jesse Wiedmeyer, a substitute teacher at Madison East High School, was handing out Madison Teachers, Inc. support stickers to fellow picketers when I asked him what the bill's passage would mean for him, personally.

"New job or a new state," he answered with a rueful chuckle. "That's what we decided, y'know? If we want to keep teaching maybe Wisconsin's not the place."

Two women who are teachers in Madison but preferred not to give their names expressed serious concerns over what the bill would mean in terms of how they actually did their jobs.

"Without collective bargaining rights we can't negotiate curriculum, other important safety and school issues that are important to students— and that's why we teach," said one.

Mostly, they were concerned with just how much remained unknown about the bill's particulars, rushed through in just under a week as it's been. If collective bargaining rights for everything but salary are to be taken away, will teachers have a say in what they teach their students? Or will the governor have the ability to legislate curriculum?

It's just one of a slew of serious questions that are being asked regarding the bill and, so far, going unanswered by Walker.

State workers have stated time and again that they're more than willing to share in the burden of balancing the budget through concessions. They made a series of them at the end of contract negotiations that were ultimately struck down by the lame-duck session of the Legislature that bowed to the wishes of the incoming administration.

This isn't about money, though. As Brad Lutes, a teacher from Sun Prairie and one of the speakers at today's rally said, "As much as this is about salaries and benefits, it's much more about the loss of workers' fundamental rights."

Stripping 50 years of established labor law in less than a week is a dangerous and frankly disgusting act of stubborn, compassionless, short-sighted governance. Walker says he doesn't want to negotiate and seems completely blind to the massive outpouring of opposition coming from his constituents. That to me indicates a person not interested in being part of a democracy, but rather someone more concerned with personal gain and autocracy.

That's not the Wisconsin I've come to love in the 10 years I've lived here, and there are tens of thousands of people (at least!) who visibly agree with me.

Keep it up, Wisconsin. Solidarity!

@bluecheddar1 blue cheddar
@athenae Some try 2 paint **#Madison** as only sandals,lattes. Well yestrday I saw WAY MORE WORK COATS & coveralls in town **#wiunion #solidarityWI**
12:44pm Feb 16

@aemilli Emily
I effing love my city and my state so much right now. **#notmywi #killthisbill #wiunion**
1:32pm Feb 16

@cruiskeen cruiskeen
RT @aemilli: Apparently Ian's Pizza brought free pizza to the protesters at 2 a.m. last night. http://huff.to/iaF9wf Will now be eating ...
1:38pm Feb 16

@JacquelynGill Jacquelyn Gill
#TAA says we're going to have another sleepover in the Capitol tonight! Bring your sleeping bags! **#wiunion**
2:57pm Feb 16

@MissPronouncer Miss Pronouncer
Just watched a report on nt'l TV about WI possibly being a "template" for other states as fight for workers' rights builds at state capitol.
3:12pm Feb 16

@swell Swell
We have to recall Scott Walker in January 2012. Even if we beat him now, imagine what he would do his last year in office! **#dumpwalker**
4:11pm Feb 16

@DefendWisconsin Defend Wisconsin
VOTE FOR THE BUDGET REPAIR BILL IS BEING PUSHED THROUGH TONIGHT. COME TO THE CAPITOL ASAP AND GET READY TO STAY OVER **#killthisbill #wiunion**
4:39pm Feb 16

@MelissaRyan Melissa Ryan
Email from @DailyKos encouraging people to come to the rallies. @ThisBowers: The battleground is in Madison.
6:16pm Feb 16

THE VIEW FROM INSIDE THE WISCONSIN STATE CAPITOL

Mike Elk

THE ATLANTIC, FEBRUARY 25, 2011

"I am suffering from audio nausea from all these drums and shouting. I am on overload. I'm exhausted," sighed 42-year-old AFSCME staff representative Edward Sadlowski. The Wisconsin Local 40 member had been sleeping on the cold marble floor of the Wisconsin state Capitol for over a week when I caught up with him. "I can barely hear, talk, or see straight," he said. "However, I am loving every moment of it and wouldn't want to be anywhere else."

Sadlowski's comments sum up what it has been like to be in the Capitol as pro-union protesters occupy it for the second week in a row. Amid the noise and confusion, it's also been an exhilarating experience for many of its participants, who feel they have found their collective voices in the banging of drums and the singing of "Solidarity Forever." Others—mainly younger—feel like they are discovering who they are as they converse with the like-minded strangers who have thronged the halls and rotunda of the Capitol.

"My father always said during a strike is when we would rebuild the labor movement," said Sadlowski, a veteran organizer whose father famously vied to head the United Steelworkers of America in the late '70s. "We are proving it right here."

Older union organizers have been sharing their experiences organizing in the workplace with students who have never before engaged with the labor movement. Some youngsters have been so inspired that they are talking about dedicating their lives to it.

"Every day I come down here I just feel like we are winning," said Andrew Cole, who is in his twenties. "We are just a bunch of people standing around a Capitol talking together and singing songs, but through this collective voice we have been able to define the national debate about unions."

Likewise, young and optimistic organizers have been giving older ones, beaten down by years of anti-union actions, new ideas—and new hope that it might be possible to rebuild the much-decimated labor movement.

Sadlowski has served as a bridge between the two groups, often coordinating communication among protesters occupying the Capitol. "I think what we created here is the first true labor temple," he said. "Coming down to the Capitol is a lot like coming to church. It's rejuvenating; it's a spiritual experience for a lot of people."

But unlike a church, where people go home at night, hundreds of protesters have turned the Capitol into their temporary home. People have been sleeping there overnight since Tuesday, Feb. 15. They eat meals there, and go to nearby houses and dormitories to take showers.

In the early days, the Capitol occupation was almost entirely coordinated by the Teaching Assistants' Association, the union of teaching assistants at the University of Wisconsin-Madison. But other unions have become more involved in occupying the Capitol since, organizing groups to clean the building and provide food and supplies for people camping out there. Local pizza businesses have been experiencing a mini-boom as people from all over the country and even the world have called in delivery orders for the protesters, while Midwestern grandmothers with thick Wisconsin accents stop by to deliver trays of food cooked at home. In one back hallway, you can find tables full of food as well as boxes of donated supplies like toilet paper, water, toothbrushes, soap, spare hats, scarves, and gloves that are free to take. This level of organization is what has made it sustainable for hundreds of people to more or less live in a Capitol of a major Midwestern state.

Activities have been organized to create a festive environment. There are bands and drum circles that play throughout the day. People put on street theater performances and organize arts and crafts projects. One night

I spotted a group of women knitting. Another night, a group of people meditating.

When everyone goes to bed, you can walk around the Capitol and find young college couples cuddling and kissing in one corner, while families with children bed down for the night in another.

The presence of blue-collar workers in the Capitol has made it more difficult for Governor Scott Walker or Capitol Police to kick protesters out. "Each night one union will take a shift and send down a hundred of its member to sleep in the Capitol. One day the firefighters will come, the next the construction unions," said Sadlowski. "The labor movement understands they have to stand in solidarity with the young people who started this occupation."

"In a struggle such as this, we have proven that numbers and masses determine what happens," said Dave Poklinkoski, president of International Brotherhood of Electrical Workers Local 2304. His union is planning to stay in the building Saturday night, when some of the rooms being occupied will become contested territory, and protesters will risk being kicked out.

As the political stalemate deepens in Wisconsin—and the size of protests dampens—the political importance of occupying the Capitol has risen. Teachers who were out on strike for the first few days of the protest have returned to the classroom, creating a sense of normalcy for most people in Wisconsin, even as the sit-in has continued.

"Right now the only thing we are disrupting is this Capitol," said Sadlowski. "As long as we hold onto this Capitol, we have a chance."

#KILLTHISBILL

@LegalEagle
They will keep the building open as long as testimony is being taken.
It's not just about your voice, it's about all of ours. **#wiunion**

DEAR SCOTT WALKER

BY THE THOUSANDS, people came to the Wisconsin Capitol to tell their stories as a way of speaking out against Governor Scott Walker's attack on workers. It was these farmers, firefighters, teachers, and students who helped catalyze the protests from just another show of activist anger to a sustained demonstration that captured the country's attention.

Over the course of the days-long hearing on the proposed bill, more than 1,000 people testified. Even after the hearing ended, a microphone was set up beneath the Capitol dome each day so that speakers could continue to address the assembled crowds.

For some it was the first time they felt their voice mattered. Videographer Matt Wisniewski, who spent weeks documenting and participating in the protests, observed how powerful it was "to have people listen to you and care about what you were saying, in a culture that doesn't always value that."

These speeches and shared testimonies were a form of resistance, of making the fight personal, and of energizing fellow demonstrators by reminding each other why they were there and what was at stake. One by one, these stories were woven together to create a narrative that was stronger than any one voice could ever be.

@LegalEagle Legal Eagle
Capitol is PACKED. I cannot move. I smell like I imagine a sumo wrestler might. I'm so sexy.
6:32pm Feb 16

@LegalEagle Legal Eagle
RT @rjetty: Scott Walker is the best union organizer that I've seen in ages.
7:17pm Feb 16

@ddayen David Dayen
Obama tells WTMJ in Milwaukee that Wisconsin bill stripping public employee rights "seems like more of an assault on unions."
7:36pm Feb 16

@MelissaRyan Melissa Ryan
900 people spoke at the hearing last night and today.
7:51pm Feb 16

@DefendWisconsin Defend Wisconsin
Dem senator says: I'm convinced that the nation if not the world is watching. **#wiunion #killthisbill**
8:06pm Feb 16

@TAA_Madison TAA Madison
Madison, Monona Grove, Verona, Oregon, Middleton Waunakee, Deforest, and Oshkosh schools will be closed tomorrow. **#wiunion**
9:03pm Feb 16

@LegalEagle Legal Eagle
Can no longer hear JFC over chants of "the people united will never be defeated." **#wisolidarity #wiunion #notmywi**
9:32pm Feb 16

@cabell Cabell Gathman
thx 4 encouragement, everyone. I broke mental promise not 2 cry, but I got through it. Woman nxt 2 me was v. nice. **#wiunion #killthisbill**
9:34pm Feb 16

IT'S A FARMERS' ISSUE

Tony Schultz
MARCH 12, 2011

Tony Schultz is a family farmer in Athens, Wisconsin, and board member of Family Farm Defenders. The following is text of a speech given by Schultz at the farmer labor solidarity "tractorcade" on March 12, 2011.

My name is Tony Schultz. I'm a member of Family Farm Defenders farmers union, and I'm a third generation family farmer, born and raised on a 50-cow dairy. Today my partner Kat and I run our farm as a 150-member CSA[1] with some beefers, maple syrup, and chickens and pigs. I came back to the family farm after college because of my values; and it's the values that I'm reminded of every time I look at our state's license plate and see that little red barn. It's values that I think overlap entirely with the values of the labor movement.

Family farmers, like the labor movement, value the dignity of being able to have some control over your work and your life, to be empowered by your work—not alienated by it. Family farmers, like the labor movement, value the means to have a beautiful and constructive setting to raise a family. Family farmers, like the labor movement, value economic democracy.

[1] Community Supported Agriculture

What is a union anyway, but working people coming together, acting together to improve their lives? And that is what we are here to do: to act together, to speak together in solidarity, saying, "We reject this union-busting bill, and we reject this budget!"

Solidarity between farmers and workers is an old and sacred alliance of producers that dates back beyond the populist movement, when workers and farmers came together to struggle for a progressive income tax, for a financial system that served the people, for unions and the eight-hour day.

Listen to these quotes. It was over 120 years ago when Tom Watson, the Georgia Populist, said—and this couldn't be truer—"The fruits of the toil of millions are boldly stolen to build up the fortunes of a few unprecedented in human history." Ignatius Donnelly, the Minnesota Populist, said in 1890, "The interests of rural and urban labor are the same. Their enemies are identical." For more than 100 years we have been fighting together, we have been picketing together, we've been dumping milk, we've been sitting in, we've been blocking traffic, and we are going to take this state back!

And yet there are those who tell us that this isn't a farmers' issue. Those people have petty resentment that is amplified by right-wing radio until they think that a fireman's pension is the problem. And then there are groups that represent this evil: The Dairy Business Association was here on Wednesday at "Ag day at the Capitol" saying, "Hooray for Walker's budget." Well, I want you to know that those aren't farmers. They're agribusiness corporations with a few factory farmers in front, and I want Wisconsin and the world to know that this is the real Ag Day at the Capitol, and this is a farmers' issue.

It's a farmers' issue because our rural schools are getting decimated by this budget, and they are the centers of our small towns and rural communities. In my hometown of Athens, 14 of 44 teachers got pink slips, and will be laid off because of this budget. It's bad for our children's education, it's bad for the stability of our town, it's bad for the very future of our school district, and we say no!

It's a farmers' issue because Scott Walker wants to hack BadgerCare. Eleven thousand Family Farm members depend on BadgerCare because of the exclusivity of for-profit health insurance companies, and because of the pathetic and volatile price we receive for milk and other commodities that don't meet the cost of our production. We depend on this, and we support BadgerCare!

It's a farmers' issue because we have been battling corporate power for more than a century—this budget could not be a clearer manifestation of corporate power, and we say no.

It's a farmers' issue because public workers are our friends, and neighbors, and our family members, and we stand in solidarity with them!

It a farmers' issue because we know that we're all in this together. We go up together or we go down together. The way I see it is we got two choices: I can have my unions busted and stand alone and be pitted against my neighbor in a desperate and unequal economy, or we can come together to say 'This is what our families need, this is what our communities need, this is what a just wage is, this is what a democracy looks like!' It's a farmers' issue because we understand that an injury to one is an injury to all! Solidarity!

@TAA_Madison TAA Madison
All of Milwaukee public schools will be closed tomorrow. **#wiunion**
#killthisbill
9:45pm Feb 16

@millbot Emily Mills
Seeing lots of blankets, pillows & sleeping bags coming out. **#wiunion**
#notmywi
10:20pm Feb 16

@KristineLZ Kristine LZ
RT @uwlaxecho: Support a teacher. Wear red tomorrow. We @WEAC"
10:34pm Feb 16

@LegalEagle Legal Eagle
Party line vote against Democratic amendment to restore collective
bargaining. Amendment fails. **#wisolidarity #notmywi**
11:11pm Feb 16

@emmahduhjemmah Emma Gibbens
HELL YEAH! You are on the wrong side of history and on the wrong side
of justice! You tell em Sen Jauch!
11:24pm Feb 16

@DefendWisconsin Defend Wisconsin
Everyone remember to register to testify in the GAR room, 4th floor north,
to keep the hearing going all night #killthisbill **#wiunion**
11:38pm Feb 16

@LegalEagle Legal Eagle
Sen Glenn Grothman just used phrase "so-called community leaders".
I hope some of those leaders organize our communities against him.
11:38pm Feb 16

@emmahduhjemmah Emma Gibbens
More and more people are arriving. I love democracy.
11:44pm Feb 16

DEAR SCOTT WALKER

Sigrid Peterson
FEBRUARY 14, 2011

Dear Governor Walker,

I doubt you remember me. In fact, we've never formally met, but you and I grew up not half a block away from each other in the small town of Delavan, Wisconsin. You were in my sister Katie's high school class, though perhaps you didn't know her then (indeed, she was a brainy punk rocker, while you were a mullet-haired jock). Six years your junior, I have only fuzzy memories of you—of riding my bike around the corner, seeing one of the "older boys" in the neighborhood walk out of his house on West Wisconsin Street, and hearing my sister say, "Hey, there's Scott Walker."

Our limited acquaintance notwithstanding, within the past four days I fear I've gotten to know you fairly well, or well enough. So perhaps it's time I introduce myself. My name is Sigrid Peterson. I'm your former neighbor from Delavan, and I'm a public-sector worker in Wisconsin.

If it isn't obvious, I'm writing to ask you, your administration, and your Republican friends in the legislature to put a swift stop to your proposed "budget-repair" bill, along with its crude and unapologetic assault on 50 years of rights and benefits granted to Wisconsin's public-sector employees. Your measure is nothing short of devastating—stripping most (in some cases, all) of our collective bargaining rights, incapacitating any future resources of our unions, and further straining the livability and reach of our compensation with steep increases in employee contributions to health care and pensions.

And you do this with nothing but unsubstantiated excuses that this is the "only alternative." And you do this with no effort (none) to meet with workers since you took office. Forgive me, but this makes you no more forthright or articulate than a tongue-tied and cowardly teenager breaking up with his girlfriend/boyfriend via text message. Does this mean you'll bring back your mullet too?

If I'm irreverent, Governor Walker, I assure you it's in service to things greater than concern over my job, alone. I write this out of respect for my late father too—your old neighbor, a lifelong Wisconsinite, and a public municipal employee. I also write this out of pride in the progressive legacy of my home state, a legacy you and your colleagues delight in dismantling.

My dad, Lyle (raised in Richland Center, Wisconsin), was living proof that a public-sector job—with its modest salary but good benefits—garners more than the sum of its parts. More importantly, he taught me that we should celebrate (versus vilify) this form of work arrangement and ensure that we fight for the same for workers in every sector of the economy.

Dad raised me and my seven brothers and sisters on a comparatively small municipal accountant's salary of $32,000 a year. That salary not only fed (with lots of spaghetti) and housed us, but slimly subsidized all eight of our undergraduate educations at the University of Wisconsin-Madison. His affordable health insurance treated eight cases of chicken pox, 33 episodes of tonsillitis, and paid for a total of 137 stitches. Most importantly, his comprehensive health care saw my mom, Shirley (raised in Muscoda, Wisconsin), through two years of chemotherapy treatments, and carried Dad to the end of his 10-year battle with cardiomyopathy.

Dad's pension with the Wisconsin Retirement System is a lifesaver to my mother in her older years. Mom had to exit the formal labor force at a young age in favor of unpaid work in the home to feed, clothe, love, and educate eight good and generous people. She still lives in Delavan, Dad's pension serving as her fixed income against the backdrop of a labor market that would have punished (if not outright dismissed) her after 40 years of bringing up kids.

Five of those kids (and their families) live in Wisconsin today. We are teachers, public attorneys, university doctors, web engineers, and business people. We give to our local communities. My mom, in particular, has spent a lifetime in volunteer service to Delavan fighting for clean watersheds, transparent city government, the preservation of public education, and accountable economic development toward quality jobs.

I'm her sixth daughter and seventh child. Two and half years ago, I left a career in New York City to be close to her in Wisconsin and to pursue my dream of getting a Ph.D. I'm currently a graduate student in our top-ranked Department of Geography, as well as an employee of the University of Wisconsin-Madison. Similarly to teaching assistants (TAs, or full-time graduate students who dedicate more than twenty hours a week to instructing undergraduates), I devote over half of my workweek as a University project assistant (PA). I am part of the staff in a policy research center in the Department of Sociology devoted to growing Wisconsin's economy through statewide partnerships between businesses and workers. That job (which grants me membership in AFT local 3220, the Teaching Assistants' Association, or TAA) provides a small take-home salary of just over $12,000 a year, along with state health insurance to help me weather winter infections and viruses. Importantly, my job also grants me a tuition waiver, without which I could never afford to pursue training in the academy. I know just how lucky I am, and my greatest goal is to repay this debt by becoming a professor in a land grant institution like the University of Wisconsin, giving back to young people seeking an affordable public education, as well as helping them get the most out of a few short years of engaging in the profound fun that is thinking and learning. Your proposal, Governor Walker, seeks to strip me of the contractual rights to the benefits allowing me to stay here, and I am frightened over what my future holds if it passes.

As ambitious as it is damaging, your bill is also of grave offense to the progressive legacy of the state of Wisconsin, a legacy my father held dear, and one I bragged wildly about in New York. While there, I worked on the physical and economic redevelopment of Lower Manhattan's central business district ("Wall Street"), following its decimation from the terrorist attacks of 9/11. As typical New Yorkers often do, my friends and colleagues would tease me for hailing from "one of those funny-shaped states in the middle." I'd always take their jab with good humor, but try to explain just how deeply proud I was of Wisconsin's good people and progressive history—the land of Bob La Follette, Gaylord Nelson, Frank Zeidler, and Russ Feingold.

My job in the city demanded I work with various CEOs and executives of major Wall Street corporations, and on limited occasions, when our job titles and ranks melted away (perhaps prior to a breakfast meeting or during a casual work gathering), we spoke candidly about personal interests. My nerdy obsession with cities and the history of workers came up frequently. And what amazed me was the reverence these otherwise powerful actors of private enterprise expressed for the city, county, and state employees who kept the Big Apple running. Maybe it's the sheer humility one feels when confronted with New York's awesome, gritty mass of physical infrastructure and embodied space, but I met power brokers who deeply respected the men and women laboring for the metropolis, day in and day out. None of the executives with whom I worked were anti-union, nor would they have ever rubber-stamped such a bold-faced erosion to public workers' basic rights and livelihoods as you endorse today.

While your version of Wisconsin's "door" may indeed be "open for business," I doubt the business people I know would care to walk through it, especially now—try as you might to steeply discount the entry ticket.

I leave in a few weeks to visit New York, to see my very good friends, and to catch them up on my goings-on in Wisconsin. I still have things to brag about, of course. I still get to live among the kind, committed, and understatedly clever folks of my upbringing everyday. And I get to work for our tremendous state university, in a department I respect immensely, and with people I love. But I regret to say, Governor Walker, I brag a bit less enthusiastically, now. You disappoint me, old neighbor. What's worse, you don't just disappoint me, you embarrass me, you embarrass my father, you embarrass Delavan, and you embarrass the state of Wisconsin.

Please stop your bill, for all our sakes.

@LegalEagle Legal Eagle
The vote is now.
11:52pm Feb 16

@LegalEagle Legal Eagle
12-4 on party lines, the budget repair bill is sent to the Legislature.
And with that, it's back to protesting.
11:53pm Feb 16

@millbot Emily Mills
Big day across Wisconsin tomorrow. Big thanks to everyone out there
fighting the good fight. See you in the morning! **#wiunion #notmywi**
12:04am Feb 17

MY MANIFESTO, OR WHY I FIGHT FOR WORKERS RIGHTS IN WISCONSIN

JOANNE STAUDACHER
MARCH 18, 2011

Joanne Staudacher posted the following as a note on Facebook.

This is the text of the sign I wore on my back when I marched at the Capitol last. It is my manifesto, my statement of purpose, and every word is truth. My manifesto was limited to the size of what I could carry on my back, could have used some better planning, had to have an amendment over my two-poster limit and I had to tie it around my throat like a cape to keep it all visible. I broke the lines in the same way that my medium and handwriting dictated.

I fight for the people I love, the people I have loved, the people I will love. I fight for the land beneath my feet. I fight for people who don't agree with me, because I still want them to have a beautiful future. Yes, some of you tagged will not agree with me. I still offer you my story, my motivation, my intent, and the better future I hope we will share.

This is why I fight. This is why I will not give up. I have made this note visible to "Everyone"—feel free to share it, to comment on it, to think about it—whatever makes you happy. This is why I fight, for better I hope, not worse. The war isn't over. In true badger fashion, we dig in and hold fast:

Dear Walker & Hopper:

I AM WISCONSIN.

Conceived, born, raised,

educated, employed + unemployed,

living still, and hope to die.

My father is a forester, methodist, veteran.

My mother is a seamstress, CCD teacher, devout Catholic.

Both sides farmed. I come from

hardworking, determined, long-lived stock.

I am unemployed. I am pro-union.

I have worked for pay in homes, yards,

restaurants, offices, computer labs, warehouses,

thrift stores, and college classrooms.

I have a Ph.D.

I have been a literacy tutor, humane society

volunteer—I've donated money, food, blood,

and time.

I am a daughter, wife, sister, aunt, niece,

cousin, friend, mentor. I will be a mother.

I will not see my children's future spoiled.

I sewed my own wedding dress + changed my alternator.

I am a deer hunter who bakes vegan cookies.

I'm equal parts June Cleaver + meat cleaver.

I am educated, creative, passionate. Complex.

I have been Chippewa Falls, Holcombe, Eau Claire,

Prairie du Chien, Milwaukee, Fond du Lac, Green Bay.

I am Oshkosh.

I stand before you in my science

camp T-shirt + thrift store skirt.

I am not a slob. If I were

lazy, I wouldn't be here.

You may not remember folks

like me, but I WILL RECALL

YOU.

I am Wisconsin, and I am

NOT alone!

@eigenjo Jo Nelson
the world has its eye on is. let's make sure it is focused on our massive peaceful demonstrations today. **#notmywi #killthisbill #wiunion**
9:13am Feb 17

@MelissaRyan Melissa Ryan
National media finally taking notice of what's happening here in Wisconsin. **#notmyWI**
9:37am Feb 17

@scoutprime scoutprime
Sign--100% of teachers better educated than Gov Walker. (he's hs grad for u out of staters)
10:15am Feb 17

@aemilli Emily
whole building just sang national anthem **#notmywi**
10:42am Feb 17

@aemilli Emily
chanting at the senators going in to vote! kill the bill! **#notmywi**
10:56am Feb 17

@emmahduhjemmah Emma Gibbens
@sentaylor you go girl! Don't tell me where you're off to! :D
11:19am Feb 17

@DefendWisconsin Defend Wisconsin
This is a great thing! The Senate will not be able to vote because they will not have quorum. STAY IN THE CAPITOL! **#killthisbill #wiunion**
11:20am Feb 17

@bluecheddar1 blue cheddar
So what I gather: A vote can't be taken if Dem Senators walk out - as they have. Needed are 20 Senators. There are only 17 now. .... :-)
11:24am Feb 17

@micahuetricht Micah Uetricht
Democratic reps just walked out of the capitol. No vote on Walker's bill. **#wiunion**
11:32am Feb 17

AMERICA IS NOT BROKE

Michael Moore
MARCH 5, 2011

Speech delivered at the Wisconsin Capitol

America is not broke.

Contrary to what those in power would like you to believe so that you'll give up your pension, cut your wages, and settle for the life your great-grandparents had, America is not broke. Not by a long shot. The country is awash in wealth and cash. It's just that it's not in your hands. It has been transferred, in the greatest heist in history, from the workers and consumers to the banks and the portfolios of the uber-rich.

Today just 400 Americans have more wealth than half of all Americans combined.

Let me say that again. Four hundred obscenely rich people, most of whom benefited in some way from the multitrillion-dollar taxpayer "bail-out" of 2008, now have more loot, stock, and property than the assets of 155 million Americans combined. If you can't bring yourself to call that a financial coup d'etat, then you are simply not being honest about what you know in your heart to be true.

And I can see why. For us to admit that we have let a small group of men abscond with and hoard the bulk of the wealth that runs our economy, would mean that we'd have to accept the humiliating acknowledgment that we have indeed surrendered our precious democracy to the moneyed elite. Wall Street, the banks, and the Fortune 500 now run this Republic—and, until this past month, the rest of us have felt completely helpless, unable to find a way to do anything about it.

I have nothing more than a high school degree. But back when I was in school, every student had to take one semester of economics in order to graduate. And here's what I learned: Money doesn't grow on trees. It grows when we make things. It grows when we have good jobs with good wages that we use to buy the things we need and thus create more jobs. It grows when we provide an outstanding educational system that then grows a new generation of inventors, entrepreneurs, artists, scientists, and thinkers who come up with the next great idea for the planet. And that new idea creates new jobs and that creates revenue for the state. But if those who have the most money don't pay their fair share of taxes, the state can't function. The schools can't produce the best and the brightest who will go on to create those jobs. If the wealthy get to keep most of their money, we have seen what they will do with it: recklessly gamble it on crazy Wall Street schemes and crash our economy. The crash they created cost us millions of jobs. That too caused a reduction in revenue. And the population ended up suffering because they reduced their taxes, reduced our jobs, and took wealth out of the system, removing it from circulation.

The nation is not broke, my friends. Wisconsin is not broke. It's part of the Big Lie. It's one of the three biggest lies of the decade: America/Wisconsin is broke, Iraq has WMD, the Packers can't win the Super Bowl without Brett Favre.

The truth is, there's lots of money to go around. LOTS. It's just that those in charge have diverted that wealth into a deep well that sits on their well-guarded estates. They know they have committed crimes to make this happen, and they know that someday you may want to see some of that money that used to be yours. So they have bought and paid for hundreds of politicians across the country to do their bidding for them. But just in case that doesn't work, they've got their gated communities, and the luxury jet is always fully fueled, the engines running, waiting for that day they hope never comes. To help prevent that day when the people demand their country back, the wealthy have done two very smart things:

1. They control the message. By owning most of the media they have expertly convinced many Americans of few means to buy their version of

the American Dream and to vote for their politicians. Their version of the Dream says that you, too, might be rich some day—this is America, where anything can happen if you just apply yourself! They have conveniently provided you with believable examples to show you how a poor boy can become a rich man, how the child of a single mother in Hawaii can become president, how a guy with a high school education can become a successful filmmaker. They will play these stories for you over and over again all day long so that the last thing you will want to do is upset the apple cart—because you—yes, you, too!—might be rich/president/an Oscar winner some day! The message is clear: Keep your head down, your nose to the grindstone, don't rock the boat, and be sure to vote for the party that protects the rich man that you might be some day.

2. They have created a poison pill that they know you will never want to take. It is their version of mutually-assured destruction. And when they threatened to release this weapon of mass economic annihilation in September of 2008, we blinked. As the economy and the stock market went into a tailspin, and the banks were caught conducting a worldwide Ponzi scheme, Wall Street issued this threat: Either hand over trillions of dollars from the American taxpayers or we will crash this economy straight into the ground. Fork it over or it's goodbye savings accounts. Goodbye pensions. Goodbye United States Treasury. Goodbye jobs and homes and future. It was friggin' awesome, and it scared the shit out of everyone. "Here! Take our money! We don't care. We'll even print more for you! Just take it! But, please, leave our lives alone, PLEASE!"

The executives in the board rooms and hedge funds could not contain their laughter, their glee, and within three months they were writing each other huge bonus checks and marveling at how perfectly they had played a nation full of suckers. Millions lost their jobs anyway, and millions lost their homes. But there was no revolt (see No. 1).

Until now. On Wisconsin! Never has a Michigander been more happy to share a big, great lake with you! You have aroused the sleeping giant known as the working people of the United States of America. Right now the earth is shaking, and the ground is shifting under the feet of those who are in charge. Your message has inspired people in all 50 states and that message is: WE HAVE HAD IT! We reject anyone who tells us America is broke and broken. It's just the opposite! We are rich with talent and ideas and hard work and, yes, love. Love and compassion toward those who have, through no fault of their own, ended up as the least among us. But they still crave what we all crave: our country back! Our democracy back! Our good name back! The United States of America. NOT the Corporate States of America. The United States of America!

So how do we get this? Well, we do it with a little bit of Egypt here, a little bit of Madison there. And let us pause for a moment and remember that it was a poor man with a fruit stand in Tunisia who gave his life so that the world might focus its attention on how a government run by billionaires for billionaires is an affront to freedom and morality and humanity.

Thank you, Wisconsin. You have made people realize this was our last best chance to grab the final thread of what was left of who we are as Americans. For three weeks you have stood in the cold, slept on the floor, skipped out of town to Illinois—whatever it took, you have done it, and one thing is for certain: Madison is only the beginning. The smug rich have overplayed their hand. They couldn't have just been content with the money they raided from the Treasury. They couldn't be satiated by simply removing millions of jobs and shipping them overseas to exploit the poor elsewhere. No, they had to have more—something more than all the riches in the world. They had to have our soul. They had to strip us of our dignity. They had to shut us up and shut us down so that we could not even sit at a table with them and bargain about simple things like classroom size, or bulletproof vests for everyone on the police force, or letting a pilot just get a few extra hours sleep so he or she can do their job—their $19,000 a year job. That's how much some rookie pilots on commuter airlines make, maybe even the rookie pilots flying people here to Madison. But he's stopped trying to get better pay. All he asks is that he doesn't have to sleep in his car between shifts at O'Hare Airport. That's how despicably low we have sunk. The wealthy couldn't be content with just paying this man $19,000 a year. They wanted to take away his sleep. They wanted to demean and dehumanize him. After all, he's just another slob.

And that, my friends, is corporate America's fatal mistake. But in trying to destroy us they have given birth to a movement—a movement that is becoming a massive, nonviolent revolt across the country. We all knew there had to be a breaking point some day, and that point is upon us. Many people in the media don't understand this. They say they were caught off guard about Egypt, never saw it coming. Now they act surprised and flummoxed about why so many hundreds of thousands have come to Madison over the last three weeks during brutal winter weather. "Why are they all standing out there in the cold? I mean there was that election in November, and that was supposed to be that!"

"There's something happening here, and you don't know what it is, do you...?"

America ain't broke! The only thing that's broke is the moral compass of the rulers. And we aim to fix that compass and steer the ship ourselves from now on. Never forget, as long as that Constitution of ours still stands, it's one person, one vote, and it's the thing the rich hate most about America—because even though they seem to hold all the money and all the cards, they begrudgingly know this one unshakeable basic fact: There are more of us than there are of them!

Madison, do not retreat. We are with you. We will win together.

#ONEDAYLONGER

@MelissaRyan
Back inside. Taking a moment to absorb everything. So many people documenting this on phones. Everyone is the media. **#notmyWI**

DO NOT RETREAT, RETWEET

EVEN AFTER THE WISCONSIN PROTESTS HIT THE PAGES
and screens of the mainstream media, it was Twitter and blogs, photos
and web videos that remained the best ways of following the latest in the
#WIunion story.

Twitter updates scrolled continuously; go-to tweeters posted photos of
the growing crowds, told followers when and where help was needed, and
solicited donations of food and supplies. They recruited speakers for television shows looking to cover the story, and challenged traditional media for
failing to cover the protests and for portraying the peaceful demonstrators
as violent troublemakers.

An outspoken group of Wisconsin bloggers called out Republican
shenanigans and helped shape the broader media's protest coverage.
Rabble-rousing and proudly progressive, the bloggers of the Wisconsin
"Cheddarsphere" turned the protests into a national story that soon drew
support from a vibrant community of netroots bloggers across the country. And it was a blogger who provided the strangest yet most revealing
moment of the whole saga, when Ian Murphy, pretending to be billionaire Republican donor David Koch, prank-called Walker. The call, if a
somewhat questionable journalistic tactic, made headlines, revealing that
Walker had considered planting "troublemakers" among the protesters

to provoke violence, and contemplated laying a trap for the Democratic senators who were on the run.

Online organizing led to real results—the millions of dollars raised nationally to help with recall elections, stories that bubbled up from Twitter and blogs to the mainstream media—while also spreading the protests' message in less tangible but equally powerful ways. Tens of thousands of people watched the videos that Matt Wisniewski filmed from inside the Capitol, and over a hundred thousand watched live video that online activist Ben Brandzel broadcast from the Capitol on his iPhone on the night of the first real conflict between police and protesters.

Just as those occupying the Capitol had found a way to take government into their own hands, these bloggers, videographers, and activists had found ways to take control of and tell their own story to the world.

@micahuetricht Micah Uetricht
Walking around Madison, the convos I'm overhearing are wild. Rank and file union workers are livid. Never seen anything like this in my life
11:50am Feb 17

@micahuetricht Micah Uetricht
More than a few people here are talking general strike. **#solidarityWI**
12:53pm Feb 17

@ThisBowers Chris Bowers
RT @Atrios i've got some extra room. the WI dems can crash at my place if they want / **#wiconsin #solidarity**
1:06pm Feb 17

@MelissaRyan Melissa Ryan
News about the 14 Senators who have left the state has everyone here at @barriques excited and re-energized. **#NotmyWI #aslongasittakes**
2:18pm Feb 17

@eigenjo Jo Nelson
huffpo wants to get in touch with a firefighter in wisconsin to interview. anyone interested? mention me and i'll DM you with info.
2:44pm Feb 17

@brianekdale Brian Ekdale
cop near us is swaying and texting **#sheswithus #wiunion**
3:23pm Feb 17

@scoutprime scoutprime
Balloons carrying poster of fist released to top pf Rotunda. Everyone went crazy. **#wiunion #killthebill**
3:31pm Feb 17

@MelissaRyan Melissa Ryan
RT @daveweigel: RT @mamaier262: RT @ufcw: Winning the internet - Wisconsin Democratic State Senator tells @govwalker she'll "brb"
4:06pm Feb 17

#WIUNION

Natasha Chart
MAY 3, 2011

Adapted from the Service Employees International Union (SEIU) Blog

So much has changed politically in Wisconsin in the last three months. It shows up clearly in one timeline of the Wisconsin union struggle, which begins with historic-low polling favorability for unions and finishes with jaw-droppingly bad polling for Wisconsin's brand new governor.

The public groundswell of opposition to Governor Scott Walker's attack on workers' rights has changed. It's gone from getting thousands of people to the Capitol every day and tens of thousands every weekend, to getting a few people there every day while mobilizing volunteers to mount and contribute to recall campaigns against Wisconsin Republicans.

The shape of national and social media interest has also changed. Last Thursday, for the first time since the February peak of the protests in Madison, "Wisconsin" dropped from the list of top tags on *Daily Kos*, the largest community blog in the progressive netroots.

The popular #WIunion tag on Twitter no longer updates too fast to read everything, though it still sees regular use, and has been superseded by the #wirecall and #wivote tags that started being used as the energy of protest politics was shifted towards electoral politics.

As we're likely to be feeling the ripple of recent events in Wisconsin for a long time to come, it's a good point at which to look back at some of the early social media milestones before they're lost in the flood. Whatever else it was and is, the #WIunion struggle was mostly a word-of-mouth popular uprising, driven in large part by citizen media and email activism, inspiring people all over the country. If we're lucky, we'll see its like again.

The list of social media milestones you'll find below could have been three times as long, or more. Hopefully, it's just long enough to capture the sense of community purpose and public conversation that made #WIunion a powerful experience.

1: The Call

The infamous call, where *Buffalo Beast* blogger Ian Murphy impersonated David Koch and recorded the 20 minutes of conversation he then had with Walker, was one of the most shocking, if not gonzo, media moments of the "budget-repair" bill fight. Listeners marveled at the amount of time the governor made available, on short notice and without an appointment, for someone that he thought was a billionaire campaign contributor of his. At the same time Walker bragged about his exploits to "Koch," almost as if he were giving a progress update to a boss, his staff was telling Democratic state senators that he was too busy to talk to them.

2: The Mistress

The report, via a chain of blog posts and a little sleuthing by *Blogging Blue*'s Zach Wisniewski, that not only was Republican state Sen. Randy Hopper living with his 25-year-old mistress in Madison, but that she was also a lobbyist, generated a media firestorm. The story was prominently picked up by *Firedoglake*, and spurred a fundraising action on *Daily Kos* to run ads on the topic to support the Hopper recall campaign.

3: They Begged To Differ

Blogger Chris Liebenthal covered the budget fight and protests through the largely editorial posts in the "solidarity" archive on *Cognitive Dissidence*.

Liebenthal's chronicling of the *Milwaukee Journal Sentinel*'s support of Walker before its eventual criticism of him over the budget fight in late February is exemplary of the way bloggers in the aggregate tend to connect these sorts of dots into larger stories, in ways that mainstream media outlets often won't. Liebenthal has countered Walker's claims about public employees and has continued to focus on issues such as alleged "cost-cutting" measures that will actually cost the state millions.

4: They Mopped the Floors

Allison Hantschel of *First Draft* started covering the protests early, with extensive photo archives on the blog and Flickr stream. Hantschel immediately got the story out that these were peaceful, positive events, striking back against the talking points of Walker's allies with personal stories and editorials, and larger photo diaries from all the big weekend rallies.

Key posts include a photo diary of protesters washing the Capitol floor and playing chess, a review of the UW-Madison privatization plan, and an eyewitness debunking of the claim that protesters took hinges off Capitol building doors.

5: They Built a Town

David Dayen of *Firedoglake* provided one of the definitive eyewitness reports on "The Incredible Ecosystem of the Wisconsin State Capitol," when the national blog decided that this was a big enough deal to send a correspondent. This is fairly rare for even large blogs, who tend not to cover events in person if they don't have writers nearby. It's likely that this wouldn't have happened if the local blogs hadn't followed the story from the beginning and helped keep it alive.

6: They Got Pizza

Word got out that Ian's Pizza on State Street was taking its leftover pizzas to the Capitol protests while the building was being occupied 24 hours a day during the Assembly Democrats' marathon budget-repair bill hearings. Some bloggers noticed and asked people to call in orders to be delivered to the protesters so that Ian's would get reimbursed. People on Twitter were made aware. The local *Journal Sentinel* and *The New York Times* heard about it.

Ian's Pizza got call-in orders for the protesters from all 50 states, Washington, D.C., Egypt, Antarctica, and dozens of other countries. A few weeks in, they got so many orders that they opened the doors and gave away their food for free to anyone who walked in and placed an order, in addition to continuing to deliver their widely-praised pizzas to the protests down the block at the Capitol.

Ian's also makes salads. They were delicious.

7: They Got Thrown Out

Madison blog *Dane 101*'s archive of state government stories featured extensive photo diaries, covered day-by-day developments at the Capitol, and put the spotlight on stories such as the illegal contributions made to Walker's campaign by wealthy railroad executives. They also posted video of some key moments, such as footage of citizens being removed from the state Assembly antechamber in advance of a March 11 vote on a stand-alone bill to strip state workers' collective bargaining rights.

8: The Whole Country Watched

Until Thursday, April 28, the "Wisconsin" tag steadily remained among the 20 most popular on *Daily Kos*. This national blog, while it didn't send a correspondent, has prominently featured diaries by community members (including teachers and other union workers) from Wisconsin and interested political enthusiasts from around the country. Front-page authors picked up the story and covered the topic daily during the height of the protests and budget standoff, as well as educating people about the recall effort.

During the first electoral contest following the peak of Capitol protests, the Wisconsin Supreme Court race between David Prosser and JoAnne Kloppenburg, a front page analysis of the procedures being followed in the investigation of vote totals in Waukesha was significant in quelling conspiracy theories about the election's outcome. And while Kloppenburg lost in the final count, many onlookers were amazed that she'd made up a 30-point deficit in the polls to come so close to unseating the incumbent, Prosser.

9: They Would Not Be Silent

#WIunion: This hashtag isn't the one that was initially favored by the unions. It was actually started by Kristian Knutsen of the *Isthmus*, Madison's alternative weekly paper, on Feb. 11 and used as a tag for their daily blog coverage, well before events in Madison became a national story. With a first-mover advantage like that in the Wisconsin Twittersphere, it was the one that stuck, even trending worldwide at one point. Although the pace has slowed considerably, it was updating on April 2 at a rate of two to three times per minute, minimum, and still gets updated with new content at least every five minutes or so during the day.

Other tags worth mentioning: #notmywi, #solidaritywi, #wirecall, and #wivote. For the nationwide fightback, #statesos and #1u have been picking up steam ever since.

Also noteworthy on Twitter, Melissa Ryan, Sen. Russ Feingold's former new media director, put together the lists of key local bloggers and #WIunion allies for others who wanted to follow their perspective on events.

10: They Took Pictures of Each Other

This list would be woefully incomplete without a mention of several independent films of the protests posted to Vimeo, by 23-year-old Matt Wisniewski (no relation to Zach Wisniewski of *Blogging Blue*), set to popular songs and cut together from his own footage of the Capitol protests. While not blog posts, as such, these video montages (though there were many others, and multiple livestreams, and many Flickr archives of still photos) will define the event for tens of thousands of people who weren't able to be there in person, and even for many who were.

When people asked if you saw "the protest videos" in Madison at the peak of the demonstrations, chances were, they meant these.

11: They Watched the World

A time-lapse video of global protests and uprisings from Dec. 18, 2010–March 7, 2011 was put together by John Caelan of *SwampPost*, and added to his site on March 9, 2011. The video link spread like wildfire over Twitter, tapping into popular sentiment among the activist community that saw protests in Madison and other state capitals as part of a global wave of populist uprisings, each unique to their situations but inspired by the same longing for more just societies.

12: They Raised Some Dough

The online fundraising driven by the #WIunion events and national publicity definitely deserves its own spotlight. As they head into an unprecedented season of recall elections, Wisconsin Democrats start with a cash advantage in excess of $1 million, and to thank for it, they can mostly look to four online activist organizations that are unaffiliated with either a Democratic Party committee or any of the unions involved (these are MoveOn.org, Democracy for America, the Progressive Change Campaign Committee, and *Daily Kos*).

As of May 2, over $3 million was raised online from more than 173,000 people, putting the average donation at a little over $17.

And then ...

Wisconsinites were so fired up that they began collecting signatures to recall six Republican state senators in special elections this summer. Soon after, Walker signed a bill that that made it more difficult for seniors, students, and people of color to be heard at the polls. In Wisconsin and around the country, conservatives are stepping up their attacks on workers and democracy following the *Citizens United* Supreme Court decision that unlimited corporate money could be poured into politics.

Increased protests over cuts to education, health care, mass transit, public safety, and job security in the #WIunion era have been met with bipartisan proposals for even bigger cuts at every level of government. Often, these cuts are offered side by side with tax cuts for millionaires and big business. These are not the results the protesters were looking for.

Still, there were results. There was intense, unfiltered public conversation through social networking sites. Volunteers were recruited on websites. Funds were raised over email. Could there be more someday?

"Whose house? Our house!" was a regular chant in Madison and, I've heard, wherever governors are launching attacks on working people. Yet, it's going to take a lot of work before the people who work in "our" houses start acting like it again.

Though once upon a time, even having unions was a pipe dream. "One person, one vote," used to be a laughable proposition. For those ideals, people past and present have faced despots and tear gas, nooses and clubs. So I have great faith that the final outcome, eventually, will be justice for all.

Because I've seen what democracy looks like. It's pretty great. I think everybody will want some.

@analieseeicher Analiese Eicher
RT @chicagobars: Free drinks on me for any WI state senators hiding out in Chicago from Gov Scott Walker's power play.
4:22pm Feb 17

@LegalEagle Legal Eagle
When all of this is over, I want to be in a dark room with a stiff drink. And also a scalp massage.
4:44pm Feb 17

@micahuetricht Micah Uetricht
Anyone who has ever complained that the American populace is too lazy to fight back should be in Madison right now. **#unionWI #killthebill**
4:45pm Feb 17

@cabell Cabell Gathman
RT @nateckennedy: 30,000 people protesting in Wisconsin and Fox News is talking about the "silent majority" who disagrees. Sheesh.
4:51pm Feb 17

@DefendWisconsin Defend Wisconsin
Please be peaceful and non-violent. This is OUR state capitol. There is food and water available. We are winning this. **#wiunion**
4:54pm Feb 17

@JacquelynGill Jacquelyn Gill
I defy anyone with a soul to feel the energy of >30,000 workers and students crying for justice & not feel moved. Walker isn't. **#wiunion**
4:57pm Feb 17

@MelissaRyan Melissa Ryan
Text from my Mom, watching cable news from KY: Watching the news. Rallies getting more and more coverage. Tons. Keep fighting! **#WIunion**
5:18pm Feb 17

@LegalEagle Legal Eagle
I am not a union member. My job doesn't provide ANY health care. I don't have a pension. I'm still in solidarity with **#notmywi #wiunion**.
5:48pm Feb 17

@bluecheddar1 blue cheddar
No profile 2 pick out I see dudes in sweatshrts n on the mullet side along w.hipsters aside oldr couples **#wiunion**
7:04am Feb 17

GIVING A FACE TO THE PROTEST: INTERVIEW WITH VIDEO-GRAPHER MATT WISNIEWSKI

Erica Sagrans
MAY 2, 2011

Matt Wisniewski is videographer and public employee at the University of Wisconsin-Madison. Wisniewski, who was 23 at the time of the protests, created powerful videos from the Capitol occupation that quickly went viral and helped spread the story of the protests around the world. His videos can be seen at Vimeo.com/mgwisni.

Erica Sagrans: I was in London during the Wisconsin protests, and people there were mentioning seeing photos and watching videos online as one of the main ways that they stayed in touch with what was going on in Wisconsin. Your videos really resonated with a lot of people who weren't able to experience the protests up close. What do you think you were able to convey to people, which perhaps wasn't being shared elsewhere?

Matt Wisniewski: The first video I put out, I think was on February 18, maybe February 17, which was about four or five days from when the rally started. And all the news coverage that came out right when it started was very factual. There were a couple pictures attached to each story. There was some video on local news, but it was mostly just people holding signs and looking at the camera, and there was also some weird stuff that was coming out from Fox News and *Drudge Report* that sort of made us look bad or inferring that we were a riotous crowd.

But what I think made the first video so successful and made it spread so quickly was that I gave a face to the protest. I showed the diversity of people that were there. And I gave it an emotional angle that the other factual information didn't really show. That first video really conveys the energy that we had the first three weeks. It was such an infectious thing because people that I knew who lived in Madison who hadn't gone would see the video and be like, "Wow, it's really great," and then they would be inspired to go down to the Capitol and they'd be like, "Holy crap, I didn't realize it was so powerful. I was so wrong to doubt this." But I think the fact that I gave it a face and I really conveyed the emotion that was happening, because the emotion was infectious, it was incredible down there, I think that really helped the first video take off.

ES: I was looking at your website and read some of what you'd written about the power of story and narrative. I'm wondering what for you is the story of these past few months, or the story that you were trying to tell with your videos?

MW: That is a difficult thing to say. That's like a book by itself. What I saw and what I got out of this—I'll tell you my story. I'm a public employee, so the budget-repair bill is directly going to affect me. It's going to take money away from the paycheck I get every month. I initially went down to the Capitol to protest the money, the monetary value of what I was losing—and then when I got down there, I saw a lot of people from unions (I'm non-union), and I started to meet people from unions, and I started to learn about the labor movement, stuff that I hadn't learned in school. I started to realize how powerful this whole thing is, the labor movement, and it started to get tied into civil rights, and labor rights are human rights. The thing that kept me coming back was this sense of community that we had. Everyone that was down there was working together—the people who were staying in the Capitol overnight, people who were delivering them food and supplies. They started to organize offices in the Capitol. There was a wing that was just for children and their parents to hang out in. There was a wing that just had a ton of food, and people were there watching it and making sure no one was coming in there and stealing it. There were people handing out food and making sandwiches. There was also an information station where people could go and ask where they could get blankets or pillows or sleeping bags. It was really like a community and everyone really cared about each other. I think that's something unique not only to the Midwest but to Madison as a city, is that people really do take stock in each other's well-being.

ES: I know that you posted your email address where people could send in messages of support for protesters. Will you talk about what kinds of messages you got and what you did with them?

MW: At first I was getting a lot of emails through my website, and those are more difficult for me to respond to because when I hit "reply" I can't reply without changing the "from." So I actually posted my email on the website, and my email blew up then, obviously. Probably for about two weeks I was getting close to 200 emails a day, and then it died down after that. I would say over the course of the last two and a half months I probably got several thousand emails. Eventually I started to post those on a website, and I would try to document where the email came from, and I'd post the comment they sent me. I got thousands of emails. I don't think I got more than five that were negative, and even those were people who disagreed but wanted to have a discussion, a civil discourse.

I was getting emails from people all over Wisconsin, people all over the United States, and I got several from outside the country. All of 'em were just like, "Keep up the fight, because we know if you guys fail, then they're going to come after us next." It was really incredible.

There was this hearing that was going on for the budget-repair bill, and the reason we could keep the Capitol open was because the hearing kept going on, and it went on for eight or nine days in a row, 24 hours a day. I signed up and gave my testimony really late on a Saturday night or Sunday morning, it was like 2 a.m. on a Sunday morning. I went up and I was reading off emails I had gotten. During it I broke down in tears, I'm not exactly sure why, but I think it was that I'd been living the entire protest through my camera lens, I hadn't really absorbed the emotion and expressed it. I felt like there was so much pressure on me to convey these messages from the thousands of people who had been sending me emails. It was a position I'd never been in before, where I was a spokesman for this huge group of people. I was really stressed out for awhile.

I read a bunch of [the messages in the hearing], but we also had this thing called the People's Mic, and people could speak on it, and I went on there probably a dozen times and read a few emails.

ES: The People's Mic seemed like a really interesting part of the whole occupation, how much people were speaking out and sharing their stories with one another at the microphone set up in the Capitol.

MW: I'm part of the organization that ran the People's Mic now, and we were talking about the People's Mic recently. We live in a country where it sort of feels like your voice doesn't matter, because there's so many of us. Someone compared it to old-school Rome, where people would speak about politics in the open and have discussions—it felt like that. People were up there and they knew that people were listening, and they cared about what they were saying, and they started to realize that their voice matters and their vote matters. It was really powerful to have people listen to you and care about what you were saying in a culture that doesn't always value that.

ES: During the protests, did you see yourself mostly as someone documenting what was going on, or as someone who was doing video and participating in other ways? Or did you see making videos as a way of protesting?

MW: The first few days I went, I just happened to have my camera with me, and I take pictures a lot. I was sort of documenting what was going on. The reason I actually made the first video was basically just so that my friends who couldn't go down there could see what was going on. I do wedding videography, and I just edited it together in the way I do wedding videos—I pick a song and then edit it to the music. Once the first video went viral and the second video was really popular, I almost felt like I had to go, because people were counting on me to show them what was going on. I also felt like if I wasn't documenting this, then no one might see it. I ended up with 200 or 400 gigabytes of video footage. I haven't even gone through any of it practically. I would sit in front of the People's Mic sometimes and just record what people were saying because I knew that if I didn't, no one would ever see it or hear what they were saying. I did feel like that was how I was participating because I hoped that the people who were seeing my videos were either protesters who were there already and using it to motivate themselves to go back every day, or people who weren't there and would use it to eventually go down to the Capitol on those big rally days. I think it was both.

ES: Had you done video of a similar event or big events like this, or had you been involved politically in something like this before?

MW: Not hardly at all. I considered myself to have pretty strong political beliefs, but I hadn't really participated in democracy in that way before. And the only videos I'd really produced were for weddings.

ES: What's next for you, either organizing-wise or video-wise?

MW: I'm part of Autonomous Solidarity Organization now, but I don't have a very senior role there. I'm trying to participate just enough so that I do what I say I can do. I don't want to be the person who says they can do something and then fails to do it, because I do have a full-time job and other stuff going on. I'm going to definitely stick with them for awhile and help 'em out as much as I can. As far as a political career or what I want to do in politics, I don't know if I want to be involved more than I really have been so far. I really like where I am an activist/documentarian. I actually got offered a job by AFSCME (American Federation of State, County and Municipal Employees) to work in Washington, D.C. as their video guy— but I just love Madison so much, and I have a full-time job that I really love to do, and I don't know if I want to have my entire life be politics. I really love what we did, and I hope that we can keep helping this change move forward, but I don't see myself as a lifetime activist or anything like that. Hopefully once we turn the tide and fix our rights I can go back to being a kid for a little longer. I haven't dressed in suits so much in my entire life as I have for the past two months.

ES: Right—as someone who's been involved with politics in D.C., I think it's great to do that, but we need people all over, doing video, doing different things all over the country. There's not just one way to effect change.

MW: That's something that was so cool about this movement—the way people were using media. There were a lot of events or periods during the rally that I only learned about through Twitter. I basically became a Twitter celebrity on accident. I had a Twitter account and the last time I used it before this started was probably a year ago, and I had 10 followers who were my friends. And then one day I logged into Twitter after this happened, and I had some 500 followers, and I was like, "What is going on?" So then I had to start using Twitter because people were listening to me.

The way people were using their camera phones, and taking video and putting it online and capturing all these moments that were really important and spreading them on Facebook—that was such a unique thing that I don't think people have really seen before. I think that it'll definitely be a case study in social media use for a long time.

ES: What do you think the role of social media was—was it a way of people capturing the protests and telling that story, or a way people organized, or what else?

MW: It was just that we could see so many more facts and events that were happening outside of only the media realm. Normally an event like this, you learn about it through either being there or reading in the newspaper. In this event, there were so many more sources of information than that, anybody who went down there was a source of information who could take pictures, or video, or tweet about it, or put it on their Facebook. It was like an aggregator, but it was also getting other people involved. It was incredibly valuable.

One of the more important nights of the rallies was the night that they passed the budget-repair bill after hours—it was on a Wednesday or a Tuesday, and the doors usually close at 5 o'clock on those days, and there was hardly anybody there, probably a few thousand people at the Capitol. Somebody tweeted, "They're trying to pass this budget bill tonight, get to the Capitol"—and thousands of people showed up. And we occupied the Capitol that night, and that was the first night the doors were open. It was crazy. I would never have known about it if it hadn't been for Twitter. I think it played an incredibly important role. And there's actually now a circle of influential Wisconsin union tweeters who are spreading knowledge out to people who are still listening and paying attention to what's going on.

ES: Who are the main tweeters you've been following?

MW: The main ones I was following closely are @bluecheddar1, who does a radio show, and an attorney named @LegalEagle, as well as her friend @edcetera who tweeted a lot during the protests. There are three reporters from Madison who were covering the protests every day and tweeting all the time and providing a lot of really good information—two were @News3David and @News3Jessica. It was really cool that there were citizen journalists providing information, but also that there were actual news journalists who were really into it and spreading knowledge more than just putting out a story. They were putting up tweets and pictures and videos on a timely basis.

ES: That's it as far as my questions go, but is there anything else you think is an important part of the story or that you'd want to share?

MW: I think something that was really important to my part of the story here was if I hadn't chosen to get involved and to do something, then none of my side of the story would have ever happened. I could have spent the whole time at home, do whatever I wanted, have all this free time—but the fact that I got involved and that I was actually doing something to try to help this movement spread, was such a fulfilling thing for me. The fact that you called me about a story for a book—that's crazy to me—no one's ever cared what I talked about before. But I think that sometimes you have to put away your personal wants for a movement that is a lot bigger than just you. I would hope that what I did did help the movement and got people to come to the Capitol—I will never know for sure if that's true, but I would hope that that's true, and all the time that I spent and all the nights that I didn't sleep, that those were all worth it because of what ended up happening and this community that we built together that isn't going to be shut down. It's just not something I've experienced before. I love what we did, and I love all the emails that I got, and I love that I got to spread that around, the love that we were all sharing. I will never forget that experience for the rest of my life.

One email that I got really resonates with me—I took video during the first really big rally with 100,000 people, and I took video of this dad, and he had his baby daughter on his back. She must have been less than two years old. When I was taking the video I was really nervous. I was think-ing, "Oh man, I'm nervous that this guy's going to think something weird about me taking pictures of his daughter." And I put it in the video because I just thought it was such a cool moment, and he ended up emailing me and was like, "Thank you for putting us in the video. It's so awesome. When she grows up I'm going to show her the video, and she's going to know she was there for this historic event." That really hit me that what I did and what I captured and created is going to be out there for the rest of my life. People are going to be watching it 10 years from now and that's so cool—they'll remember what happened in Madison and look back on it and say, "We started something there that changed things."

@WEAC WEAC
RT @wendykloiber: RT @thebookpolice: Am I to believe that not a single friend of the worker in WI has a damn vuvuzela? **#solidarity**
7:11pm Feb 17

@bluecheddar1 blue cheddar
@sentaylor Thank you Senator Taylor for everything. You are our hero. I hope things R well w. U & all the Senators **#wiunion**
8:11pm Feb 17

@eigenjo Jo Nelson
RT @WiStateJournal: BREAKING: Madison schools to close Friday amid calls for more protests http://dlvr.it/GtH8w
8:37pm Feb 17

@LegalEagle Legal Eagle
RT @pourmecoffee: Governor Walker will regret radicalizing teachers. When they come for him, all he will see is rulers and then darkness.
9:41pm Feb 17

@JacquelynGill Jacquelyn Gill
@karamartens The Packers issued a statement of solidarity - they're publicly owned, and unionized, and they stand with us! **#wiunion**
9:50pm Feb 17

@JacquelynGill Jacquelyn Gill
Or, if food and beer don't tempt you to protest, come for the hot union men and women in uniform! **#whatisitaboutfirefighters?** **#wiunion**
10:01pm Feb 17

@DefendWisconsin Defend Wisconsin
We have been testifying for over 60 hours and counting! If you haven't had your voice heard, head to room 328 NW **#killthisbill** **#wiunion**
10:03pm Feb 17

@LegalEagle Legal Eagle
HUGE thanks to the Capitol cleaning crew - on day 4, bathrooms clean & completely stocked with all your necessities. **#wiunion #wisolidarity**
10:12pm Feb 17

@cabell Cabell Gathman
Dudes, I <3 HAVING A BULLHORN. I used to think what was missing from my life was a giant flag, but now I know it's a flag AND a bullhorn.
10:33pm Feb 17

PRANKSTER IAN MURPHY TALKS ABOUT CALLING WALKER

Elizabeth DiNovella
The Progressive, March 7, 2011

Prank caller Ian Murphy, who pretended to be right-wing billionaire (and Governor Scott Walker supporter) David Koch, visited Madison this weekend and took in the protests. Murphy was invited to Wisconsin by a schoolteacher from Fond du Lac, Wisconsin, who flew him out to the Badger state.

Murphy is a folk hero around here. His punking of the governor gave huge momentum to the burgeoning pro-democracy movement. People began protesting at the Koch brothers' lobbying offices here in Madison and elsewhere. More importantly, by releasing the audio of Walker speaking candidly about the crisis, Murphy changed the narrative. Walker's naked corporate agenda was revealed for what it was, bursting the "budget crisis" storyline.

The role of right-wing money in funding anti-union efforts often goes unnoticed by the press. But even the corporate media had to take notice. And it gave proof to what many of us had suspected—Walker is in for the long haul and will start layoffs in an attempt to crush bargaining rights. Walker went so far as to admit he considered inserting provocateurs in the peaceful protests.

Murphy's an editor of the *Buffalo Beast*, and unlike many out-of-towners who have descended upon Madison recently, he knows how to dress for the cold. He's stocky, with a round face and shaggy brown hair underneath a big fuzzy hat. He totally looked like a Wisconsinite.

Mike, the teacher from Fond du Lac, took him to the Capitol rotunda, which had just reopened the day before. He introduced Murphy, and the crowd cheered him and shouted chants of "Beast! Beast! Beast!"

Murphy is a fan of *The Progressive*, and he and his entourage stopped by the office to say hello. After our chat, they headed down to State Street Brats, you know, to get some sausage.

Q: How did you decide to be David Koch, rather than someone else?

Ian Murphy: I came across a quote from Tim Carpenter, one of the 14 Democratic state senators who left the state, about Walker not talking to the Dems.

["He's just hard-lined—will not talk, will not communicate, will not return phone calls," said Carpenter.]

I read this in a piece by Amanda Terkel on *Huffington Post*. Walker wouldn't talk to them. He wouldn't pick up the phone. So I thought, whose call would he take?

I had been following Koch brothers. I knew they had been involved with union-busting. The choice was obvious.

Q: Were you surprised that the prank worked?

Ian Murphy: Very. I was a little unprepared. I thought the jig would be up each time I called.

Q: You made more than one call?

Ian Murphy: Yes. The first call answered by a male secretary. He knew the name David Koch. He transferred me over to Walker's executive assistant, Dorothy Moore. She told me my name sounded familiar and asked me to please call back.

I called back and spoke to Keith Gilkes, Walker's chief of staff. He was expecting me to call. He was thrilled to talk to me. I told him I had to talk to Scott.

He said that could be arranged and that I should just leave my number.

One problem was that I was using Skype. So I told them my maid Maria washed my cell phone. I would've had her deported, I said, but she works for close to nothing. Gilkes thought this was funny.

He checked the governor's schedule and told me to call back at 2 p.m. And I did and I got through to the governor.

With pranks, you have to tip your hand a little. I tipped my hand with the maid, so they kind of deserved it.

Q: Were you surprised by what Walker said?

Ian Murphy: Yes. The part about planting provocateurs was really amazing. And disturbing.

Murphy put the prank call on the *Buffalo Beast* website. The rest is history. Now every day I see an anti-Koch protester sign. One of the funniest is, "Scott, your Koch dealer is on line 2."

KOCH WHORE

Wisconsin Governor Scott Walker answers his master's call

Ian Murphy
BUFFALO BEAST, FEBRUARY 23, 2011

"David Koch": We'll back you any way we can. What we were thinking about the crowd was, uh, was planting some troublemakers.

Wisconsin Governor Scott Walker: You know, well, the only problem with that—because we thought about that…

WHAT YOU ARE ABOUT TO WITNESS IS REAL. NO NAMES HAVE BEEN CHANGED TO PROTECT THE INNOCENT. THERE ARE NO INNOCENT. –MURPHY

"He's just hard-lined—will not talk, will not communicate, will not return phone calls."
　　–Wisconsin state Sen. Tim Carpenter (D) on Walker

Carpenter's quote made me wonder: who could get through to Walker? Well, what do we know about Walker and his proposed union-busting, no-bid "budget-repair" bill? The obvious candidate was David Koch.

　　I first called at 11:30 a.m. CST, and eventually got through to a young, male receptionist who, upon hearing the magic name Koch, immediately transferred me to executive assistant Dorothy Moore.

"We've met before, Dorothy," I nudged. "I really need to talk to Scott—Governor Walker." She said that, yes, she thought she had met Koch, and that the name was "familiar." But she insisted that Walker was detained in a meeting and couldn't get away. She asked about the nature of my call. I balked, "I just needed to speak with the governor. He knows what this is about," I said. She told me to call back at noon, and she'd have a better idea of when he would be free.

I called at noon and was quickly transferred to Moore, who then transferred me to Walker's chief of staff Keith Gilkes. He was "expecting my call."

"David!" he said with an audible smile.

I politely said hello, not knowing how friendly Gilkes and Koch may be. He was eager to help. "I was really hoping to talk directly to Scott," I said. He said that could be arranged and that I should just leave my number. I explained to Gilkes, "My goddamn maid, Maria, put my phone in the washer. I'd have her deported, but she works for next to nothing." Gilkes found this amusing. "I'm calling from the VOID—with the VOID, or whatever it's called. You know, the Snype!"

"Gotcha," Gilkes said. "Let me check the schedule here... OK, there's an opening at 2 o'clock Central Standard Time. Just call this same number, and we'll put you through."

Could it really be that easy? Yes. What follows is a rushed, abridged transcript of my—I mean, David Koch's conversation with Walker.

Walker: Hi; this is Scott Walker.

Koch: Scott! David Koch. How are you?

Walker: Hey, David! I'm good. And yourself?

Koch: I'm very well. I'm a little disheartened by the situation there, but, uh, what's the latest?

Walker: Well, we're actually hanging pretty tough. I mean—you know, amazingly there's a much smaller group of protesters—almost all of whom are in from other states today. The state Assembly is taking the bill up—getting it all the way to the last point it can be at where it's unamendable. But they're waiting to pass it until the Senate's—the Senate Democrats, excuse me, the Assembly Democrats have about a hundred amendments they're going through. The state Senate still has the 14 members missing but what they're doing today is bringing up all sorts of other non-fiscal items, many of which are things members on the Democratic side care about. And each day we're going to ratchet it up a little bit. ... The Senate majority leader had a great plan he told about this morning—he told the Senate Democrats about and he's going to announce it later today, and that is: The Senate organization committee is going to meet and pass a rule that says if you don't show up for two consecutive days on a session day—in the state Senate, the Senate chief clerk—it's a little procedural thing here, but—can actually have your payroll stopped from being automatically deducted—

Koch: Beautiful.

Walker: —into your checking account and instead—you still get a check, but the check has to be personally picked up and he's instructing them—which we just loved—to lock them in their desk on the floor of the state Senate.

Koch: Now you're not talking to any of these Democrat bastards, are you?

Walker: Ah, I—there's one guy that's actually voted with me on a bunch of things I called on Saturday for about 45 minutes, mainly to tell him that while I appreciate his friendship and he's worked with us on other things, to tell him I wasn't going to budge.

Koch: Goddamn right!

Walker: His name is Tim Cullen—

Koch: All right, I'll have to give that man a call.

Walker: Well, actually, in his case I wouldn't call him and I'll tell you why: he's pretty reasonable but he's not one of us…

Koch: Now who can we get to budge on this collective bargaining?

Walker: I think the paycheck will have an impact. ... Secondly, one of the things we're looking at next ... we're still waiting on an opinion to see if the unions have been paying to put these guys up out of state. We think there's at minimum an ethics violation if not an outright felony.

Koch: Well, they're probably putting hobos in suits.

Walker: Yeah.

Koch: That's what we do. Sometimes.

Walker: I mean paying for the senators to be put up. I know they're paying for these guys—I mean, people can pay for protesters to come in and that's not an ethics code, but, I mean, literally if the unions are paying the 14 senators—their food, their lodging, anything like that ... [*** Important regarding his later acceptance of a Koch offer to "show him a good time." ***]

[I was stunned. I am stunned. In the interest of expediting the release of this story, here are the juiciest bits:]

Walker: I've got layoff notices ready. ...

Koch: Beautiful; beautiful. Gotta crush that union.

Walker: [bragging about how he doesn't budge]... I would be willing to sit down and talk to him, the Assembly Democrat leader, plus the other two Republican leaders—talk, not negotiate and listen to what they have to say if they will in turn—but I'll only do it if all 14 of them will come back and sit down in the state Assembly. ... Legally, we believe, once they've gone into session, they don't physically have to be there. If they're actually in session for that day, and they take a recess, the 19 Senate Republicans could then go into action and they'd have quorum. ... So we're double-checking that. If you heard I was going to talk to them that's the only reason why. We'd only do it if they came back to the Capitol with all 14 of them...

Koch: Bring a baseball bat. That's what I'd do.

Walker: I have one in my office; you'd be happy with that. I have a slugger with my name on it.

Koch: Beautiful.

Walker: [union-bashing...]

Koch: Beautiful.

Walker: So this is ground zero, there's no doubt about it. [Talks about a "great" *New York Times* piece of "objective journalism." Talks about how most private blue-collar workers have turned against public, unionized workers.] ... So I went through and called a handful, a dozen or so lawmakers I worry about each day and said, "Everyone, we should get that story printed out and send it to anyone giving you grief."

Koch: Goddamn right! We, uh, we sent, uh, Andrew Breitbart down there.

Walker: Yeah.

Koch: Yeah.

Walker: Good stuff.

Koch: He's our man, you know.

Walker: [Blah about his press conferences, attacking Obama, and all the great press he's getting.] Brian [Sandoval], the new governor of Nevada, called me last night. He said—he was out in the Lincoln Day Circuit in the last two weekends and he was kidding me, he said, "Scott, don't come to Nevada because I'd be afraid you beat me running for governor." That's all they want to talk about is what are you doing to help the governor of Wisconsin. I talk to Kasich every day—John's gotta stand firm in Ohio. I think we could do the same thing with Rick Scott in Florida. I think, uh, Snyder—if he got a little more support—probably could do that in Michigan. You start going down the list there's a lot of us new governors that got elected to do something big.

Koch: You're the first domino.

Walker: Yep. This is our moment.

Koch: Now what else could we do for you down there?

Walker: Well the biggest thing would be—and your guy on the ground [Americans For Prosperity president Tim Phillips] is probably seeing this [stuff about all the people protesting, and some of them flip him off].

[Abrupt end of first recording, and start of second.]

Walker: [Bullshit about doing the right thing and getting flipped off by "union bulls," and the decreasing number of protesters. Or some such.]

Koch: We'll back you any way we can. What we were thinking about the crowd was, uh, was planting some troublemakers.

Walker: You know, well, the only problem with that—because we thought about that. The problem—the, my only gut reaction to that is right now the lawmakers I've talked to have just completely had it with them, the public is not really fond of this. ... [Explains that planting troublemakers may not work.] My only fear would be if there's a ruckus caused is that maybe the governor has to settle to solve all these problems. ... [something about '60s liberals.] ... Let 'em protest all they want. ... Sooner or later the media stops finding it interesting.

Koch: Well, not the liberal bastards on MSNBC.

Walker: Oh yeah, but who watches that? I went on "Morning Joe" this morning. I like it because I just like being combative with those guys, but, uh. You know they're off the deep end.

Koch: Joe—Joe's a good guy. He's one of us.

Walker: Yeah, he's all right. He was fair to me. ... [bashes NY Sen. Chuck Schumer, who was also on the program.]

Koch: Beautiful; beautiful. You gotta love that Mika Brzezinski; she's a real piece of ass.

Walker: Oh yeah. [Story about when he hung out with human pig Jim Sensenbrenner at some D.C. function, and he was sitting next to Brzezinski and her father, and their guest was David Axelrod. He introduced himself.]

Koch: That son of a bitch!

Walker: Yeah no kidding huh?...

Koch: Well, good; good. Good catching up with ya.

Walker: This is an exciting time [blah, blah, blah, Super Bowl reference followed by an odd story of pulling out a picture of Ronald Reagan and explaining to his staff the plan to crush the union the same way Reagan fired the air traffic controllers]. ... That was the first crack in the Berlin Wall because the Communists then knew Reagan wasn't a pushover. [Blah, blah, blah. He's exactly like Reagan. Won't shut up about how awesome he is.]

Koch: [Laughs] Well, I tell you what, Scott: Once you crush these bastards I'll fly you out to Cali and really show you a good time.

Walker: All right, that would be outstanding. [*** Ethical violation much? ***] Thanks for all the support. ... It's all about getting our freedoms back.

Koch: Absolutely. And, you know, we have a little bit of a vested interest as well. [Laughs]

Walker: [Blah] Thanks a million!

Koch: Bye-bye!

Walker: Bye.

So there you have it, kids. Government isn't for the people. It's for the people with money. You want to be heard? Too fucking bad. You want to collectively bargain? You can't afford a seat at the table. You may have built that table. But it's not yours. It belongs to the Kochs and the oligarch class. It's guarded by Republicans like Walker, and his Democratic counterparts across that ever-narrowing aisle that is corporate rule, so that the ever-widening gap between the haves and the have-nots can swallow all the power in the world. These are known knowns, and now we just know them a little more.

But money isn't always power. The protesters in Cairo and Madison have taught us this—reminded us of this. They can't buy a muzzle big enough to silence us all. Share the news. Do not retreat; ReTweet.

The revolution keeps spinning. Try not to get too dizzy.

#WISHYOUWEREHERE

@emmahduhjemmah
Sen Dems leaving the state? Hell yeah!

THE WISCONSIN 14

ON FEBRUARY 17, the fourth day of massive protests in the Madison Capitol, all 14 of Wisconsin's Democratic state senators disappeared. State troopers were sent to track them down, but it soon became clear that they had left the state and regrouped at an undisclosed location across the border in Illinois, where Wisconsin police had no jurisdiction.

The 14 Democratic senators had taken the extreme measure of fleeing Wisconsin in order to block Governor Walker's bill from being brought to a vote by the Legislature, where Republicans were trying to pass it as quickly as possible despite the outpouring of opposition. By bringing the legislative process to a halt, the senators opened up a space for the protesters to keep the momentum of the occupation going strong in their absence.

Republicans held a 19-14 majority in the state Senate, but a quorum of 20 senators is required by law in order to hold a vote on financial matters. Republicans needed only to persuade a single Democrat to return—but all 14 remained together and on the run for more than three weeks, longer than anyone expected. When they finally did return, the group was welcomed home by over 100,000 supporters who cheered and held signs saying, "Thank You Fab 14," "We Heart the Wisconsin 14," and "Fighting 14."

This dramatic action, where Democratic senators stood with the protesters demanding the bill be stopped, didn't just energize Wisconsin progressives. It fired up people all over the country who had become disillusioned by Democrats' reluctance to stand up and fight for their principles. Since the election of President Barack Obama in 2008, progressives had become frustrated with an administration and Democrats who seemed too willing to compromise in the face of Republican extremism. But for several weeks this winter, the Wisconsin 14 set an example for the country, showing how progressives and elected officials could work together, and how Democrats could fight back.

@micahuetricht Micah Uetricht
Fox is really saying WI protests are violent? I'M IN MADISON, AND
THERE IS NOT A SHRED OF VIOLENCE. Absolutely, positively none.
#Wlunion
10:54pm Feb 17

@eigenjo Jo Nelson
it is amazing to see the outpouring of national attention. i remember 9pm
on tuesday 2/15 we feared our voices would not be heard!
11:13pm Feb 17

@micahuetricht Micah Uetricht
CONFIRMED: Further violence in Capitol.A woman just entered,
unsolicited, and gave us all homemade cookies **#Wlunion**
11:22pm Feb 17

@liz_gilbert Liz Gilbert
"Great sign: the national guard can't teach organic chemistry"
-@M_Pomerantz **#killthebill #wiunion #notmywi**
11:29pm Feb 17

@LegalEagle Legal Eagle
May or may not have announced to my friends my plan to run for office
tonight. Wisconsin, you inspire me. **#wisolidarity**
12:44am Feb 18

@bluecheddar1 blue cheddar
I am toast. G'night.
12:58am Feb 18

THE SENATOR FROM BAY VIEW: CHRIS LARSON FIGHTS FOR WORKER RIGHTS IN WISCONSIN

David Dayen

FIREDOGLAKE, FEBRUARY 22, 2011

Wisconsin state Sen. Chris Larson (D-Milwaukee) is one of 14 Democrats hiding out in Illinois, participating in a "filibuster with our feet" to slow down the "budget-repair" bill, which would strip collective bargaining rights from public employees, among other things. By walking out of the state, Senate Democrats have denied Republicans the 3/5 quorum needed for passing legislation with a fiscal intent. Larson and his 13 colleagues and their whereabouts have become a major part of this unfolding story, but he'd rather the focus go to the legislation on offer, and the constituents out in the streets in Madison and elsewhere.

"Ever since we stepped away, there's been a lot of attention on us," said Larson in an interview last night from his undisclosed location in Illinois. "We're trying to focus it back on this ridiculous legislation."

Despite the disadvantage of being outside the state, Larson believes that he and his colleagues have been able to get their message out. "There have been huge rallies in Wisconsin. Not just in the Capitol, but in our districts in support of us and against this legislation," Larson said. He believes that the stalemate has forced a spotlight on what Governor Scott Walker and his fellow Republicans have been doing since taking office. Trying to ram this budget-repair bill through the Legislature in a matter of days, with radio and TV ads on the air from the Club for Growth, before Democrats ever got a chance to see it, is a symptom of how Walker and the Republicans, who control both houses of the Legislature, have been operating.

"This has been happening since they got in there," Larson said, referring to several bills rubber-stamped by the Legislature in January, including a series of corporate tax cuts totaling over $140 million at a time when Walker and his party keep talking about a budget crisis. "Frankly, there hadn't been much public outcry because of the Packers. People weren't paying attention. It's not a coincidence that it's a week after the Super Bowl when people wake up and say, 'What the hell is going on?'"

Contrary to the opinions of A.G. Sulzberger in an article in *The New York Times* today, Larson said that his constituents fully understand the difference between labor concessions on pension and health-care contributions, given the tough economic and budget environment, and the stripping of virtually all collective bargaining rights. Most labor groups have agreed to the givebacks but not the loss of their bargaining rights. Larson attributes this awareness from the public to the long tradition of organized labor in the state. He cited one event in particular that sticks in the minds of Wisconsinites:

> My district is in Bay View, south of Milwaukee. A hundred and twenty-five years ago, workers there decided to strike for eight-hour workdays and weekends. They had enough of 16-hour days and poor work conditions. The governor said at the time that if they strike and march on the factory they'll get shot. Seven people died at Bay View. We started this back then. We were the first state in the nation to provide public employee bargaining rights. The first AFSCME local is here. People get workers' rights in Wisconsin.

The Bay View Massacre of 1886, coming up on its 125th anniversary on May 5, is an important corollary to what's happening in Madison today. The striking workers spent two years building their movement for an eight-hour workday, warning noncompliant businesses that they would call a nationwide strike if they didn't meet the demand by May 1886. When that date rolled around, labor leaders spent several days marching through Milwaukee, picking up new recruits at each factory and workplace along the way. The strikers shut down every factory in Milwaukee except for one, the North Chicago Railroad Rolling Mills Steel Foundry in Bay View. They could not get entry into Rolling Mills, and after a one-day standoff, Governor Jeremiah Rusk gave the order:

> Rusk called the Mills and told Captain Treaumer of the Lincoln Guard, "If the strikers try to enter the mill, shoot to kill." Captain Treaumer then ordered his men to pick out a man, concentrate, and kill him when the order is given. The strikers spent the night in open fields nearby while the militia camps stayed at the Mills with sentries posted. During the night the sentries were shooting at anything that moved. A Navy tug brought provisions for the guard.

> May 5: Around nine in the morning the strikers gathered again chanting, "Eight hours." A reporter who slept with them reported that it was odd that this was a group with no real leadership, but everyone was united in one single purpose.

> The crowd approached the mill and faced the militia, who were ready to fire. Before Treaumer knew the crowd's real intentions he ordered halt, but the strikers, who were about two hundred yards away, did not hear him.

> He ordered the militia to fire. The crowd was in chaos as people fled the scene. *The Milwaukee Journal* reported that six were dead and at least eight more were expected to die within 24 hours.

> Meanwhile, some strikers called for revenge on the militia but to no avail. For several days afterwards a few strikers were still marching throughout the city but no one would join them. The dead included a 13-year-old boy who tagged along with the crowd wondering what was going on and a retired worker who lived in Bay View. He was struck down by a stray bullet, as he was getting water and was not part of the strike. - *Libcom.org*

Public sympathy after the massacre (and others like it, such as the Haymarket Riot in Chicago) eventually led to widespread change in

THE SENATOR FROM BAY VIEW | 123

Milwaukee county and city governments. Socialists were voted in during the next election in 1888. Eventually, workers won the right to an eight-hour day. They did it through collective action. These are the hard-fought rights that Walker's measure would basically take away from public employees—the ability to bargain in their interest for appropriate pay, benefits, and working conditions. These rights were won with blood.

There's a kind of eternal recurrence here. Mike Elk reports that the Southern Central Federation of Labor (SCFL), a 45,000-member AFL-CIO local in the Madison area, just endorsed a general strike if Walker signs the budget-repair bill and strips workers' rights. Only individual unions and not the labor federation can call a strike, so the SCFL announcement takes care to say it will "begin educating affiliates and members on the organization and function of a general strike." Many public-sector unions and some construction unions could go out on strike as part of this effort.

Larson did feel a certain burden as part of the group of senators leading what has become a nationwide effort to fight back against an assault on workers' rights. The state Senate committee in Wisconsin has raised $330,000 in a matter of days in online contributions from ActBlue, thanks largely to efforts by the netroots and progressive groups. But Larson said he was trying not to let that go to his head, believing instead that he was part of a continuum with the Bay View marchers.

"People have always stood up for labor," Larson said. "This has happened for 50 years. People have been spit on, beat up, punched, shot at for protecting their rights. We're just one piece of that."

He said he understood the plight of those workers who had decent wages, health insurance, and a good pension, and lost it during the Great Recession. "Those people look at the public sector and its union protections. They can either say, 'I hope everyone rises up to that level,' or 'I hope no one does.' I don't fault people who get frustrated, but I hope they say, 'I don't have that but I'd like to.' The right wing's counting on the middle class fighting among themselves and the rich getting richer."

Larson continued: "Scott Walker is trying to pit the middle class against itself. If anything it's brought the middle class together. I'm getting emails and phone calls, people stopping by my office, people who never would stop by my office, people who aren't in unions are coming out. Walker doesn't get it. He's not understanding why we're upset."

@LegalEagle Legal Eagle
RT @analieseeicher: My republican gpa says he'll walk the streets (w/bad knees) to collect sigs for Walkers recall. <3 my family
11:22am Feb 18

@DefendWisconsin Defend Wisconsin
Come outside of the Capitol after speeches at 1 PM to help us clean. Show @GovWalker that we take care of WI. Look for yellow vests **#wiunion**
11:33am Feb 18

@finnryan Finn Ryan
Yes, I will lose $4000-$5000 from my annual salary if this bill passes, but I WILL ALSO LOSE MY RIGHTS AS A PUBLIC WORKER **#wiunion**
12:01pm Feb 18

@WEAC WEAC
You can hear the crowd roar as Russ Feingold walks by.**#wiunion**
12:18pm Feb 18

@eigenjo Jo Nelson
Ian's Pizza says people are calling from all over country to order pizza to deliver to the protesters as thanks. :)
1:56pm Feb 18

@eigenjo Jo Nelson
change fb status to "Today I stand with the teachers, nurses, and all public employees of Wisconsin who are fighting for their rights." **#fb**
2:06pm Feb 18

@bluecheddar1 blue cheddar
@mommelissab Many teachers. Yes. But also PLENTY of men in Carhart jackets - the universal workman coat. **#wiunion**
2:38pm Feb 18

@WEAC WEAC
RT @stanscates: Mother Jones reporter @AndrewKroll is on his way 2 Wisconsin. Follow him & @MotherJones **#wiunion**
2:52pm Feb 18

LIVE FROM AN UNDISCLOSED LOCATION

Wisconsin State Senator Kathleen Vinehout
February 23, 2011

"Get back to work," the man told me. He listened to the radio all afternoon and was convinced I needed to be in Madison to do my job. At the same time, my constituents pleaded with me to fight for workers' rights.

Leaving Madison was the only way my colleagues and I could stop a bill that would fundamentally change Wisconsin. We needed time for the people's voice to be heard.

On Feb. 11 Governor Scott Walker introduced a bill to make sweeping changes in the state's Medicaid system, chip away at the civil service system, and do away with public-workers' rights.

The bill is fast-tracked; the only committee hearing was the following Tuesday. Public testimony was halted with still hundreds waiting to testify. The bill passed out of committee at 12 a.m. Thursday morning and was scheduled for a final Senate vote the same day.

Invoking a Wisconsin Constitution provision, my Senate Democratic colleagues and I decided to move our base of operations to Illinois. By crossing state lines we were outside the reach of the majority party who would have compelled us to vote. We did not take this decision lightly. We chose our only option to slow the process and work toward honest negotiations.

The governor says the proposed law is necessary to balance the budget. Last Friday state and local public-employee union leaders agreed to all financial aspects of the bill. Still the governor claims he must eliminate public-employee unions to resolve the budget deficit.

Two years ago Wisconsin faced a $6.6 billion budget hole. We filled the deficit with a balanced approach to spending and taxes that protected vital services and infrastructure. We cut spending by more than $3 billion—the deepest cut in Wisconsin history. We closed tax loopholes and made other tax changes to bring an additional $1.6 billion to the state coffers. We cut government programs by $2 billion, making nearly every aspect of government do more with less. Now the state faces a deficit of less than half that amount.

According to the non-partisan Legislative Fiscal Bureau the state isn't even required to pass a "budget-repair" bill. But if the governor wants to get the state's fiscal house in order by the end of this fiscal year, he could call for passing parts of the bill dealing only with fiscal matters.

There is absolutely no need to destroy Wisconsin's traditions of civil service, clean government, quality public schools, and peaceful labor relations.

The governor called on public employees to pay more for their health care and pensions. In good faith, public-employee union leaders agreed to those financial concessions. Now it is time for Walker to negotiate in good faith.

My Democratic colleagues and I respectfully asked the governor to negotiate. We reminded him that a large coalition of religious leaders asked that he sit down with leaders.

But the governor refuses to sit down with labor leaders, refuses to acknowledge the concessions made by those leaders, and refuses to negotiate at all.

My office phone has rung continuously for over a week. The calls run 10 to one opposed to the bill. I received more contact from constituents on this bill than all other issues in the past four years combined. Cities, counties, and school boards are passing resolutions asking that parts of the bill eliminating public-workers' rights be removed. Many local officials expressed dismay over the way the bill usurps local control. Some mayors who complained unions gained too much power say the governor's bill is too extreme.

Even though I write this from an undisclosed location in Illinois, I continue to talk with constituents, local government officials, and local media.

I work with my staff to respond to thousands of constituents who write or called about this bill. And I continue to represent the people of our Senate district.

People asked me when we will return to Madison. Right now the ball is in the governor's court. He has the power to end the strife by simply calling all sides to the table.

Something so far he has refused to do.

@LegalEagle Legal Eagle
Just saw myself in a mirror. I look like a person who hasn't slept in days.
So worth it though. **#wiunion #wisolidarity**
3:04pm Feb 18

@LegalEagle Legal Eagle
It's cold and windy in Milwaukee. Kind of wish I was wearing socks.
3:40pm Feb 18

@LegalEagle Legal Eagle
Angry man 2 inches from my face tells me to "get some skin in the game"
instead of being protected by union. I'm not a union member. **#weac**
4:14pm Feb 18

@eigenjo Jo Nelson
At capitol now. We are getting this party started.
4:43pm Feb 18

@micahuetricht Micah Uetricht
Stayed up all night in capitol,drove to Chicago at 5am, worked an 8 hour
day, and now leaving to return to Madison. and I'm pumped! @Wlunion
5:08pm Feb 18

@eigenjo Jo Nelson
Dear dem senators, we love you but please dont come home. Love the
masses. thanks for being our fearless leaders and advocates! **#wiunion**
5:17pm Feb 18

@JacquelynGill Jacquelyn Gill
RT @millbot: Jesse Jackson just called the protests the "Super Bowl of
worker's rights." Awesome. **#wiunion #notmywi**
6:12pm Feb 18

@jjoyce Jason Joyce
Jackson: "This is a Ghandi moment. This is a King moment." **#wiunion
#notmywi**
6:21pm Feb 18

IF DC DEMOCRATS WANT TO FIRE UP THE BASE, THEY HAVE TO PICK A FIGHT

Chris Bowers

DAILY KOS, MARCH 20, 2011

Over the past five weeks, tens of thousands of grassroots progressives have hit the streets, and made political contributions totaling in the millions, in support of the fight for workers' rights in Wisconsin. As a political organizer, I can't help but wonder why a simultaneous spending fight in the U.S. Congress—one which impacts far more people—hasn't resulted anywhere near the same amount of activist outpouring.

Certainly, the relative lack of an existential threat is one of the key differences, as unions are fighting for their lives in Wisconsin and Ohio. While some organizations are faced with the void in the D.C. spending fight, most notably Planned Parenthood and NPR, there isn't a strong belief they will disappear entirely while Democrats control the Senate and the White House.

A second important difference between the Wisconsin and D.C. fights is the relative lack of pageantry inside the beltway. Among all center-left constituencies, labor remains the undisputed champion in its ability to turn people out to events not hosted by a candidate for president. The sheer energy of the protests in Wisconsin, spurred on by the existential threat to labor lacking in the D.C. fight, inspired many people around the country to take action themselves.

However, a third, more fundamental reason for the relative lack of grassroots activism is that Democratic leaders in Congress and the White House haven't picked a fight with Republicans. Starting in late November, when President Barack Obama backed a pay freeze for federal workers, Democratic leaders in the White House and Senate made it plain that they agreed with the basic Republican campaign premise of slashing non-defense discretionary spending. While Democrats have some differences with Republicans over the quality and quantity of the cuts they desire, the line between the two parties is pretty blurry right now. Vagaries such as "winning the future" aren't clearing up the picture.

In the same vein as inching toward Republicans on policy, almost everyone believes the White House would rather give Republicans most of what they want than go through a government shutdown. If Obama presents himself as anything, he presents himself as a bipartisan deal-maker. This has been central to his image since he launched his campaign for president more than four years ago. He burnished this image back in December, cutting a number of deals with Republicans during the lame-duck session, most notably an extension to all of former President George W. Bush's tax cuts.

The idea that Obama will suddenly make a break from his longstanding motif to engage in a high-stakes fight over a government shutdown comes off as ludicrous. Who would believe he would do that? As such, on at least an unconscious level we all know there is not going to be a big public fight, a.k.a. a government shutdown, over spending cuts in D.C. The most likely outcome is what happened in December: The White House is going to work out some deal with Republicans behind closed doors, giving them most of what they want. Aside from the debatable question about whether or not that's good politics, forging bipartisan deals behind closed doors unques-tionably functions as a severe dampener on grassroots activism.

The exact opposite happened in Wisconsin. Instead of pleading for bipartisanship, the Senate Democrats there left the state in order to deny Senate Republicans the quorum needed to pass the "budget-repair" bill. By doing so, the Wisconsin 14 launched national activist efforts into high gear, quickly raising more than three-quarters of a million dollars from 30,000 donors. A couple of weeks later, the Democratic Party of Wisconsin fol-lowed suit by officially backing recall efforts against all eight Republican state senators who were eligible. It wasn't long before a couple million bucks poured in. The whole time, the crowds on the ground in Madison—and around the country—kept getting bigger and bigger. The Wisconsin Democrats picked real fights, and the activism flowed freely as a direct result.

Democrats in D.C. could experience a similar windfall in activist support during the spending fight. To do so, they would likely have to say "no" to some specific Republican demands and suffer through a government shutdown. This line of action would definitely be risky. If Democrats appeared to be the unreasonable party, as Governor Scott Walker and Senate Republicans did in Wisconsin, they would take a significant hit in the polls and Obama's re-election would be imperiled. However, if it succeeded, and Republicans were viewed as the unreasonable party, then Democrats would simultaneously fire up their base and receive a nice bump in the polls. High risk, high reward.

Back when I was a consultant, clients repeatedly asked me how they could get some of that "internet magic," by which they meant lots of buzz, supporters, and money. When I told them it usually required becoming a leader in a big national fight, more often than not they demurred. In most cases, this wasn't due to shyness, but instead because it simply wasn't an option open to them (going viral isn't easy). It is, however, an option open to Democratic leaders in D.C., especially Obama. They can choose to walk through it if they wish, but right now there is no good reason to believe they will.

@gregtarnoff
Wow. **#wiunion** is trending on twitter. Kinda makes me feel like a rebel in Egypt.

FROM THE MIDDLE EAST TO THE MIDWEST

THE REVOLUTIONS THAT SWEPT ACROSS TUNISIA AND EGYPT this winter were clear inspiration for the tens of thousands of people who occupied the Wisconsin Capitol just weeks afterward. "Hosni Walker," "Walker is the Mubarak of the Midwest," and "March Like an Egyptian," read the signs that demonstrators waved in the air at rallies and posted throughout the statehouse.

There were distinct similarities. In both the Egyptian and Wisconsin uprisings, occupying a physical location—Tahrir Square in Cairo and the Capitol in Madison—was key. In both, the use of Twitter and social media played a central role in organizing the action and keeping participants informed about the latest developments. While some called it the "Twitter Revolution" in Egypt, the Wisconsin protests may have been the United States' first popular movement captured with and largely driven by social media tools. The Republican leadership in Wisconsin even appeared to take a page directly from Egypt's playbook, when access to DefendWisconsin.org, one of the major organizing and information sites that protesters had created, was blocked from within the Capitol. In both the Middle East and the Midwest, citizens began to feel as though their bold actions were bringing about unlikely yet profound changes in the world.

Despite the connections, however, some felt that comparing the Wisconsin uprising to the Egyptian revolution did not fairly reflect the staggering nature of what had just taken place in the Middle East. In Tunisia, the revolt began when a fruit vendor set himself on fire; there and in Egypt, people overthrew brutal U.S.-backed dictators after decades of repression, and hundreds were killed over the course of the protests. Comedian Jon Stewart put things in perspective by joking that while protesters in Egypt risked being shot, protesters in Madison risked being caught up in a drum circle.

And yet, there was no denying that Egypt was very much alive and in the air as an inspiration for the protesters in Wisconsin. From pizza orders called in from Cairo to mutual demonstrations of solidarity, there was a distinct—if complex—connection between the Wisconsin uprising that unfolded just weeks after the Egyptian revolution.

@TAA_Madison TAA Madison
At the U. of Kentucky, Geography graduate students are taking up a collection to support us. Thank you U. of Kentucky Geographers! **#wiunion**
6:25pm Feb 18

@abeckettwrn Andrew Beckett
Funniest part of the day? Watching people in the Assembly gallery get admonished for doing "jazz hands" instead of applauding. **#wibudget**
6:35pm Feb 18

@LegalEagle Legal Eagle
@jenniebrand I haven't heard anything official, but EVERYONE I've talked to says they're willing to contribute/make sacrifices
8:00pm Feb 18

@micahuetricht Micah Uetricht
Finally time to sleep. Tomorrow, Breitbart and Tea Partiers descend on Madison. **#wiunion**
1:09am Feb 19

WE STAND WITH YOU AS YOU STOOD WITH US

Kamal Abbas
FEBRUARY 21, 2011

The following is a statement to workers of Wisconsin from Kamal Abbas, the general coordinator of Egypt's Centre for Trade Unions and Workers Services.

KAMAL ABBAS: "I am speaking to you from a place very close to Tahrir Square in Cairo, 'Liberation Square,' which was the heart of the revolution in Egypt. This is the place were many of our youth paid with their lives and blood in the struggle for our just rights.

From this place, I want you to know that we stand with you as you stood with us.

I want you to know that no power can challenge the will of the people when they believe in their rights, when they raise their voices loud and clear, and struggle against exploitation.

No one believed that our revolution could succeed against the strongest dictatorship in the region. But in 18 days the revolution achieved the victory of the people. When the working class of Egypt joined the revolution on Feb. 9 and 10, the dictatorship was doomed, and the victory of the people became inevitable.

We want you to know that we stand on your side. Stand firm and don't waiver. Don't give up on your rights. Victory always belongs to the people who stand firm and demand their just rights.

We and all the people of the world stand on your side and give you our full support.

As our just struggle for freedom, democracy, and justice succeeded, your struggle will succeed. Victory belongs to you when you stand firm and remain steadfast in demanding your just rights.

We support you. We support the struggle of the peoples of Libya, Bahrain and Algeria, who are fighting for their just rights and falling martyrs in the face of the autocratic regimes. The peoples are determined to succeed no matter the sacrifices, and they will be victorious.

Today is the day of the American workers. We salute you American workers! You will be victorious. Victory belongs to all the people of the world, who are fighting against exploitation, and for their just rights."

@MelissaRyan Melissa Ryan
#Wlunion RT @knitmeapony: Holy crap. I love the universe today. Egypt supports Wisconsin Workers: http://t.co/JNhAO1E @muskrat_john.
9:11am Feb 19

@cjliebmann cjliebmann
RT @Cog_Dis: Remind the teabaggers that they are enjoying their Saturday off thanks to the blood, sweat and tears of union workers. **#wiunion**
9:46am Feb 19

@MelissaRyan Melissa Ryan
Welcome "counter" protesters. Nice of you to join us on day 6. **#notmywi #wiunion**
10:52am Feb 19

@MelissaRyan Melissa Ryan
All 300 of you. **#wiunion #notmyWI**
10:53am Feb 19

@cjliebmann cjliebmann
RT @Cog_Dis: @ChrisJLarson and @sentaylor Just stay low. We got this one for you. **#solidarityWI #wiunion**
11:38am Feb 19

@micahuetricht Micah Uetricht
Madison summarized in one sentence: Wisconsin is in the middle of a class war--and we will hold the line. --Capitol rally speaker **#wiunion**
11:40am Feb 19

CAIRO IN WISCONSIN
Eating Egyptian Pizza in Downtown Madison

Andy Kroll
TomDispatch, February 27, 2011

The call reportedly arrived from Cairo. Pizza for the protesters, the voice said. It was Saturday, Feb. 20, and by then Ian's Pizza on State Street in Madison, Wisconsin, was overwhelmed. One employee had been assigned the sole task of answering the phone and taking down orders. And in they came, from all 50 states and the District of Columbia, from Morocco, Haiti, Turkey, Belgium, Uganda, China, New Zealand, and even a research station in Antarctica. More than 50 countries around the globe. Ian's couldn't make pizza fast enough, and the generosity of distant strangers with credit cards was paying for it all.

Those pizzas, of course, were heading for the Wisconsin state Capitol, an elegant domed structure at the heart of this Midwestern college town. For nearly two weeks, tens of thousands of raucous, sleepless, grizzled, energized protesters have called the stately building their home. As the police moved in to clear it out on Sunday afternoon, it was still the pulsing heart of the largest labor protest in my lifetime, the focal point of rallies and concerts against a politically-charged piece of legislation proposed by Governor Scott Walker, a hard-right Republican. That bill, officially known as the Special Session Senate Bill 11, would, among other things, eliminate collective bargaining rights for most of the state's public-sector unions, in effect eviscerating the unions themselves.

"Kill the bill!" the protesters chant en masse, day after day, while the drums pound and cowbells clang. "What's disgusting? Union-busting!"

One World, One Pain

The spark for Wisconsin's protests came on Feb. 11. That was the day the Associated Press published a brief story quoting Walker as saying he would call in the National Guard to crack down on unruly workers upset that their bargaining rights were being stripped away. Labor and other left-leaning groups seized on Walker's incendiary threat, and within a week there were close to 70,000 protesters filling the streets of Madison.

Six thousand miles away, Feb. 11 was an even more momentous day. Weary but jubilant protesters on the streets of Cairo, Alexandria, and other Egyptian cities celebrated the toppling of Egyptian President Hosni Mubarak, the autocrat who had ruled over them for more than 30 years and amassed billions in wealth at their expense. "We have brought down the regime," cheered the protesters in Cairo's Tahrir Square, the center of the Egyptian uprising. In calendar terms, the demonstrations in Wisconsin, you could say, picked up right where the Egyptians left off.

I arrived in Madison several days into the protests. I've watched the crowds swell, nearly all of those arriving—and some just not leaving—united against Walker's "budget-repair" bill. I've interviewed protesters young and old, union members and grassroots organizers, students and teachers, children and retirees. I've huddled with labor leaders in their Madison "war rooms" and sat through the governor's press conferences. I've slept on the cold, stone floor of the Capitol (twice). Believe me, the spirit of Cairo is here. The air is charged with it.

It was strongest inside the Capitol. A previously seldom-visited building had been miraculously transformed into a genuine living, breathing community. There was a medic station, child day care, a food court, sleeping quarters, hundreds of signs and banners, live music, and a sense of camaraderie and purpose you'd struggle to find in most American cities, possibly anywhere else in this country. Like Cairo's Tahrir Square in the weeks of the Egyptian uprising, most of what happens inside the Capitol's walls is protest.

Egypt is a presence here in all sorts of obvious ways, as well as ways harder to put your finger on. The walls of the Capitol, to take one example, offer regular reminders of Egypt's feat. I saw, for instance, multiple copies of that famous photo on Facebook of an Egyptian man, his face half-obscured, holding a sign that reads, "EGYPT Supports Wisconsin Workers: One World, One Pain." The picture is all the more striking for what's going on around the man with the sign: A sea of cheering demonstrators are waving Egyptian flags, hands held aloft. The man, however, faces in the opposite direction, as if showing support for brethren halfway around the world was important enough to break away from the historic celebrations erupting around him.

Similarly, I've seen multiple copies of a statement by Kamal Abbas, the general coordinator for Egypt's Center for Trade Unions and Workers Services, taped to the walls of the Capitol. Not long after Egypt's January revolution triumphed and Wisconsin's protests began, Abbas announced his group's support for the Wisconsin labor protesters in a page-long declaration.

Then there's the role of organized labor more generally. After all, widespread strikes coordinated by labor unions shut down Egyptian government agencies and increased the pressure on Mubarak to relinquish power. While we haven't seen similar strikes yet here in Madison—though there's talk of a general strike if Walker's bill somehow passes—there's no underestimating the role of labor unions like the AFL-CIO, the Service Employees International Union (SEIU), the American Federation of State, County, and Municipal Employees, and the American Federation of Teachers in organizing the events of the past two weeks.

Faced with a bill that could all but wipe out unions in historically labor-friendly states across the Midwest, labor leaders knew they had to act—and quickly. "Our very labor movement is at stake," Stephanie Bloomingdale, secretary-treasurer of Wisconsin's AFL-CIO branch, told me. "And when that's at stake, the economic security of Americans is at stake."

"The Mubarak of the Midwest"

On the Sunday after I arrived, I was wandering the halls of the Capitol when I met Scott Graham, a third grade teacher who lives in Lacrosse, Wisconsin. Over the cheers of the crowd, I asked Graham whether he saw a connection between the events in Egypt and those here in Wisconsin. His response caught the mood of the moment. "Watching Egypt's story for a week or two very intently, I was inspired by the Egyptian people, you know, striving for their own self-determination and democracy in their country," Graham told me. "I was very inspired by that. And when I got here I sensed that everyone's in it together. The sense of solidarity is just amazing."

A few days later, I stood outside the Capitol in the frigid cold and talked about Egypt with two local teachers. The most obvious connection between Egypt and Wisconsin was the role and power of young people, said Ann Wachter, a federal employee who joined our conversation when she overheard me mention Egypt. There, it was tech-savvy young people who helped keep the protests alive and the same, she said, applied in Madison. "You go in there everyday and it's the youth that carries it throughout hours that we're working, or we're running our errands, whatever we do. They do whatever they do as young people to keep it alive. After all, I'm at the end of my working career; it's their future."

And of course, let's not forget those almost omnipresent signs that link the young governor of Wisconsin to the aging Mubarak. They typically label Walker the "Mubarak of the Midwest" or "Mini-Mubarak," or demand the recall of "Scott 'Mubarak.'" In a public talk on Thursday night, journalist Amy Goodman quipped, "Walker would be wise to negotiate. It's not a good season for tyrants."

One protester I saw on Thursday hoisted aloft a "No Union Busting!" sign with a black shoe perched atop it, the heel facing forward—a severe sign of disrespect that Egyptian protesters directed at Mubarak and a symbol that, before the recent American TV blitz of "rage and revolution" in the Middle East, would have had little meaning here.

Which isn't to say that the Egypt-Wisconsin comparison is a perfect one. Hardly. After all, the Egyptian demonstrators massed in hopes of a new and quite different world; the American ones, no matter the celebratory and energized air in Madison, are essentially negotiating loss (of pensions and health-care benefits, if not collective bargaining rights). The historic demonstrations in Madison have been nothing if not peaceful. On Saturday, when as many as 100,000 people descended on Madison to protest Walker's bill, the largest turnout so far, not a single arrest was made. In Egypt, by contrast, the protests were plenty bloody, with more than 300 deaths during the 29-day uprising.

Not that some observers didn't see the need for violence in Madison. Last Saturday, Jeff Cox, a deputy attorney general in Indiana, suggested on his Twitter account that police "use live ammunition" on the protesters occupying the state Capitol. That sentiment, discovered by a colleague of mine, led to an outcry. The story broke on Wednesday morning; by Wednesday afternoon Cox had been fired.

New York Times columnist David Brooks was typical of mainstream coverage and punditry in quickly dismissing any connection between Egypt (or Tunisia) and Wisconsin. On The Daily Show, Jon Stewart spoofed and rejected the notion that the Wisconsin protests had any meaningful connection to Egypt. He called the people gathered here "the bizarro Tea Party." Stewart's crew even brought in a camel as a prop. Those of us in Madison watched as Stewart's skit went horribly wrong when the camel got entangled in a barricade and fell to the ground.

As far as I know, neither Brooks nor Stewart spent time here. Still, you can count on one thing: If the demonstrators in Tahrir Square had been enthusiastically citing Americans as models for their protest, nobody here would have been in such a dismissive or mocking mood. In other parts of this country, perhaps it still feels less than comfortable to credit Egyptians or Arabs with inspiring an American movement for justice. If you had been here in Madison, this last week, you might have felt differently.

Pizza Town Protest

Obviously, the outcomes in Egypt and Wisconsin won't be comparable. Egypt toppled a dictator; Wisconsin has a democratically-elected governor who, at the very earliest, can't be recalled until 2012. And so the protests in Wisconsin are unlikely to transform the world around us. Still, there can be no question, as they spread elsewhere in the Midwest, that they have re-energized the country's stagnant labor movement, a once-powerful player in American politics and business that's now a shell of its former self. "There's such energy right now," one SEIU staffer told me a few nights ago. "This is a magic moment."

Not long after talking with her, I trudged back to Ian's Pizza, the icy snow crunching under my feet. At the door stood an employee with tired eyes, a distinct five o'clock shadow, and a beanie on his head.

I wanted to ask him, I said, about that reported call from Cairo. "You know," he responded, "I really don't remember it." I waited while he politely rebuffed several approaching customers, telling them how Ian's had run out of dough and how, in any case, all the store's existing orders were bound for the Capitol. When he finally had a free moment, he returned to the Cairo order. There had, he said, been questions about whether it was authentic

144 | FROM THE MIDDLE EAST TO THE MIDWEST

or not, and then he added, "I'm pretty sure it was from Cairo, but it's not like I can guarantee it." By then, another wave of soon-to-be disappointed customers was upon us, and so I headed back to the Capitol and another semi-sleepless night.

The building, as I approached in the darkness, was brightly lit, reaching high over the city. Protesters were still filing inside with all the usual signs. In the rotunda, drums pounded and people chanted and the sound swirled into a massive roar. For this brief moment at least, people here in Madison are bound together by a single cause, as other protesters were not so long ago, and may be again, in the ancient cities of Egypt.

Right then, the distance separating Cairo and Wisconsin couldn't have felt smaller. But maybe you had to be there.

@micahuetricht Micah Uetricht
One contingent not seen here: anarchists in black. One contingent
representing heavily: middle-aged teachers w/families. **#wiunion**
12:00pm Feb 19

@ryan_rainey Ryan Rainey
#tea party here not as numerous but just as passionate as **#wiunion**
protesters
12:14pm Feb 19

@cjliebmann cjliebmann
#wiunion is trending third in U.S. but i'm wondering why "national
christmas tree" is trending at all?
12:15pm Feb 19

@KyleMianulli Kyle Mianulli
Opposing side of capitol has light and celebratory sense. Teabaggers
seem tense and angry.
12:19pm Feb 19

@ryan_rainey Ryan Rainey
After speaking with police and **#wiunion** supporters it appears a visit from
pres Clinton is still a rumor. Can anyone confirm?
1:06pm Feb 19

@MelissaRyan Melissa Ryan
@leftofthehill You're welcome! WI bloggers have been working nonstop
to cover this and deserve all the love, support, and props we can give.
1:07pm Feb19

@JacquelynGill Jacquelyn Gill
Remember: If things start getting heated near you, start the crowd
chanting "peaceful!" Don't let the bullies incite the crowd. **#wiunion**
1:07pm Feb19

@WEAC WEAC
Counter-protesters wearing red @SEIU shirts in hopes to incite.
Actual @SEIU members are wearing PURPLE shirts, not red. **#wiunion**
1:15pm Feb19

@WEAC WEAC
Good Facebook status:"Tweeting the **#wiunion** revolution. *brb*"
1:28pm Feb19

AN EGYPTIAN SPRING AND A WISCONSIN WINTER

Alexander Hanna

June 12, 2011

The Cairo evening seeped with optimism and joy, with dancing punctuated by shouts of Egyptian pride, and people waving the red, white, and black flag with the eagle emblazoned in the center. I was nearly breathless when I reached the Qasr al-Nil bridge that led to Tahrir Square after running from my hotel wearing oversized khakis and uncomfortable shoes with no socks, equipped with only my two cell phones (American and Egyptian), which I had assembled hastily minutes after Egypt's vice president had announced that President Hosni Mubarak had stepped down and subsequently bolted out the door.

I had flown to Cairo five days earlier, after nearly two weeks of staying up late at night, eyes glued to my computer, focusing on Twitter and Al Jazeera. As a sociology Ph.D. student at the University of Wisconsin, my research is on activists who use social media in Egypt; now bloggers and citizen journalists I had tracked for months had abandoned their computers and were fighting against Mubarak's regime in the streets, although still tweeting and blogging from smartphones.

Two days later, on my way back to Wisconsin, I rested on an airport floor in Istanbul, using my backpack as a pillow after sleeping little on the plane. I posted on Facebook, "Egyptians faced and won against the notorious Central Security Forces. State employees can do the same against measly Wisconsin National Guard troops," in response to Governor Scott Walker's threat of calling in the National Guard if corrections employees went on strike.

And on Sunday, Feb. 13, I was back in Madison, in the office of my union, the Teaching Assistants' Association. I chuckled at a website that photoshopped Mubarak's face onto that of Dr. Evil from Austin Powers, and Scott Walker's face onto that of Mini-Me's. I joked that someone should create an image of the two shaking hands. But stationed in the overflow room of the Wisconsin Capitol during the first day of mass protests in Madison, I puzzled over the waving of Egyptian flags and signs that read, "Walk Like an Egyptian," hoisted by a few in the thousands of pro-labor protesters stationed in front of the statehouse.

I'm somewhat less Pollyannaish than many others when it comes to making the connection between Cairo and Madison, a comparison that was in vogue during the early days of the Wisconsin protests. The "From Cairo to Madison" meme became a common part of the protest discourse, used by many, including Wisconsin state Sen. Lena Taylor and activist Medea Benjamin, the only other person I know of that was at the heart of both events.

I initially smirked at the comparisons of Cairo to Madison, of Mubarak to Walker. It may have merited a tweet or a Facebook status update. I did, after all, just come from Egypt, so the connection seemed to be a funny coincidence, like a red string I had threaded from Cairo to Madison. It certainly was coincidental that large protests in Madison had come shortly after those in Cairo brought to an end Mubarak's regime, but did the two really have anything to do with each other? Yes, there were occupations in both. Yes, many people participated. Yes, youth and social media did help catalyze action. But my latter and much more long-held sentiment was that of distaste and annoyance with the continued comparison. How can you compare the struggle in Egypt, wherein a popular movement forced the hand of a dictator who had held onto the reins for 30 years—to a struggle against a fairly-elected governor who had only been in office for three months? Could you actually compare the deaths of over 800 Egyptian martyrs to a situation in which your greatest threat was perhaps, as labor journalist Micah Uetricht noted, being assaulted with homemade cookies?

I don't want to belabor the obvious differences or similarities here. But making the comparison has some serious implications for how we do politics in the United States.

First off, it belittles and trivializes the efforts and struggles of Egyptians. Against enormous odds, Egyptians emerged en masse on Jan. 25 and eventually held Tahrir Square, braving attacks by Central Security Forces, State Security Investigations (the infamous *mukhabarrat*, an organization that brutally abducted political dissenters in the middle of the night), plainclothes thugs, and Mubarak supporters riding on horses and camels. Compare this to Wisconsin-based police forces that were broadly in favor of protest action. Off-duty police officers frequently participated in the protests, holding "Cops for Labor" signs, even though they had been exempted from the effects of Walker's collective bargaining law. Capitol Police had daily meetings with protest organizers and the Capitol occupants to ensure clear lines of communication and so that cleaning operations could take place each evening. Madison protesters, in participating, at most risked their jobs—especially in the case of Madison teachers "sicking out"—but did not risk life nor limb in their involvement. The flip side of this is self-aggrandizement by the Wisconsin protesters. Between the two, which will be remembered as a world-changing event decades from now?

Furthermore, although on the surface we may be seeing a new opening for political possibility, we see each movement heading in radically different directions. While the Egyptian movement seems new, it is emerging from a vibrant history of human rights work and labor struggles. This movement is finally bearing political fruit, breaking down a stagnant political regime and culture of fear. In Wisconsin, the labor movement is decades-old but is almost at its nadir. Public-sector unionism has been on the decline for the past 30 years, marred now by aged, creaky institutions, an ugly public image of union thugs, Cadillac health care and pension plans, and, possibly most damning, a service model of unionism in which members see their own union as merely "insurance" against abuse by The Boss. Gone seem to be the days of social movement unionism in which the "haves" feared the collective power and solidarity of the "have-nots." Now we're fighting with our backs against the wall.

Finally, the comparison itself signals a lack of political imagination, one that must resort to farfetched comparisons to justify its relevancy. I don't agree with the now-infamous sign, held by Egyptian Muhammad Saladin Nusair to show support for Wisconsin workers, that it is "One World, One Pain." While it's good to see solidarity alive and well, and that it is true that "the whole world is watching," hope is a thin thread on which to connect movements. It seems more apt for Wisconsinites to look towards inspiration from American labor's heyday, when there were few guarantees of rights and the ability to organize, when unions weren't insurance and, to quote the singer Travis Morrison, "Being union got you dead." That's more like what the situation looks like now for an increasing number of states, of which Wisconsin is the opening salvo in a full-on attack by the right. As unionists, our own vision of American labor should place it in proper historical context, and rebuild and reorganize our unions from there.

And so Egypt has seen a spring, while in Wisconsin it's become winter. The buds of the Egyptian spring are trying to survive against whipping winds and torrential downpours. But the reprieve between the storms may allow time for development, for the creation of a more democratic political regime. On the other side of the world, in Middle America, we huddle together against ice and snow, against the northern wind that cuts to the bone, that chatters the teeth and freezes the hair in our nostrils. It will take organizing and self-criticism of what in our unions and political organizations is awry. It's going to take a lot of time and energy to actively stoke the stove fire and remodel the log cabin, maybe more than we are willing to admit.

But if there's one thing that Wisconsinites have done well for years, it's weathering winters.

Alexander Hanna is a Ph.D. student in sociology at the University of Wisconsin-Madison and co-president of the graduate student union, the Teaching Assistants' Association (TAA).

@micahuetricht Micah Uetricht
RT @MikeElk: @mmflint (Michael Moore) paying for me to come up to Wisconsin and cover **#notmywi #wiunion**
2:53pm Feb 19

@micahuetricht Micah Uetricht
May be 1000s of Tea Partiers here,but I honestly haven't seen em. A few marching around, a couple hundred at both capitol entrances **#wiunion**
2:57pm Feb 19

@KyleMianulli Kyle Mianulli
So proud of the state of Wisconsin. Peaceful protests with health dose of passionate democratic discourse.
3:03pm Feb 19

@JacquelynGill Jacquelyn Gill
Don't tell my fellow thugs, but after six days of **#wiunion**, I just broke down in tears with the positive emotion at this Capitol.
3:17pm Feb 19

@WEAC WEAC
RT @charlesmonaco: I'm a Maine legislator - coming cross country by Uhaul to Madison with food and solidarity. **#WIunion**
4:15pm Feb 19

@MelissaRyan Melissa Ryan
RT @actblue: 1,000 donors, $16k for the Wisconsin Senate Democrats in just one hour: http://actb.lu/ai2Jrl **#WIunion #solidarityWI**
4:29pm Feb 19

@JacquelynGill Jacquelyn Gill
Want to help #wiunion from afar? Call major media outlets and ask them why Twitter is doing a better job of the news than they ate.
4:47pm Feb 19

@micahuetricht Micah Uetricht
TAs wandering arnd Capitol,rounding up Hitler signs, patiently explaining that comparisons to genocide are inappropes **#boutdamntime #wiunion**
5:05pm Feb 19

THE CAIRO-MADISON CONNECTION

Noam Chomsky

MARCH 11, 2011

On Feb. 20, Kamal Abbas, Egyptian union leader and prominent figure in the Jan. 25 movement, sent a message to the "workers of Wisconsin": "We stand with you as you stood with us."

Egyptian workers have long fought for fundamental rights denied by the U.S.-backed Hosni Mubarak regime. Kamal is right to invoke the solidarity that has long been the driving force of the labor movement worldwide, and to compare their struggles for labor rights and democracy.

The two are closely intertwined. Labor movements have been in the forefront of protecting democracy and human rights and expanding their domains, a primary reason why they are the bane of systems of power, both state and private.

The trajectories of labor struggles in Egypt and in the U.S. are heading in opposite directions: toward gaining rights in Egypt, and defending rights under harsh attack in the U.S.

The two cases merit a closer look.

The Jan. 25 uprising was sparked by the Facebook-savvy young people of the April 6 movement, which arose in Egypt in spring 2008 in "solidarity with striking textile workers in Mahalla," labor analyst Nada Matta observes.

State violence crushed the strike and solidarity actions, but Mahalla was "a symbol of revolt and challenge to the regime," Matta adds. The strike became particularly threatening to the dictatorship when workers' demands extended beyond their local concerns to a minimum wage for all Egyptians.

Matta's observations are confirmed by Joel Beinin, a U.S. authority on Egyptian labor. Over many years of struggle, Beinin reports, workers have established bonds and can mobilize readily.

When the workers joined the Jan. 25 movement, the impact was decisive, and the military command sent Mubarak on his way. That was a great victory for the Egyptian democracy movement, though many barriers remain, internal and external.

The external barriers are clear. The U.S. and its allies cannot easily tolerate functioning democracy in the Arab world.

For evidence, look to public opinion polls in Egypt and throughout the Middle East. By overwhelming majorities, the public regards the U.S. and Israel as the major threats, not Iran. Indeed, most think that the region would be better off if Iran had nuclear weapons.

We can anticipate that Washington will keep to its traditional policy, well-confirmed by scholarship: Democracy is tolerable only insofar as it conforms to strategic-economic objectives. The United States' fabled "yearning for democracy" is reserved for ideologues and propaganda.

Democracy in the U.S. has taken a different turn. After World War II the country enjoyed unprecedented growth, largely egalitarian and accompanied by legislation that benefited most people. The trend continued through the Richard Nixon years, which ended the liberal era.

The backlash against the democratizing impact of '60s activism and Nixon's class treachery was not long in coming: a vast increase in lobbying to shape legislation, in establishing right-wing think tanks to capture the ideological spectrum, and in many other measures.

The economy also shifted course sharply toward financialization and export of production. Inequality soared, primarily due to the skyrocketing wealth of the top 1 percent of the population—or even a smaller fraction, limited to mostly CEOs, hedge fund managers and the like.

For the majority, real incomes stagnated. Most resorted to increased working hours, debt, and asset inflation. Then came the $8 trillion housing bubble, unnoticed by the Federal Reserve and almost all economists, who were enthralled by efficient market dogmas. When the bubble burst, the economy collapsed to near-Depression levels for manufacturing workers and many others.

Concentration of income confers political power, which in turn leads to legislation that further enhances the privilege of the super-rich: tax policies, deregulation, rules of corporate governance, and much else.

Alongside this vicious cycle, costs of campaigning sharply increased, driving both political parties to cater to the corporate sector—the Republicans reflexively, and the Democrats (now pretty much equivalent to the moderate Republicans of earlier years) following not far behind.

In 1978, as the process was taking off, United Auto Workers President Doug Fraser condemned business leaders for having "chosen to wage a one-sided class war in this country—a war against working people, the unemployed, the poor, the minorities, the very young, and the very old, and even many in the middle class of our society," and having "broken and discarded the fragile, unwritten compact previously existing during a period of growth and progress."

As working people won basic rights in the 1930s, business leaders warned of "the hazard facing industrialists in the rising political power of the masses," and called for urgent measures to beat back the threat, according to scholar Alex Carey in *Taking the Risk Out of Democracy*. They understood as well as Mubarak did that unions are a leading force in advancing rights and democracy. In the U.S., unions are the primary counterforce to corporate tyranny.

By now, U.S. private-sector unions have been severely weakened. Public-sector unions have recently come under sharp attack from right-wing opponents who cynically exploit the economic crisis caused primarily by the finance industry and its associates in government.

Popular anger must be diverted from the agents of the financial crisis, who are profiting from it; for example, Goldman Sachs, "on track to pay out $17.5 billion in compensation for last year," the business press reports, with CEO Lloyd Blankfein receiving a $12.6 million bonus while his base salary more than triples to $2 million.

Instead, propaganda must blame teachers and other public-sector workers with their fat salaries and exorbitant pensions—all a fabrication, on a model that is all too familiar. To Governor Scott Walker, to other Republicans, and many Democrats, the slogan is that austerity must be shared—with some notable exceptions.

The propaganda has been fairly effective. Walker can count on at least a large minority to support his brazen effort to destroy the unions. Invoking the deficit as an excuse is pure farce.

In different ways, the fate of democracy is at stake in Madison, Wisconsin, no less than it is in Tahrir Square.

@WEAC WEAC
We say again, with hearts full, how proud we are that you are in this fight with us. Solidarity! **#wiunion**
5:08pm Feb 19

@ryan_rainey Ryan Rainey
Large **#wiunion** crowd chanting "@foxnews lies" near their camera
5:12pm Feb 19

@WEAC WEAC
RT @YoProWI: A man in Cairo Egypt just called Ian's pizza ordering food for the rallyers here in Madison. hmm...
5:34pm Feb 19

@micahuetricht Micah Uetricht
Just ate two pieces of pizza paid for by anonymous generous union supporters somewhere in America.It was really good. **#solidarityWI**
10:34pm Feb 19

@micahuetricht Micah Uetricht
Sign in rotunda: Obama come to Madison
1:34pm Feb 20

@micahuetricht Micah Uetricht
Just occurred to me: the most striking part of these protests is massive amounts of young ppl fired up abt labor mvt, w no prior labor ties
2:40pm Feb 20

@micahuetricht Micah Uetricht
For the 2nd time since I've come, I spent 20mins hearing testimony from everyday WI citizens abt effects of bill. So, so powerful. **#wiunion**
5:19pm Feb 20

@micahuetricht Micah Uetricht
Leaving the state capitol, i can't shake the sense that i'm walking away from one of the more impt events in recent american history
7:59pm Feb 20

FROM CAIRO TO MADISON: HOPE AND SOLIDARITY ARE ALIVE

MEDEA BENJAMIN
THE HUFFINGTON POST, FEBRUARY 21, 2011

Here in Madison, Wisconsin, where protesters have occupied the state Capitol to stop the pending bill that would eliminate workers' right to collective bargaining, echoes of Cairo are everywhere. Protesters here were elated by the photo of an Egyptian engineer named Muhammad Saladin Nusair holding a sign in Tahrir Square saying, "Egypt Supports Wisconsin Workers: One World, One Pain." The signs by protesters in Madison include "Welcome to Wiscairo," "From Egypt to Wisconsin: We Rise Up," and "Government Walker: Our Mubarak." The banner I brought directly from Tahrir Square saying, "Solidarity with Egyptian Workers," has been hanging from the balcony of the Capitol alongside solidarity messages from around the country.

My travels from Cairo to Madison seem like one seamless web. After camping out with the students and workers in the Capitol, I gave an early-morning seminar on what it was like to be an eyewitness to the Egyptian revolution and the struggles that are taking place right now in places like Libya, Bahrain, and Yemen. Folks told me all day how inspiring it was to hear about the uprisings in the Arab world.

Some took the lessons from Cairo literally. Looking around at the Capitol that was starting to show the wear and tear from housing thousands of protesters, I had mentioned that in Cairo the activists were constantly scrubbing the square, determined to show how much they loved the space they had liberated. A few hours later, in Madison's rotunda, people were on their hands and knees scrubbing the marble floor. "We're quick learners," one of the high school students told me, smiling as she picked at the remains of Oreo cookies sticking to the floor.

I heard echoes of Cairo in the Capitol hearing room where a nonstop line of people had gathered all week to give testimonies. The Democratic Assembly members have been giving folks a chance to voice their concerns about the governor's pending bill. In this endless stream of heartfelt testimonies, people talk about the impact this bill will have on their own families—their take-home pay, their health care, their pensions. They talk about the governor manufacturing the budget crisis to break the unions. They talk about the history of workers' struggles to earn living wages and have decent benefits. And time and again, I heard people say, "I saw how the Egyptian people were able to rise up and overthrow a 30-year dictatorship, and that inspired me to rise up and fight this bill."

Solidarity is, indeed, a beautiful thing. It is a way we show our oneness with all of humanity; it is a way to reaffirm our own humanity. CODEPINK sent flowers to the people in Tahrir Square—a gesture that was received with kisses, hugs, and tears from the Egyptians. The campers in Madison erupted in cheer when they heard that an Egyptian had called the local pizza place, Ian's, and placed a huge order to feed the protesters. "Pizza never tasted so good," a Wisconsin fireman commented when he was told that the garlic pizza he was eating had come from supporters in Cairo.

Egyptian engineer Muhammad Saladin Nusair, the one whose photo supporting Wisconsin workers went viral, now has thousands of new American Facebook friends. He wrote in his blog that many of his new friends were surprised by his gesture of solidarity, but he was taught that "we live in ONE world and under the same sky."

"If a human being doesn't feel the pain of his fellow human beings, then everything we've created and established since the very beginning of existence is in great danger," Muhammad wrote. "We shouldn't let borders and differences separate us. We were made different to complete each other, to integrate and live together. One world, one pain, one humanity, one hope."

From the trenches of Wisconsin's Capitol, hope—and solidarity—are alive and well.

@MelissaRyan
"Our State motto is Forward. This is backward." **#notmyWI**

WHAT'S THE MATTER WITH WISCONSIN?

THERE'S ALWAYS BEEN SOMETHING ABOUT WISCONSIN.
John Nichols, political writer and seventh-generation Wisconsinite, says that people from his state deeply believe that it is the greatest in the nation, and with good reason. Wisconsin has been a pioneer in promoting justice and equality—often serving as a model for other states around the country.

In the 1860s, Wisconsinites helped runaway slaves travel north to freedom in Canada and proudly fought in the Civil War in order to help bring about the end of slavery. Wisconsin was the birthplace of the progressive movement under Governor "Fighting Bob" La Follette, who became a national icon for progressive reform, introducing the "Wisconsin Idea" that institutions should be controlled by voters, not special interests. The progressive movement helped Wisconsin become the first state to pass child-labor laws and one of the first states that ratified the amendment that gave women the right to vote.

In 1911, Wisconsin was the first state to enact workers' compensation, and in 1932, it was the first to pass unemployment insurance. Much of President Franklin Delano Roosevelt's New Deal legislation was inspired by the work of Wisconsin progressives. In 1959, Wisconsin became the first state in the nation to allow public workers to join unions and bargain collectively, and it was the home of the country's first public-employees union, the American Federation of State, County and Municipal Employees (AFSCME).

More recently, Wisconsinites protesting apartheid in South Africa occupied the Capitol in the 1980s, and in the 2000s the antiwar movement gained momentum when cities and even small towns around Wisconsin passed antiwar resolutions. As John Nichols explains, "If you could come out as against the war back then, it's not that hard to come out in support of state workers now."

Yet the strong labor movement that grew throughout the years in Wisconsin didn't come without a price. When Governor Scott Walker threatened to deploy the National Guard to prevent a potential strike, he recalled one of the state's most violent episodes in labor history. In 1886, workers across the country marched and went on strike for the eight-hour workday. When 15,000 workers gathered outside the Bay View steel foundry to urge the workers inside to join them, Governor Jeremiah Rusk called in 250 members of the National Guard to quell the uprising. In the end, seven protesters were shot and killed in what is now known as the Bay View Massacre.

It was this progressive history that helped foster the conditions that led to the 2011 Capitol occupation. And it was Madison's vibrant left-leaning infrastructure and institutions, as well as its global outlook and high concentration of students and teachers that all combined to create an environment where a diverse coalition could come together, and subsist, in defense of long-held values and shared identity.

@MikeElk Mike Elk
Wow no metal detrectors at Wisconsin state Capitol just a sign that says please no firearms total Midwest nice **#wiunion #notmywi**
10:38pm Feb 20

@LegalEagle Legal Eagle
RT @DefendWisconsin: defendwisconsin.org is being BLOCKED on the Capitol's wireless network. DM @TAA_Madison TAA Madison if you help set up mirrors
11:34am Feb 21

@bluecheddar1 blue cheddar
Somewhere in my many tweets, I learned that 300 California nurses are flying to Wisconsin to rally with us. Amazing **#wiunion**
1:57pm Feb 21

@WEAC WEAC
RT @eigenjo: The vuvuzela might be counterproductive. Just saying.
2:32pm Feb 21

@bluecheddar1 blue cheddar
I see many signs w this sentiment"My teachers taught me 2 stand up 4 myself now I stand up 4 them" **#wiunion**
4:02pm Feb 21

@LegalEagle Legal Eagle
Crowd is cheering. Constantly. Walker press conference set to start. It's a battle of wills & a battle of decibels. **#wiunion #wisolidarity**
4:50pm Feb 21

@thesconz The Sconz
jesus! the daily show brought in a camel that got its leg stuck and fell down!
4:57pm Feb 21

@WEAC WEAC
RT @wiartteacher: I can feel the heartbeat of Wisconsin in the Capitol. **#wiunion**
5:02pm Feb 21

ALL'S NOISY
ON THE MIDWESTERN FRONT

ANDREW E. KERSTEN
DISSENT, FEBRUARY 21, 2011

As I sit here at my computer, the button I wore today is still on my shirt. It was given to me by the American Federation of Teachers-Wisconsin organizer on my campus so I could show my solidarity with others who are protesting our newly-elected governor's agenda this afternoon in Green Bay, in Madison, and across the state. It has a picture of Wisconsin's Capitol with a question in bold above it: **"W.T.F?"** Those who know me know I rarely swear. But really, W.T.F.? There is no other way to put what is going on in this state. W.T.F., like those other great cursing acronyms—S.N.A.F.U. and F.U.B.A.R.—says it all.

In all seriousness, and with tears in my eyes, I am trying to make sense of this, and it's hard to do.

As a historian of the United States who has written about unions and working people, I know the history. Since last November, I've been reading about how a blue state has gone red. That's too simplistic and an inaccurate characterization of the past and present. Rather, we need to see Wisconsin as a front in the political and economic war that has swept through our nation. It has a very long history—if only it were new!—in this country and in Wisconsin.

The struggle between the rich and their politicians and the working class was there at the beginning of the state. The first labor union in

Wisconsin predated the state's admission into the Union by a year. Wisconsinites were always active partisans in the struggle to shape the political economy. At times, this struggle was peaceful; at other times, it was not. In 1886, while workers in Chicago were fighting for an eight-hour day and in the midst of the Haymarket Massacre, workers outside Milwaukee were staging their own protests for industrial democracy at the Bay View rolling mill. On May 4, 1886, National Guardsmen fired into the crowd of strikers, killing seven.

The Bay View Massacre—which is memorialized every year—was just one episode in the labor battles in Wisconsin. Twelve years later in Oshkosh, there was a general strike by woodworkers laboring in the town's factories. "Saw Dust City" was a world leader in the production of doors, windows, and sashes. The mill owners were among the nation's most callous and cruel. They crushed the strike and brought the strike leaders up on charges of conspiracy. Clarence Darrow, the great labor lawyer, came to their defense and quite rightly pronounced to the jury and by extension the entire American public that the case was not merely about the grievances of abused workers. (They had indeed been abused.) By winning in court, the mill owners hoped to smash all unions in Wisconsin and in the United States. As Darrow said, the case was "but an episode in the great battle for human liberty, a battle which was commenced when the tyranny and oppression of man first caused him to impose upon his fellows and which will not end so long as the children of one father shall be compelled to toil to support the children of another in luxury and ease." If his defendants went to jail for conspiracy, Darrow declared, "then there never can be a strike again in this country where men cannot be sent to jail as well." Darrow won freedom for his clients, but the bigger fight went on.

With or without Darrow, the war raged in Wisconsin. There were victories such as the nation's first workers' compensation law in 1902 and stunning defeats like the successful open-shop movement in the 1920s, which stunted the Wisconsin Federation of Labor and its member unions. The war continued unabated during the Great Depression. Wisconsin's Baby Wagner Act of 1937, a milestone law providing state workers the same rights and guarantees as the national New Deal labor law, did not go unchallenged. And in 1939, conservatives won a major victory with the passage of the Employment Peace Act, which curtailed the right to strike and picket and opened new avenues to shut down militancy. Weakened but not destroyed, workers kept fighting through the Cold War years. In 1959, Wisconsin was the first state to allow its public-sector employees to form unions and bargain collectively. In the last 30 years, even while labor has been flat on its back, there were major workers' struggles and strikes in the core industries in Wisconsin. In my hometown of Green Bay in the late 1970s and through the 1980s, there were four significant strikes: at Nicolet Paper, at KI Industries, at Schneider Trucking, and, of course, at Lambeau Field.

And now, in this new Gilded Age of corporate greed, bailouts, upper-bracket tax cuts, corporate subsidies, deregulation, and disinvestment, we are witnessing yet another historic frontal assault on workers' rights in Wisconsin. It's all predicated upon the elections last November, which swept the radical right wing into office. Why did this happen? The Democrats' plan for prosperity did not work fast enough. Certainly we can say that recalcitrant Republicans and their Blue Dog Democrat friends are partly to blame. They greatly limited President Barack Obama's "Summer of Recovery." But I say too that the Democrats missed an opportunity. The stimulus package along with the bailouts helped to create wealth and restart the economy, but these measures did not go far enough in creating prosperity. Obama should have taken a page out of President Franklin Delano Roosevelt's playbook and had Congress pass the Employee Free Choice Act, along with the stimulus. Sure, the federal government can help create wealth, but they should also help empower workers to go and get it! It worked for the Greatest Generation; it would have worked for us. Instead, we got half a stimulus and a corporate bailout without workers' rights.

The Summer of Recovery wasn't what its name promised, and voters across the nation were mad and again sought change. In Wisconsin, a majority of voters threw out the incumbents and endorsed those with a new plan for wealth. Last week, the plan was revealed: Destroy unions, prevent new ones from forming (like faculty unions in the University of Wisconsin system), and slash wages and benefits.

And that is just for starters. Read the 140-page "budget-repair" bill and you'll see that the fix is in. The Republicans plan to gut both K–12 and higher education, and erode business and environmental regulation. Personally, I expect that once the Republicans are done it will cost me a lot more to be an employee of the University of Wisconsin-Green Bay. I also expect that my wife will lose her part-time job at our local elementary school (hence, my tears). And yet, we will probably be OK. I worry more about those around me. The husband of a close friend of mine who also works in the Green Bay public schools stands a good chance of losing his full-time job. If he keeps it, he can expect a dramatically enlarged classroom. A new friend of mine at UW-Green Bay said the cuts in his pay likely mean he will lose his home.

What's happening is not isolated, not new, and as vicious as before: Smash unions, drive workers into the ground, and reap profits from the lowly. But Wisconsin blue has not become Badger red. Far from it. The war rages on. If anything, the events of these last weeks have shown that although the Republicans have captured the statehouse and the governor's mansion, they have not captured the hearts and minds of average citizens, who have for almost two weeks been keeping a peaceful and joyful vigil. Workers and citizens across the state have joined them in solidarity. Although we here in Green Bay are quite reticent, today there was a student rally and teach-in on my campus. The last time there was any mass, on-campus student demonstration here was in 1970 when faculty, staff, and students protested President Richard Nixon's bombing of Cambodia and Laos. Thus, the protesters seem to come out when the time is just right and the stakes are high.

Will we win? It's going to be tough. Just like in 1898, the conservatives are on the verge of destroying unionism, and this time we don't have Darrow on our side. But like Darrow, I'm a hopeful pessimist. The other side has the money; they've got the points of power. We have the nerve to say no and the courage to stick together.

The Republicans have gone over the top here in Wisconsin and are running through our lines in hopes of a final victory. All's not quiet on the Midwestern Front; it's noisy. What happens over the next few weeks will make or break the lives of workers all over the state. But this class war from above won't end in Wisconsin or elsewhere in the United States, where Republicans are poised to launch similar attacks using these Cheesehead battle plans. A friend of mine who has had a bird's-eye view of the demonstrations in Madison emailed me today with photos. He wished that I were there seeing labor history unfold and asked if I thought this was the beginning of the end for unions. I replied it was not; it's the end of the beginning, as it always is. As such, we look to the future. FORWARD!, we say in Wisconsin.

Friends who know my passion for Darrow's life and legacy ask me: What would he counsel? As he once famously said, "The best proof of the usefulness of the union is that the employers don't want it." If Darrow were still among the living, his advice would be: FORM A UNION! He would also give some advice that many might not want to hear: STOP VOTING FOR YOUR ENEMIES! In 1897, the year after the Populists went down in flaming defeat, Darrow lambasted the working-class voters who elected and endorsed politicians "who entirely subverted the liberties of the people." Darrow would be clear: Fight like your very life depended on the outcome.

Andrew E. Kersten is a professor of U.S. history in the Department of Social Change and Development at the University of Wisconsin-Green Bay. His book Clarence Darrow: American Iconoclast *was published earlier this year.*

@millbot Emily Mills
Walker poo pooing out of state support, still thinks majority of WI supports him. Polling & protests suggest otherwise. **#wiunion**
5:10pm Feb 21

@MelissaRyan Melissa Ryan
The fighting 14 are closing in on $300,000 raised online! Put them over the top already. http://bit.ly/ff8aqz
5:34pm Feb 21

@LegalEagle Legal Eagle
Have any recall petitions been started? I know they can't be FILED yet, but seems like the time to get signatures if that's allowed.
5:36pm Feb 21

@LegalEagle Legal Eagle
RT @IsthmusTDP: As the **#sleepinginthecapitol** and **#floorcheckin** crowd starts up, we're wondering if any romances are blossoming via **#wiunion**
7:58pm Feb 21

@LegalEagle Legal Eagle
We have wristbands. Our fists are up in solidarity. This protest just keeps getting more and more legit. **#wiunion #wisolidarity**
8:09pm Feb 21

@MSpicuzzaWSJ Mary Spicuzza
RT @MissPronouncer: Chalkboard showing people from all over the world donate Ians Pizza to protesters in Madison
8:13pm Feb 21

@LegalEagle Legal Eagle
@sentaylor Thank you. I can't say it enough. Thanks to every last one of you. We'll be here until you can come back. **#wiunion #wisolidarity**
8:34pm Feb 21

@LegalEagle Legal Eagle
Kid you not, @tmorello is reading a letter to WI from one of the organizers of the Egypt protests. **#wiunion**
8:56pm Feb 21

LA FOLLETTE'S WISCONSIN IDEA

PETER DREIER
DISSENT, APRIL 11, 2011

In February 2011, more than 15,000 Wisconsinites marched on the state Capitol in Madison. By the middle of March, more than 100,000 protesters had joined this challenge to Governor Scott Walker's steep budget cuts, his proposal to strip public employees of collective bargaining rights, and his threat to use the National Guard if government workers go on strike. Many at these rallies called upon the memory of a Republican progressive whose bust stands inside the Capitol: Robert M. La Follette, Sr., who spent his long political career—as a U.S. congressman (1885–1890), governor of Wisconsin (1901–1906), U.S. senator (1907–1925), and candidate for president (1924)—consistently and effectively challenging militarism and corporate power. Signs asked, "What Would Bob Do?" and proclaimed, "La Follette forever." A professor at the University of Wisconsin told *The Wall Street Journal* that La Follette would "be standing with the protesters, screaming 'Right on!'" Who was this man called "Fighting Bob," who influenced so many reformers and radicals during his life and after his death?

Born in Dane County's Primrose township, La Follette worked as a farm laborer before enrolling at the University of Wisconsin. After his graduation, he ran successfully for district attorney. In 1884, he was elected to Congress as a Republican. After an electoral defeat in 1890 he returned to Wisconsin. Philetus Sawyer, a leading state Republican, offered La Follette a bribe to fix a court case against several former state officials. La Follette not only refused the bribe, but took the opportunity to publicly decry the corrosive effect of money in democratic politics. The incident lit a spark, and La Follette spent the next ten years touring Wisconsin denouncing the political influence of the railroad and lumber barons who dominated his own party. In 1900, he ran for governor on a pledge to clean up the corruption. He gave 208 speeches in 61 counties—sometimes 10 or 15 speeches a day—and won handily.

Upon taking office, he denounced the "corporation agents and representatives of the machine," who had "moved upon the Capitol." As a corrective, he promoted the "Wisconsin Idea," making the state a laboratory for reforms that would prove highly influential. He created state commissions on the environment, taxation, railroad regulation, transportation, and civil service, recruiting experts (especially from the University of Wisconsin) to provide ideas and information. To weaken the political influence of big business and party machines, he successfully pushed for campaign spending limits and direct primary elections, which gave voters the right to choose their own candidates for office. He supported measures that doubled the taxes on the railroads, broke up monopolies, preserved the state's forests, protected workers' rights, defended small farmers, and regulated lobbying to curtail patronage politics.

Elected to the U.S. Senate in 1906, La Follette became a leader of the Senate's progressive wing. In 1909, as the progressive spirit spread to cities and states around the country, La Follette launched a publication that soon became a major outlet for the movement's ideas. *La Follette's Weekly Magazine* was edited by his wife, Belle, and featured articles by leading journalists such as Lincoln Steffens, Ray Stannard Baker, and William Allen White, as well as by La Follette himself. Its goal, La Follette wrote, was "winning back for the people the complete power over government—national, state, and municipal—which has been lost to them." To this end, the magazine championed women's suffrage, led the fight to stay out of World War I, criticized the postwar Palmer Raids as a violation of civil liberties, and supported workers' rights and control of corporate power. Never a commercial success, the magazine gained popularity among progressive farmers and working people and raised La Follette's national profile. (After his death, the publication was renamed *The Progressive*. Still published in Madison, Wisconsin, it remains a major voice of dissent.)

Breaking again with the Republican Party, La Follette supported Democrat Woodrow Wilson in the 1912 presidential election over Theodore Roosevelt (an erstwhile Republican running on the Progressive, or Bull Moose, Party ticket), the Republican William Howard Taft, and the Socialist Eugene Debs. But La Follette later risked his political career opposing Wilson, becoming one of only six senators to vote against Wilson's war declaration. On April 4, 1917, two days after Wilson called for the United States to enter the war, La Follette delivered a forceful speech in the Senate. "The poor ... who are always the ones called upon to rot in the trenches, have no organized power," he told the chamber. "But oh, Mr. President, at some time they will be heard. ... There will come an awakening. They will have their day, and they will be heard."

After the war, La Follette stuck to his principles. He found new outlets for his lifelong struggle against corporate power as a close ally of the labor movement and a supporter of farm loan programs. He called for investigations of corporate "war profiteers" and defended the victims, including Debs, of Wilson's wartime crackdown on dissent. As the Red Scare continued with the notorious Palmer Raids, La Follette became the dissidents' biggest advocate. "Never in all my many years' experience in the House and in the Senate," he told his colleagues, "have I heard so much democracy preached and so little practiced as during the last few months."

Some Wisconsinites, and many Washington insiders and newspapers, condemned him as a traitor. In 1921, the 65-year-old La Follette had to decide whether to seek re-election. He was scheduled to give a major speech before the Wisconsin Legislature, and his aides urged him to tone down the fiery antiwar rhetoric.

La Follette opened his speech by acknowledging old supporters in the room and recognizing that this was an important turning point in his political career. Then, suddenly, he pounded the lectern and stretched his clenched fist into the air. "I am going to be a candidate for re-election to the United States Senate," he boomed. "I do not want the vote of a single citizen under any misapprehension of where I stand: I would not change my record on the war for that of any man, living or dead."

After a moment of stunned silence, the crowd erupted into thunderous applause. Even one of his staunchest critics, standing at the back of the chamber with tears running down his cheeks, told a reporter, "I hate the son of a bitch. But, my God, what guts he's got."

Or perhaps La Follette simply had a better understanding of Wisconsin voters. They re-elected him that year with 80 percent of their votes.

Many La Follette-watchers viewed his momentous 1922 re-election victory as a vindication of his antiwar and anti-corporate stances. The Conference for Progressive Political Action, a coalition of unions, socialists, and farmers, convinced him to run for president in 1924 as an independent progressive. La Follette, historically a Republican, selected Montana Sen. Burton Wheeler, a Democrat, as his running mate.

La Follette's platform called for government takeover of the railroads, elimination of private utilities, the right of workers to organize unions, easier credit for farmers, a ban on child labor, stronger protection for civil liberties, and an end to U.S. imperialism in Latin America. He pledged an expansion of democracy, condemning reactionary Supreme Court rulings and advocating a plebiscite before any declaration of war. He promised to "break the combined power of the private monopoly system over the political and economic life of the American people" and denounced, far ahead of most political figures, "any discrimination between races, classes, and creeds."

La Follette won almost 5 million votes (about one-sixth of the popular vote), running first in Wisconsin, second in eleven Western states, and winning working-class districts of major cities. Journalist John Nichols called this "the most successful left-wing presidential campaign in American history."

Though he died of a heart attack less than a year after the election, La Follette's success inspired other progressive movements and campaigns around the country, including farmer-labor parties in Minnesota and North Dakota, the Progressive Party in Wisconsin, and the American Labor Party in New York City. La Follette's ideas as governor, senator, and presidential candidate helped lay the groundwork for Franklin Roosevelt's reforms in the 1930s. Harold Ickes, Sr., an influential adviser on the 1924 campaign, became part of President Franklin Delano Roosevelt's inner circle and a major architect of the New Deal. La Follette's progressive political offspring also include Floyd Olson of Minnesota, perhaps the most radical governor of any state; Upton Sinclair, whose 1934 campaign for California governor borrowed many of La Follette's ideas; and New York Congressman (later Mayor) Fiorello La Guardia, who nominated the senator for president in 1924, declaring, "I speak for Avenue A and 116th Street, instead of Broad and Wall."

Decades after La Follette's courageous opposition to World War I, a U.S. president once again asked Congress for an authorization to go to war—this time in Vietnam. Ernest Gruening (D-Alaska) and Wayne Morse (R-Ore.), the only senators to vote against the Gulf of Tonkin Resolution, shared something else in common. Gruening had served as spokesman for La Follette's 1924 campaign. Morse, a Wisconsin native, told *Time* magazine in 1956 that his fondest memory as a young man was lapping up liberal philosophy "at the feet of the great Robert La Follette, Sr."

And, even before the current protests broke out, La Follette's specter haunted Wisconsin's Walker. Breaking with convention, Walker held his inauguration in a part of the Capitol rotunda far from La Follette's bust, avoiding the possibility that he might be photographed sharing a frame with the progressive stalwart.

Among La Follette's political heirs are also several literal descendants, who have served Wisconsin as senator, governor, secretary of state, and activists. His son Phil, elected Wisconsin governor in 1930, ushered in what some have called a "little New Deal" during the Depression. In 1931, the state enacted its first labor code, declaring that all workers had the right to form unions and to picket, four years before the federal Wagner Act. That year, too, Phil La Follette pushed through Wisconsin's unemployment compensation system, the first in the nation. Doug La Follette, a veteran environmental activist, is Wisconsin's current Secretary of State. His great-grandfather and La Follette were brothers.

The revival of Wisconsin's radical spirit, so evident in the massive and sustained mobilizations in Madison, suggests that it will take more than these ceremonial logistics for conservatives to erase the legacy of La Follette.

Peter Dreier is E.P. Clapp Distinguished Professor of Politics at Occidental College. This essay is adapted from The 100 Greatest Americans of the 20th Century, *due to be published in November by Nation Books.*

@cjliebmann cjliebmann
RT @markos: Daily Kos community breaks $100K raised for Wisconsin
Senate Dems. They've raised $317K from overall netroots.
8:59pm Feb 21

@millbot Emily Mills
RT @IsthmusTDP: Wisconsin Dems say protest website
@DefendWisconsin blocked in Capitol http://isthmus.com/r/?r=1365
#wiunion #notmywi
11:47am Feb 22

@bluecheddar1 blue cheddar
If a vote strips collec. bargaining-next-general strikes. Repub. Senator
recall is/are inevitable.Votes do have consequences.
12:22pm Feb 22

@millbot Emily Mills
Rotunda now chanting "Recall!" at rep now speaking in session.
12:37pm Feb 22

@MikeElk Mike Elk
Walker Pulls a "Mubarak" and Cut off Internet to Capitol Protestors as
Poll Shows Drop of Support http://bit.ly/hsN2aB **#wiunion**
12:52pm Feb 22

THE WISCONSIN UPRISING: WHY MADISON?

Dan S. Wang
MARCH 20, 2011

Picture this.

I'm pedaling downtown from my home on Madison's West Side for a show on a summer evening, past modestly sized mid-century homes tucked into the slopes. Getting there early, I walk up State Street and around the square. Students in town for the summer are out entertaining themselves with burgers and ice cream while their professors dine on Nepali food. A man with a guitar, who resembles the other man with a guitar a little further down the street, tunes his beat-up instrument. Near the steps of the Capitol, homeless gentlemen make their beds in spacious intervals along the square, in peaceful coexistence with the cop zipping by the lit-up Capitol on a bicycle and the patrons of upscale locavore restaurants strolling to and from their car parks. Hardly noticed are a couple of teens on the lawn and, playing roles we can only imagine, a lone suit working late—an aide, lawyer, or lobbyist—who crosses the square from office to condo. After the band is done at the Orpheum or the Majestic, I munch a fresh donut at the Greenbush Bakery to fuel my return passage through the quiet dark streets and leafy bike paths, seemingly far from the turmoil of the world.

This funky idyll is—or was—the norm in Madison. It is that kind of placid Midwestern town: well-educated, competently governed, economically stable, and full of intelligent diversions—which is to say, it is not a normal place at all. It is a Rust Belt city enjoying the trappings of a modest 20th-century affluence while hundreds of cities, towns, and villages throughout the region deal with economies that have gone down the greased chute of globalization, leaving behind wrecked communities. It is this comparatively intact economy and community—and the peculiar abnormalities of Madison that have flourished as a result—that are worth considering following the events of February and March.

In the age of clicktivism and depoliticized sites like malls, airports, and urban entertainment districts, place and space in political movements matter more than ever. Madison was the natural focus of early and continued action for the obvious reason that it is the capital, where the governor and the state assembly do their work. The Capitol is where people came to personally confront the extremists in power. But the size and the sustained nature of the outpouring of discontent begs the question: What is it about this particular city that surrounds the square that allowed for this possibility?

For one thing, Madison has long been one of those places where you don't have to look very hard to see the globe, in a sort of distorted reflection; the city suffers from a conceit of cosmopolitanism, a scene where sporting Guatemalan pants or quaffing Belgian lambic can be passed off for consciousness and connection. Needless to say, in normal times this tendency is irritating to the critical eye. But in extraordinary times the substance behind the superficiality does make a difference. For example, Madison is a favorite stop on the left-wing circuit, always supplying national movement figures a reliable audience. When Noam Chomsky wrote an analysis for *Truthout* in which he linked the Cairo and Madison movements, he was thinking about the friendly town he has visited regularly over the years—in 2009 and 2010 he lectured to packed houses at the Orpheum Theatre. Even better, a *Wisconsin State Journal* profile of Madison native Evan Hill, who had gone to report from Tahrir Square for Al Jazeera, was published on Feb. 8, just days before the Wisconsin uprising broke out. The internationalist awareness of the local populace worked to the movement's advantage over the first week in the many echoes of Cairo, and then through to the Ian's Pizza phenomenon (where supporters from every state and over twenty countries ordered hot pies for the frozen demonstrators), before fading as the political narrative split into different storylines. Whether and how that internationalism will be re-injected into the language of the movement is unknown, but internationalist terms remain as a potential advantage and cannot be erased for as long as the movement's demonstration element is located primarily in Madison.

A key factor in how the movement materialized over the first weeks of the uprising is that Madison is a people's city, not a police state. Madisonites take it for granted, but nearly all the out-of-state visitors I met mentioned the unbelievably low and friendly police presence, especially over the first two weeks. Speaking from a Chicago perspective, where the cops routinely don $700 worth of hard-shell riot gear to contain depressingly small anti-war demonstrations, I can say that by comparison Madison has thus far successfully fended off the pressure to militarize America's police forces.

There are reasons for this. One, the Madison Police Department is strongly committed to a trust-based and non-confrontational philosophy. Two, it is a comparatively well-educated force, without the egregious corruption that plagues the departments of so many cities. And three, Madison's main public security threat is the crowds of out-of-control drunk college football fans and the regular party atmosphere in the city's drinking district. Even in terms of outside agitators, it is the bars that attract the out-of-town rabble, not the demonstrations. The city police know this, and so does county law enforcement.

The consciousness of the police and county sheriff bled over into open sympathy for the forces opposed to Walker early on, thus depriving the governor of a ready onsite tool of enforcement. In time both Chief Noble Wray and Sheriff Jim Mahoney publicly questioned and/or criticized the governor in their capacity as public security professionals. Their statements damaged Walker, further (and correctly) painting him as a hyper-partisan extremist, and reinforced the broad unity of public opposition. So when right-wing outsiders were baffled by Walker's tolerance of the occupation, they did not understand that in Madison the police have different and more intelligent priorities, unlike the authoritarian law enforcement most Americans now accept. The lesson here is that building the conditions for large social movements that can assemble in spectacular and peaceful masses includes working to civilize your local police.

Another thing about Madison is its progressive and countercultural infrastructure. Over a couple of generations at least, people in Madison have built up a functioning network of co-ops and enlightened businesses, a healthy local alternative media in print, radio, and online, several locally-based but internationally-networked progressive organizations, and thriving local food and bike cultures. This infrastructure is maintained and used by a population of graduate students, educators, sort-of-creative types, and lots of people who work secure, moderately compensated state jobs. On the whole, this is a population that has, compared to the big-city rat racers, a good deal of free time. To put it negatively, Madison is one of those enclaves where "artist" is not a meaningful professional category, the local currency project trades heavily in "bodywork," and an awful lot of residents seem to have the time and narcissism to "work" on themselves.

But a friend once said to me, as awful as the prospect may be, the hippie freaks just might be humanity's last and best hope. By essentially hosting the Wisconsin uprising, the hippie element of Madison did in fact prove its worth. Without the laid-back vibe and good humor, the anger might have gotten out of control. Without the easy generosity expressed in a thousand little ways (I did my part early on with a midnight delivery of five dozen donuts to the occupied rotunda—the pleasure is truly in the giving), the welcome would have stayed theoretical. And most importantly, it was the people of Madison, dedicated and available, who kept the attendance of the weekday rallies at respectable and sometimes very impressive numbers for four weeks. Unions and student organizations bused in people from Milwaukee and other parts of the state for a day at a time, but without the thousands of Madison residents holding down the square during the week in frigid temperatures, the movement would not have gained the respect that durability commands.

After the rallies on the square took a backseat to the statewide April 5 election for the Wisconsin Supreme Court, the dispersed recall campaigns, and the localized struggles around the wider region (working to defeat new mining initiatives in northern Wisconsin, resisting emergency privatization powers in Benton Harbor, Michigan, and so forth), for people who live in Madison additional questions concern the lasting effects on our city of this historic uprising. Will the nascent police state patched together by Scott Walker to maintain control of the Capitol become a permanent feature of our town? What sorts of punitive measures will the conservatives aim at the workers and students of Madison? Will the events of the past few weeks open opportunities to bring the segregated communities of Madison—all of which will suffer under the Walker agenda—into substantive contact? How will the Generation Y students, who played powerful roles and gained real political experience, move forward as radicalized adults facing much greater personal uncertainties than those before them?

Although much in this struggle has yet to be settled, we can be sure that the old "normal" of Madison is gone. Walker's attacks have revealed what used to be normal as a temporary arrangement. It lasted for decades and the people and institutions of Madison on balance benefited from it, but if Madison was a pocket of comfort, health, and freedom in the Midwestern geography of deindustrialization and global reordering, then the conservative offensive has turned that pocket inside out. Over the first four months of 2011, the people of Madison rejoined the people of Detroit, Youngstown, Rockford, Flint, Janesville, and the rest of the Midwest as a front in the global class war. Now it is up to those of us who call Madison home to take those progressive achievements and privileges afforded by the decades of stability—and to put them to use in the shared struggle that has landed on our doorstep and is not going away.

Dan S. Wang is a writer, artist, and activist who lives in Madison and teaches in Chicago.

#STATESOS

@MikeElk
In the wake of Wisconsin, three states have backed off anti-union bills Florida, Indiana, Michigan, will Ohio be next? **#wiunion**

RESISTANCE IS SPREADING

INSPIRED BY THE EVENTS IN WISCONSIN—and provoked by similar attacks on workers' rights in their states—people across the United States are standing up and fighting back. The resistance that began in Wisconsin emboldened citizens to occupy state capitols in Washington state and California, energized student sit-ins from Texas to New Jersey, and prompted New Yorkers to "take the spirit of Wisconsin to Wall Street" to protest their city's budget cuts. In Ohio, more than 1.3 million people signed in opposition to a bill that closely resembles the one Governor Scott Walker put forward—enough to place repeal on the ballot for this November's elections.

On Feb. 26, the newly-formed group US Uncut held its first national day of protests, where activists targeted Bank of America for having paid no federal taxes in 2009. Inspired by UK Uncut, Britain's successful anti-government cuts group, the U.S. version similarly argued that government shouldn't be cutting basic services for people in need while simultaneously cutting taxes for corporations and the rich. Fueled in part by the momentum of Wisconsin, US Uncut has organized hundreds of sit-ins and fostered civil disobedience of a kind not often seen in the United States.

Also on Feb. 26, while tens of thousand gathered in Madison, 55,000 people joined solidarity rallies organized by MoveOn.org in front of every state capitol in the country. Demonstrators wore red and white—University of Wisconsin colors—to show their support for the Badgers' fight. Out of these protests has emerged a new push to "Rebuild the American Dream," an effort led by MoveOn and green jobs leader Van Jones that aims to build a "Tea Party for the left" by connecting various progressive fights under one recognizable banner, building a stronger and more cohesive movement as a result.

While it may be impossible to "plan" protests similar to the spontaneous Wisconsin uprising, the demonstrations there have inspired experienced activists and everyday citizens alike with a fresh vision of what is possible. In a speech laying out his vision for the American Dream Movement, Van Jones said, "The fight back has begun. It's not just Madison—as extraordinary as Madison was. That's not the great exception, that's the great example."

@MoveOn MoveOn.org
Emergency Call to Action: 50-State Wisconsin solidarity rally this Saturday
at noon: http://bit.ly/gPac2J **#wiunion**
1:18pm Feb 22

@millbot Emily Mills
Koch Industries registered SEVEN lobbyists in Wisconsin in January
alone. Assuming this is only the beginning. **#wiunion**
2:06pm Feb 22

@WEAC WEAC
I see a new sign: "I'm really from WI, and am really against this bill."
Or something like that. **#wiunion**
4:24pm Feb 22

@MelissaRyan Melissa Ryan
Wisconsin bloggers have created a site to aggregate their content.
http://solidaritywisconsin.com/ **#Wiunion**
4:53pm Feb 22

@millbot Emily Mills
Appreciate greatly what the Fab 14 are doing for WI right now, but still
hope this brings out good, new leadership for future. **#wiunion**
8:08pm Feb 22

@MelissaRyan Melissa Ryan
You know what @govwalker? It's not about the cheddar. This is about
fighting for working families. **#Wlunion**
8:44pm Feb 22

OCCUPY WA

Statement from protesters occupying the Washington state Capitol

APRIL 15, 2011

Today, April 15, 2011, we will be continuing our opposition to the budget cuts which will, if passed, leave many people in Washington more desperate and hurting than at any other time in the past 30 years.

Too often in our society we are told that we ought to look out for only ourselves. Our sense of real community has been broken down with that constant mantra and the false representations of community which corporations continually throw at us. Enough is enough! It is time that we stand together in unity and solidarity. "An injury to one is an injury to all." Our personal well-being is tied to the collective well-being of our communities. In order to win this fight we must stand together, link our arms and our wills to create a chain so strong that no one will be able to break it.

Too long we have allowed this class war to continue with the rich in constant offensive position, taking and taking what they want, while there has been very little defense from the working classes. G. K. Chesterton said, "Among the rich you will be hard pressed to find a really generous man even by accident. They may give their money away, but they will never give themselves away; they are egotistic, secretive, dry as old bones. To be smart enough to get all that money, you must be dull enough to want it." We must remember that there will be few if any from the upper classes who do not have a stake in the budget cuts. This is why we are seeing the cuts come to those of us in the more vulnerable sects of society, while the things that meet the ruling class' wants and needs go untouched.

In the Seattle workers' struggles for dignity, justice, and freedom around the turn of the century, Mr. Doodley, a Washington union activist said, "Do not ask for your rights; take them. There is something the matter with the right that is handed to you." The time we've been waiting for is here! People young and old have had enough. In the past six years more and more occupations have sprung up. First it began with occupations of Rochester University, then NYU, The New School, UC Berkeley, UCLA, UC Santa Cruz, UC Davis, UC Irvine, Evergreen State College, and LSU. Now we are seeing it with the occupations of state capitols, Wisconsin state Capitol, Washington state Capitol, and today the capitols of California and Hawaii will be occupied. We are not alone!

Mario Savio once famously said while standing on the steps of Berkeley, "There is a time when the machine becomes so odious, makes you so sick at heart, that you can't take part! You can't even passively take part! And you've got to throw yourself upon the gears, upon the wheels, upon the leavers, upon all the apparatuses! And you've go to indicate to the people who run it, to the people who own it, that unless you're free, the machine will be prevented from working at all!" And that's what this is all about. If we believe that we live in a democracy, then we've got to realize that living in a healthy democratic state means people from all classes, all races, all groups of society having a constant say and stake in what happens. This means we need to be in the streets. As it stands, simply voting every once in a while is no longer cutting it. We need to vote with our bodies in the streets of Washington and the halls of the Capitol. Let us lift our voices so that we might be heard. Let us no longer ask for our rights, but demand them!

The time has come! The time is now!

Come down to the state Capitol today at 2 p.m.!

THE PEOPLE UNITED WILL NEVER BE DEFEATED!

@MelissaRyan Melissa Ryan
Boom! @news3jessica Gov's office confirms it is Walker in recorded interview circulating online.
10:19am Feb 23

@millbot Emily Mills
Of course Walker fell for Koch prank call. Guy is megalomaniac enough to expect random chatty calls from Koch brother re: **#wiunion**
10:56am Feb 23

@MelissaRyan Melissa Ryan
RT @ttagaris: So, Wisconsin legislature shuts down its comment line, but Governor immediately takes a call from a Kansas oil billionaire
12:40pm Feb 23

@bluecheddar1 blue cheddar
I just chewed out a CNN reporter. He's was setting up a story I thought was bullshit, and I said as much. He got pissed when I told him..
1:57pm Feb 23

@micahuetricht Micah Uetricht
Almost 11pm. Lazy,overpaid teacher in front of me correcting huge stack of papers while observing legislators.She is clearly destroying WI
10:57pm Feb 23

@micahuetricht Micah Uetricht
Just walked by WI protester soundly slumbering on floor of capitol w/copy of The Shock Doctrine next to them. Fitting. **#wiunion** @NaomiAKlein
2:04am Feb 24

WISCONSIN: THE FIRST STOP IN AN AMERICAN UPRISING?

SARAH VAN GELDER
YES! MAGAZINE, FEBRUARY 18, 2011

It took a while, but Wisconsin shows that the poor and middle class of the U.S. may be ready to push back. Madison may be only the beginning.

The uprising that swept Tunisia, Egypt, and parts of Europe is showing signs of blossoming across the United States.

In Wisconsin, public employees and their supporters are drawing the line at Governor Scott Walker's plan to eliminate collective bargaining and unilaterally cut benefits. School teachers, university students, firefighters, and others descended on the Capitol in the tens of thousands, and even the Superbowl champion Green Bay Packers have weighed in against the bill. Protests against similar anti-union measures are ramping up in Ohio.

Meanwhile, another protest movement aimed at protecting the poor and middle class is in the works. Cities around the country are preparing for a Feb. 26 Day of Action, "targeting corporate tax dodgers."

Learning from the UK

The strategy picks up on the UK Uncut campaign, begun when a group meeting at a London pub—a firefighter, a nurse, a student, and others—came up with an idea that is part flash mob, part sit-in. In an article published in *The Nation*, reporter Johann Hari tells the story of the group's frustration about government cutbacks. If Vodafone, one corporation with a huge back-tax bill, paid up, the cutbacks wouldn't be needed. The group spread the word over social media, and held loud, impolite demonstrations. The idea quickly went viral, and flash mobs/sit-ins materialized at retail outlets across Britain, shutting many of them down.

Now, a US Uncut group has formed and announced a Feb. 26 Day of Action here to coincide with UK Uncut's planned protests on the same day. Already, a dozen local events are planned [UPDATE: As of Feb. 21, there are 30 local events listed on the US Uncut website]. Some groups are keeping quiet about their targets, but several are targeting Bank of America. The goal, according to a statement on the US Uncut website, is "to draw attention to the fact that Bank of America received $45 billion in government bailout funds while funneling its tax dollars into 115 offshore tax havens. ... And to highlight the fact that the poor and middle class are now paying for this largess through drastic government cuts."

The Politics of Class Warfare

Across the country, the poor and middle class have suffered from the economic collapse: Jobs disappeared, mortgages sank underneath debt, and opportunities for a college education evaporated. Much of the bailout that was supposed to fix the economy went to the very institutions that caused the collapse. Many of these institutions are now using tax loopholes and offshore tax shelters to avoid paying taxes.

The poor and middle class, those who didn't cause the collapse but have felt the most pain from the poor economy, are now being asked to sacrifice again.

It took some time for a political response to coalesce. The Tea Party movement was able to direct discontent away from the Wall Street titans who brought the economy to its knees. Funding from the Koch brothers' petro-fortune along with fawning attention from Fox News helped get the libertarian movement off the ground. But progressives remained fragmented and few built active, organized bases. Many waited for President Barack Obama to act.

The tide may now be turning. Inspired by people-power movements around the world, people in the United States are beginning to push back. The poor and middle class, those who didn't cause the collapse but have felt the most pain from the poor economy, are now being asked to sacrifice again.

Politicians are scurrying to cut spending, but fewer than one in five Americans say the federal budget deficit is their chief worry about the economy, according to a new poll by the Pew Research Center; 44 percent say they're most worried about jobs. Polls show that Americans also want spending for education, investment in infrastructure, and environmental protection. Yet spending in all these areas is up for drastic cuts in state and federal budgets.

Likewise, on the tax side, 59 percent of Americans opposed extending the Bush tax cuts for the wealthiest, according to a Bloomberg poll. Congress cut the taxes anyway, and the package will cost $800 billion over just two years.

Until now, polls have been one of the few places where anger at government policies that favor the rich while cutting service to the middle-class has been visible. But the crowds in Madison and the momentum of US Uncut tell us that may be about to change.

As a statement on the US Uncut website puts it: "We demand that before the hard-working, tax-paying families of this country are once again forced to sacrifice, the corporations who have so richly profited from our labor, our patronage, and our bailouts be compelled to pay their taxes and contribute their fair share to the continued prosperity of our nation. We will organize, we will mobilize, and we will NOT be quiet!"

@DefendWisconsin Defend Wisconsin
If you're on the first floor of the Capitol, please don't stand on the Bob La Follette statue! Thanks! **#wiunion**
2:05pm Feb 24

@cabell Cabell Gathman
Metro driver of this bus just honked #solidarity at firefighters for labor. **#wiunion #killthisbill**
2:08pm Feb 24

@scoutprime scoutprime
This crowd is middle class America. Looks like same crowd as a Packer game. **#wiunion #solidaritywi**
6:20pm Feb 24

@WEAC WEAC
RT @mikeelk: John Nichols takes the stage greeted to the sound of vuvuzuelas - quite a greeting for a labor journalist **#wiunion**
7:38pm Feb 24

@MikeElk Mike Elk
Weather observers at antarctica sent a pizza to the protestors in the Capitol yesterday. **#wiunion**
7:55pm Feb 24

@jjoyce Jason Joyce
Motion to remove speaker pro tem fails. Discussion is now on passage of the bill.
11:37pm Feb 24

@LegalEagle Legal Eagle
@JErickson85 The bill passes the Assembly. Senate must now approve.
1:31am Feb 25

@thomasmbird Thomas Bird
Don't even know the full details of what they pulled procedurally. But they will regret it. We responded with peace and love. **#wiunion**
2:30am Feb 25

THE RESISTANCE HAS BEGUN

Allison Kilkenny
The Nation, April 4, 2011

For the past week, I've been documenting the plethora of nonviolent protests breaking out across the country in opposition to the government's proposed radical budget cuts. In another typically excellent article, Chris Hedges recently declared that the resistance he's been calling for has finally begun. The powerful elite got too greedy and took too much from average Americans, who are now fighting back.

Hedges announced he will be joining protesters in Union Square for a planned tax-weekend protest in front of Bank of America.

"The political process no longer works," Kevin Zeese, the director of Prosperity Agenda and one of the organizers of the April 15 event, told me. "The economy is controlled by a handful of economic elites. The necessities of most Americans are no longer being met. The only way to change this is to shift the power to a culture of resistance. This will be the first in a series of events we will organize to help give people control of their economic and political life."

Hedges implores the one in six workers in this country who does not have a job and the "6 million people who have lost their homes to repossessions" to join the protest. And this isn't the only event of its kind in the works. Resistance cells have been springing up across the country—some planned, some seemingly spontaneous acts of desperation from citizens at their breaking points.

Albany is braced for a "Wisconsin-style" takeover of its Capitol. The "People Power Rally" includes union members representing state university professors, public school teachers, and human services group, who say the state budget will cripple classroom programs, health services, and low-income New Yorkers.

In New Hampshire, the Capitol witnessed budget-cut protests that organizers claim was the largest gathering of people on statehouse grounds in 25 years.

A similar gathering, though this time protesters actually occupied the Capitol, occurred in Mississippi.

Meanwhile, students in Illinois are organizing to oppose the House of Representatives' recent actions cutting federally-funded Pell Grants by 15 percent in 2011. The "Pell Yes!" campaign is designed to heighten awareness of the issue and "help students take a stand."

In all of these cases of resistance, the participants heed the advice from Hedges, who writes that citizens don't need leaders, directives from above, or formal organizations.

"We don't need to waste our time appealing to the Democratic Party or writing letters to the editor. We don't need more diatribes on the internet. We need to physically get into the public square and create a mass movement."

That physical action of leaving the computer at home and occupying the bank, street, or Capitol is beginning to happen.

@MelissaRyan Melissa Ryan
Heartened to see all the emails today promoting Solidarity rallies across
the country. Thank you @MoveOn @dailykos @ProgressivesUtd etc.!
11:54am Feb 25

@bluecheddar1 blue cheddar
RT @gottalaff: RT @ddayen: John Nichols predicts 1 million ppl across
the country tomorrow in solidarity with **#wiunion**
1:04pm Feb 25

@DefendWisconsin Defend Wisconsin
Vols needed to live-stream Saturday 3:00 PM rally. Must have iphone (or
similar) or laptop w/aircard. Contact: brandzel@gmail.com **#wiunion**
1:17pm Feb 25

@DefendWisconsin Defend Wisconsin
ANNOUNCEMENT: Senator Taylor will be phoning at 3:00pm. Silence is
requested in the rotunda at that time. **#wiunion**
2:45pm Feb 25

@EricKleefeld Eric Kleefeld
NEWS: Capitol Police announce building will CLOSE 4 p.m. Sunday -
they're easing this process down.
4:40pm Feb 25

@WEAC WEAC
Great sign: Walker, let's be friends with benefits. **#wiunion**
9:51pm Feb 25

HOW WISCONSIN GAVE BIRTH TO THE AMERICAN DREAM MOVEMENT

BILLY WIMSATT

JULY 17, 2011

My wife Lenore Palladino—who is MoveOn.org's field director—and I were on the train, coming home from a visit with family. It was late February, and protesters in Wisconsin had been occupying their state Capitol for a week. I overheard Lenore talking on the phone with MoveOn's campaign director, Daniel Mintz. They were trying to figure out what they could do to help.

They landed on the idea of organizing rallies that weekend, at all 50 state capitols, so people across the country could have a way to show their solidarity with the Wisconsin protesters. This was Monday, Feb. 21. The rallies would take place on Saturday, Feb. 26, just five days away—a huge undertaking in such a short amount of time. They decided to go for it.

The next day, Van Jones wrote an article for *The Huffington Post* called "Introducing the American Dream Movement," framing these rallies as the beginning of a larger fight. The idea was to say, "There's a movement here, but it doesn't see itself most of the time." The response was overwhelming.

By Thursday, over 40 groups had signed on, from ColorOfChange.org to the AFL-CIO. MoveOn's field team and our partners had organized rallies at every state capitol, complete with permits and sound systems. Glenn Beck did a special broadcast about it. He had all the logos of the partner organizations in the background, and went into a bizarre rant attacking the American Dream: "How did Van Jones and MoveOn organize this in three days? The answer is they didn't. They've been planning this since 2008!"

But it really was organized in three days: I saw it with my own eyes. By that Saturday, Lenore and her staff, their networks of local volunteers, and partner organizations had 50,000 people show up in 50 states, not including the 70,000-100,000 in Madison. MoveOn sent signs: "Save The American Dream." The American Dream movement was born.

Wisconsin was a turning point. The attacks were so extreme, people decided they had to go to extreme lengths to stand up for themselves. I think their original idea was to do a two-day rally. Then they thought maybe it could extend to three days. Then someone tweeted "as long as it takes," and people began to put their entire lives on hold to spend a month living in the state Capitol. No one could have predicted it. It was unbelievable. It gave the progressive movement hope again. It was... awesome.

The question everyone is asking ourselves now is "How do we build on this momentum? How can we keep the movement expanding?" I think part of the answer lies in asking the question—and asking that question over and over again with millions of people. "How do we build on this movement?"

The simple act of asking that question empowers each of us to take ownership. The answer is that we need to do this locally where we live. We need to connect it all in a way that lets people see that it's all one struggle. It's bigger than any one of us.

And we have to do this everywhere. We're facing similar attacks everywhere, but we haven't had a similar breakthrough like Wisconsin. That's what we need to do now.

What the American Dream movement is doing is challenging us all to think about how to tell the story and brand all of this as one big effort, in the same way the Tea Party has done. The American Dream movement is working with MoveOn, the Campaign for America's Future, the Center for Community Change, with labor, with so many groups. And there's a parallel sister effort, "We Are One," that's come out of the Leadership Conference on Civil Rights. We're all working together, saying that we have to protect the progress of the 20th century and put forward a vision for a great 21st century where everyone gets to win together. Wisconsin has been the inspiration for these efforts, and has helped bring all of these various groups together as one.

Just this weekend, July 16-17, the American Dream movement organized more than 1,500 house meetings in more than 400 congressional districts nationwide to create a "Contract for the American Dream," a progressive economic agenda written and voted on collectively by more than 100,000 people.

Van's suggestion that we begin to see ourselves as part of a larger movement has been met with an incredible—really an unbelievable—chorus of "Yes, let's do that," which is pretty uncharacteristic of how the progressive movement has been operating up until this point. Most people think, "We already have our brand, our name, or our message, or we're going to come up with our own." But instead of the usual mode that we operate in, I think that people are so terrified of what's happening and there's such a recognition that the good work we've been doing isn't enough, there's now a profound openness to sticking together and trying this radical experiment of acting like we're all on the same team.

What happened in Wisconsin has been compared to the Seattle WTO protests, which also took place during a very dark time (during another Democratic administration) when we felt like the powers that be and the multinational corporations were destroying everything we loved. That's when you first saw these really bold, unlikely coalitions—of turtles and Teamsters, blues and greens—that was really game-changing when it happened. People forget, but a whole series of these huge mobilizations happened with tens and even hundreds of thousands of people, all over the world, that came together as part of a new global justice movement a decade ago. When 9/11 happened, that energy was redirected into the peace movement—and then eventually into voter mobilization in 2004, 2006, and 2008 in Obama's election—then it was finally demobilized in 2010 because we got confused by having Obama in office and started thinking that we didn't still need to fight for our lives.

What the brave folks in Wisconsin did was say: "We're back, we're here, we're not dead, we haven't gone anywhere." It's the same movement, and it's been reawakened, like someone kicked the sleeping giant. And we woke up. It's very exciting.

Billy Wimsatt is Strategic Partnerships Director at Rebuild the Dream (RebuildtheDream.com), and the author, most recently, of Please Don't Bomb the Suburbs: A Midterm Report on My Generation and the Future of Our Super Movement.

@bluecheddar1 blue cheddar
@weep4humanity The 4pm closing on Sunday is solid. That's not conjecture.**#wiunion**
11:18am Feb 26

@MelissaRyan Melissa Ryan
Starting to see **#Wlunion** related merch show up on the street and in stores. Sadly most of it isn't union made. **#SolidarityFAIL**
11:42am Feb 26

@bluecheddar1 blue cheddar
Sky thick w snowflakes rt now **#wiunion**
1:23pm Feb 26

@bluecheddar1 blue cheddar
High of 15 degrees down here Wearing 2 pair of pants & earflap hat **#wiunion**
1:25pm Feb 26

@AFLCIO AFL-CIO
RT @VanJones68: this isn't about a shift to the political left or the political right, it is about a return to America's moral center.
2:22pm Feb 26

@millbot Emily Mills
Hearing reports from Madison police of something like 100k people for rally. Hasn't even started yet! **#wiunion**
2:29pm Feb 26

@LegalEagle Legal Eagle
Kids in snowpants are adorable. And here in large numbers. **#wiunion** @WEAC
2:43pm Feb 26

@micahuetricht Micah Uetricht
Have no idea how big this crowd is. It's incredible. So damn cold, so snowy, yet the streets are packed. **#wiunion**
3:37pm Feb 26

@micahuetricht Micah Uetricht
Also interviewed guy with sign: "Republican against the bill." Everyone wanted to shake his hand, thank him. **#wiunion #wearewi**
3:53pm Feb 26

TIME TO RECLAIM
THE AMERICAN DREAM

Van Jones
YES! MAGAZINE, FEBRUARY 22, 2011

In the past 24 months, those of us who longed for positive change have gone from hope to heartbreak. But hope is returning to America—at last—thanks largely to the courageous stand of the heroes and heroines of Wisconsin.

Reinvigorated by the idealism and fighting spirit on display right now in America's heartland, the movement for "hope and change" has a rare, second chance. It can renew itself and become again a national force with which to be reckoned.

Over the next hours and days, all who love this country need to do everything possible to spread the "spirit of Madison" to all 50 states. This does not mean we need to occupy 50 state capitols; things elsewhere are not yet that dire. But this weekend, the best of America should rally on the steps of every statehouse in the union.

MoveOn.org and others have issued just this kind of call to action; everyone should prioritize responding and turning out in large numbers.

On Saturday, the powers-that-be (in both parties) should see a rainbow force coming together: organized workers, business leaders, veterans, students and youth, faith leaders, civil rights fighters, women's rights champions, immigrant rights defenders, LGBTQ stalwarts, environmentalists, academics, artists, celebrities, community activists, elected officials, and more—all standing up for what's right.

Defending—and Defining—the American Dream

And we should announce that our renewed movement is more than just a mobilization to back unions or oppose illegitimate power grabs (as important as those agenda items are). Something more vital is at stake: Our country needs a national movement to defend the American Dream itself. And the fight in Wisconsin creates the opportunity to build one.

After all, it is the American Dream that the GOP's "slash and burn" agenda is killing off. We need a movement dedicated to renewing the idea that hard work pays in our country; that you can make it if you try; that America remains a land committed to dignity, justice, and opportunity for all. Right now, this very idea is on the GOP chopping block. And we must rescue it now—or risk losing it forever.

America will not make it through this crisis healthy and whole if—at the first sign of trouble—we are willing to throw away millions of our everyday heroes. Our teachers, police officers, firefighters, nurses, and others make our communities and country strong. Their daily work is essential to the smooth functioning and long-term success of our nation. An attack on them is an attack on the backbone of America.

Nobody objects to politicians cutting budgetary fat. But the GOP program everywhere is so reckless that it would actually cut muscle, bone, and marrow, too. This approach is both shortsighted and immoral. We should rise up against it—in our millions.

Both parties should be taking steps to solve the country's problems in a balanced, fair, and rational way. If deficits are truly the issue, then raising taxes and cutting spending both should be on the table, as tools. But Wisconsin's governor recently handed out massive corporate tax breaks, reducing the state's revenues. That move greatly added to the problem he now wants to fix by attacking essential services with a meat axe. A slew of GOP governors in places like Ohio are gearing up to take similar approaches.

If a foreign power conspired to inflict this much damage on America's first responders and essential infrastructure, we would see it as an act of war.

And if a foreign dictator unilaterally announced that his nation's workers no longer had a seat at the bargaining table in their own country, the U.S. establishment would rightfully go bananas.

If Republicans would oppose that kind of thuggery abroad, how can they champion it here at home?

How can they accept for the American people what they would denounce for the people of any other nation on Earth?

GOP governors in multiple states are advancing schemes to erase the long-standing rights of American employees to choose a union and bargain collectively. We need to call these outrageous plots what they are: un-American and unacceptable. They are not just assaults on workers; they are assaults on the American Way itself.

This Is Our "Tea Party" Moment

It is time to draw a line in the sand—nationally. Someone has to stand up for common sense and fairness. It is time to use all nonviolent means to defend the American people and our American principles from these abuses.

If we take a bold and courageous stand, over time, we can win. Make no mistake about it: this is our "Tea Party" moment—in a positive sense.

In fact, we can learn many important lessons from the recent achievements of the libertarian, populist right. Don't forget: even after the Republican's epic electoral defeat in 2008, a right-wing uprising was still able to smash public support for "new New Deal" economics. Along the way, it revived the political fortunes of the GOP.

A popular outcry from the left could just as easily shatter the prevailing bipartisan consensus that America is suddenly a poor country that cannot possibly help its people meet our basic needs.

The truth is that we don't live in Bangladesh or Malawi. America is not a poor country. The public has just been hypnotized into believing that the richest and most creative nation on Earth has only two choices in this crisis: massive austerity (as championed by the Tea Party/Republicans) or semi-massive austerity (as meekly offered by too many D.C. Democrats). It is ridiculous.

Fortunately, the people in Wisconsin know that. So they are fighting courageously. Their efforts could blossom into a compelling, national force for the good—offering a powerful alternative to those false choices.

And while our re-born movement needs to be as clear and bold as the Tea Parties, we must base our efforts on a deeper set of American values.

The Tea Party attached itself to only a single American principle. And it identifies itself with only one moment in our distant past: the Boston Tea Party, symbolizing "no taxation without representation."

"American Dream" Movement Rooted in a Deeper Patriotism

That is an important moment and concept. But the notion of negative liberty ("Don't tread on me!") is only one principle among many that makes our country great. Other equally vital American values and ideals (like justice, opportunity, fairness, and democracy) have gone largely undefended and unheralded in this recent crisis. That ends—now. Our rising movement should stand for the full suite of American values and principles.

And the American ideal most in need of defense is our most essential one: the American Dream.

The steps needed to renew and redeem the American Dream are straightforward and simple:

- Increase revenue for America's government sensibly by making Wall Street and the super-rich pay their fair share.
- Reduce spending responsibly by cutting the real fat—like corporate welfare for military contractors, big agriculture, and big oil.
- Simultaneously protect the heart and soul of America—our teachers, nurses, and first responders.
- Guarantee the health, safety, and success of our children and communities by leaving the muscle and bone of America's communities intact.
- Maintain the American Way by treating employees with dignity and respecting their right to a seat at the bargaining table.
- Rebuild the middle class—and pathways into it—by fighting for a "made in America" innovation and manufacturing agenda, including trade and currency policies that honor American workers and entrepreneurs.
- Stand for the idea that, in a crisis, Americans turn TO each other—and not ON each other.

A Return to the Moral Center

By standing up for dignity, equal opportunity, and fair play, the Wisconsin workers have found their way to America's great moral center. By standing with them, we reclaim what is best in our country.

These are not radical notions. They are the common sense ideas that form the core of who we are as a nation. We can rally Americans, once again, to stand up for these values. We can make America, once again, a land where it is safe for everyday people to dream.

We will prevail because—in truth—we are not in a right-wing period of American history, nor are we in a left-wing period. We are simply in a volatile period.

And during times like these, we can take comfort in knowing that a great nation will ultimately pull its answers—not from its ideological extremes—but from its deep, moral center.

By standing up for dignity, equal opportunity, and fair play, the Wisconsin workers have found their way to America's great moral center. They have shown us all, at last, the way back home. By standing with them, we reclaim what is best in our country.

April 15, 2009, marked the beginning of the national movement to remember the Tea Party and pull America to the ideological right.

Let Saturday, Feb. 26, 2011, mark the beginning of the national movement to renew the American Dream and return us to the moral center—where everybody counts, and everybody matters.

#ASLONGASITTAKES

@MikeElk
Madison Teachers just voted to go on general strike tomorrow
#notmywi

THE REVOLUTION WILL NOT BE PHONEBANKED

IN THE WORLD OF ELECTORAL POLITICS, mounting an historic effort to recall six Wisconsin Republican state senators from office *is* a radical act. In all of Wisconsin history, only four previous recalls have ever been attempted. Yet there is a contingent of activists who have taken issue with the way Democrats and union leaders have channeled the remarkable momentum of the uprising into the narrow and limited sphere of electoral politics.

They object to politicians and union leaders' efforts to harness and sanitize the energy of a spontaneous movement toward their own long-standing objectives. Rather than simply trying to shift the balance of power from one party to another, radical grassroots activists saw in the uprising the potential to bring about fundamental change to larger political and economic systems. And in the face of Governor Scott Walker's extreme actions, they felt that union leaders blinked by failing to call a general strike or use civil disobedience to continue or even escalate the struggle.

In an uprising marked by diversity and solidarity, these competing visions created an undercurrent of tension throughout. From the attempts to negotiate a wind-down of the Capitol occupation to the discussions of what comes next, there remain larger questions of power, control, and the meaning of the movement that has grown out of the Wisconsin struggle.

@millbot Emily Mills
Coldest, snowiest day of the last two weeks. Biggest rally turnout in support of workers to date. God love you, Wisconsin. **#wiunion #wearewi**
4:05pm Feb 26

@millbot Emily Mills
Inspired by huge turnout today in Madison & solidarity rallies all over country. Thanks for keeping it up, all! **#wiunion #wearewi**
5:19pm Feb 26

@bluecheddar1 blue cheddar
Guy's sign has shoes hanging from it, says: Obama-Here's yer comfortable shoes Where are you?
6:10pm Feb 26

@LegalEagle Legal Eagle
Day 13. We're still here. We've multiplied. And you can close the Capitol tomorrow, but our voices won't stop.
6:15pm Feb 26

@cabell Cabell Gathman
I've heard estimates up to 150K & I'd believe it. RT @AFLCIO: RT @wisaflcio: More than 100,000! http://bit.ly/h57ikr **#WIunion #WeAreWI**
6:39pm Feb 26

@bluecheddar1 blue cheddar
@purrplecatmama Now home. Damn cold there. Amazing turn-out, people just getting covered in a heavy snow. Completely unfazed. **#wiunion**
7:07pm Feb 26

@micahuetricht Micah Uetricht
Town hall mtg going on in capitol rotunda. Trying to get a sense of what will happen tomorrow at 4pm, when police kick folks out **#wiunion**
8:10pm Feb 26

LESSONS OF THE CAPITOL STRUGGLE

ELIZABETH WRIGLEY-FIELD
MARCH 9, 2011

Adapted from an article first published at SocialistWorker.org

The round-the-clock occupation of the Wisconsin state Capitol ended March 3 amid stark strategic debates on how to take the struggle forward. The fault lines of that debate continue to separate two poles of the movement in Wisconsin today.

On one side is the strategy backed by the largest unions and organizations: exclusive focus on elections to recall Republican state senators. On the other are those of us who see the central strategic issue as creating new networks focused on escalating direct, mass pressure on the state government and its corporate backers. As a proponent of the later approach, I want to share how these debates played out at the crucial moments that determined when and how the Capitol occupation would continue.

For 16 days, the Capitol occupation had been the most visible symbol of the remarkable series of protests for workers' rights in Wisconsin and a focal point for solidarity from around the world. At a more practical level, it was also the space where activists met one another, debated strategies and ideas, and organized. That occupation played a crucial role in maintaining the momentum of the protests after Madison teachers ended their sickout and returned to work during the second week of protests.

With the occupation now over, in part due to Governor Scott Walker's illegal restrictions on access to the building, activists are regrouping and developing new strategies. But the last five days of the occupation—in particular, the debates over when and how to stay or leave—revealed differences that will inform the strategies to come.

The division appeared most sharply on the first day that the police ordered the Capitol cleared—Sunday, Feb. 27—and the last day of the 16-day continuous occupation, on Thursday, March 3.

On Feb. 27, this divergence took the form of struggle for democracy within the movement as much as for the Capitol itself. Democrats, most labor union leaders and staffers, and the activists who saw themselves as running the Capitol occupation directed everyone to leave as ordered by the police at 4 p.m., while a pre-selected group was to stay behind to be arrested with a carefully constructed media message. According to Capitol Police Chief Charles Tubbs, labor leaders and the police had negotiated this exit plan—though this was news to many union members and activists involved in the occupation. Union staffers and other activists widely presented the situation as though all decisions were made: The building would inevitably be shut down and all those left in it arrested, and the only decision left was whether to join the planned protests—on its terms—or to leave quietly.

As the 4 p.m. deadline approached, Democratic state Rep. Brett Hulsey sauntered past a long line of people waiting to speak and occupied the microphone for 12 minutes, telling the crowd, "And now I want you to do the most important thing in this campaign, which is to follow me out of that door at 4 o' clock." Hulsey's lengthy speech was facilitated by self-appointed MCs who had taken control of the building's main microphones as the deadline neared; one told me he was "just doing what he was told" though he couldn't say who had told him to do what.

But rather than follow Hulsey out of the Capitol, a small group of activists had organized a different strategy: Pack the building with people refusing to leave at the deadline in the hopes that if the numbers were large enough, no one would be arrested, and the building would remain ours. In this context, those of us who fought to continue the occupation felt that we were fighting just as much for democracy within the movement as we were to continue the occupation.

In the course of this effort, we met and joined with other small groups with the same goal. One network organized in the Capitol, which later began calling itself A People's Movement, had met over several days and headed into Sunday with a plan to try to keep the building open. Correctly guessing that the police would prevent people from entering the building as the afternoon wore on, this group organized to bring crowds of people inside the Capitol to the building's entrances to protest the doors being closed to the outside. The contingents chanting, "Let them in!" helped to focus anger at the Capitol being closed, rather than acceptance of the restrictions coming from the police.

As the 4 p.m. deadline hit, instead of leaving, hundreds of activists, including many union members, decided to stay inside the Capitol. After having claimed that arrest was imminent, Capitol Police decided to avoid arrests by leaving the building open: a huge victory for protesters.

On the last day of the occupation, the same constellations of forces emerged. By this time, Walker had kept the building under illegal lockdown for four days, beginning the morning after the Feb. 27 victory. This was in violation of an explicit promise made to protesters by Chief Tubbs that the building would reopen as usual the following morning.

By Thursday, March 3, the core of activists inside the building had dwindled to fewer than 50 people, as thousands of others—in violation of the state Constitution—were kept from joining them by restrictions put on entering the Capitol. Activists knew they could not hold on indefinitely in these circumstances, so discussions inside the building turned to how to resist the police clampdown.

Over several days, activists tested the limits of the police and developed their own confidence and initiative. On Tuesday, March 1, after police set up "checkpoints" in the building, a small group of protesters moved to sit just outside the allowed area. This provoked debate inside the building about whether resisting police directives threatened the occupation—a debate that ended after half an hour, when the police decided to respond by moving the rope barrier so that those sitting were once again inside it. Then the activists moved to the other side again, establishing that even though they were flagrantly violating the rules, the police did not intend to arrest them.

As Student Labor Action Coalition member Scot McCullough explained, "It was big because they said, 'You can't cross this line,' and then we did, and they didn't do anything. ... We showed that the police don't have supreme rule here."

On Thursday, March 3, activists hatched a more daring plan. To get protesters inside the building despite police efforts to limit access, a small group inside rushed an under-guarded Capitol door and held it open at the precise moment that thousands of people had gathered for a "No Concessions" rally on the other side. Hundreds of union members streamed into the statehouse in the minutes before police managed to shut the doors again.

The mood was jubilant—for about 15 minutes, before Rep. Hulsey returned to lead people out once again. This time, the group inside advocating to stay was too small to effectively influence what happened, and by this point it was clear that to fully cooperate with the police was incompatible with maintaining the occupation. As most people filed out, what remained was a core of only about 20 activists, faced with a court order ordering them to leave.

Late that night, after hours of discussion, the small group remaining in the Capitol marched out singing, greeted by hundreds of supporters. The 16-day occupation of the Capitol had ended.

No one can fault activists—some of whom had been in the Capitol continuously for four days or longer—for choosing to leave on March 3. As the Capitol became more restricted, holding the space increasingly became a source of exhaustion rather than of creativity and networking, making it hard for activists to formulate longer-term strategies.

In that sense, the key moment was not the decision to leave the Capitol late on Thursday night. Rather, it was a long series of decisions up to that point that led to the end of the occupation: activists accepting every restriction made by the police, and the lack of an effective plan to resist, outside the courtroom, Walker's illegal restrictions on entry.

The direct action that had brought hundreds into the Capitol only hours before the occupation ended, the successful occupation on the night of Sunday, Feb. 27, and the smaller actions inside the Capitol last week showed that activists could effectively resist police orders. But this lesson was absorbed too late to bring sufficient people into the Capitol to hold it in the face of the decision of much of organized labor to scuttle the occupation.

The fault lines exposed in the Capitol debates will reassert themselves in the post-occupation strategies for taking the movement forward. The unions' strategy is to focus everything on efforts to recall the Republican senators. The idea is that special elections can elect Democrats who will modify Walker's attacks on collective bargaining, maintaining unions' legal existence—and their campaign contributions.

A recall effort could put pressure on Republican legislators to back away from their harshest demands. But it is no substitute for the kind of struggles—the teachers' sickouts and the Capitol occupation—that have propelled the struggle forward.

And in practice, the push for the recall strategy is explicitly being counterposed to action. Thus, the recall strategy relegates the hundreds of thousands of people who have protested Walker's so-called "budget-repair" bill to an almost wholly passive role. At best, they will be phone-bankers and signature-gatherers for an electoral campaign focused in eight relatively conservative districts.

Instead of building the mass movement to stop the cuts now, the Democrats and union leaders are willing to take the risk of the cuts going through, based on the hope that they will recapture the state Senate in a few months' time. But given that Walker will remain in office and the state Assembly will remain in Republican hands, it will be almost impossible to reverse those cuts once they've passed.

The cost of the Democrats' strategy of counterposing recall elections to mass action can already be seen, from the constant—and frankly condescending—admonitions to "be peaceful" to the attempts to carefully manage a media message. In fact, union leaders preferred to split the March 5 rally rather than let Michael Moore speak from their stage, for fear that he'd call for a general strike. This reflects a deep distrust of rank-and-file workers and the power of their self-organization.

But that power is what has propelled the movement forward over the last three weeks in Wisconsin. This has been seen from the regular mass demonstrations to the self-organization of Capitol City, when the hundreds of us sleeping in the Capitol managed to run it better than normal. It was direct action by large numbers of people who occupied the Capitol, spearheaded by teachers.

The most effective strategy for building a new labor movement will involve organizing the direct power of the masses of angry, hopeful, fright-

212 | THE REVOLUTION WILL NOT BE PHONEBANKED

ened and inspired people whose lives Walker is planning to wreck. The teachers gave us a glimpse of that power when they shut down schools for four days and led the blockade of the state Legislature that launched the occupation of the Capitol.

But all this hasn't been enough to stop Walker. A disruption serious enough to make Walker and his corporate backers think twice would have to involve mass action that could shut down multiple sectors of the state at once.

That vision can sometimes feel impossible to realize, even to those of us who favor it. But occupying the Capitol for over two weeks sounded just as crazy—before we did it. The question being posed to all of us in Wisconsin is whether we are going to make the most of this historic opportunity and try to organize, from the bottom up, a labor movement that fights—or fritter it away because of the fear that things will get out of hand.

Elizabeth Wrigley-Field is a graduate student at the University of Wisconsin-Madison and a member of the Teaching Assistants' Association, the Wisconsin Resists coalition, and the International Socialist Organization.

@micahuetricht Micah Uetricht
Church service about to start in the rotunda.
10:05am Feb 27

@micahuetricht Micah Uetricht
Word from several sources in capitol is if there are enough protesters in building, police won't arrest them all. **#wiunion**
#notmywi #wearewi
11:03am Feb 27

@cabell Cabell Gathman
Members of marginalized groups (POC, LGBTQ, low-income, etc.) risk greater consequences for civil disobedience. **#WeAreWI**
1:15pm Feb 27

@DefendWisconsin Defend Wisconsin
They are restricting access to the Capitol. Line formed at the King Street entrance. **#wiunion #wearewi**
1:40pm Feb 27

@MelissaRyan Melissa Ryan
RT @ddayen: My sense is that the Capitol police don't quite know yet how they will clear this building **#wiunion**
1:44pm Feb 27

@LegalEagle Legal Eagle
If the Capitol is "open to the public" until 4, but they won't let the public in, how is that open? **#wiunion**
2:27pm Feb 27

@LegalEagle Legal Eagle
I haven't felt this rushed and panicky since my first contested hearing.
2:43pm Feb 27

@ddayen David Dayen
Release from protesters: "citizens to remain in Capitol" more in a minute **#wiunion**
2:54pm Feb 27

WISCONSIN'S LOST STRIKE MOMENT

Dan S. Wang and Nicolas Lampert

April 28, 2011

Versions of this essay were originally published on Daily Kos, Proposition Press, *and the Justseeds blog.*

Two months into the Wisconsin uprising a movement still exists, but where it goes from here is unclear. The "budget-repair" bill that will end collective bargaining rights for most public employees in Wisconsin is currently tied up in the courts. Legal challenges will likely go on for several months, maybe longer. In the meantime, risks, challenges, and contradictions loom within a movement that can be described as painfully moderate. Wisconsin citizens have arisen and protested in massive numbers. The sleeping giant that is the labor movement plus working class solidarity has awoken. But the outlook is not entirely optimistic.

The Wisconsin uprising has reflected the strengths and weaknesses of the organized labor movement. Organized labor has mobilized huge numbers of people and demonstrated the collective power of public and private unions to combat Governor Scott Walker, the GOP, and corporate greed. But the movement has also become sadly reflective of the labor's leaders— cautious, allergic to direct action and civil disobedience, and most of all, averse to calling a strike. Labor leadership has instead curtailed a movement that had real potential to defeat Walker and real potential to demand

and create a more just and equal society, and transformed it into a movement that has become all about protest marches, recall efforts, and votes for Democrats.

This is a shame. For the first week, the Wisconsin uprising was all about taking risks, the eminent power of self-organized action, and the snowballing impacts of tactical escalation. Even the flight of Wisconsin's 14 Democratic senators to Illinois—to break the quorum needed for the Legislature to vote on the union-busting bill—was an act of aggression, a true counterattack that served as an *escalation*. Every escalation risks a loss of support, a desertion of the nervous, the unsure, and the moderate. But in each of the earlier escalations—the student walkouts, teachers' sickouts, the Capitol occupation, resolve stiffened and excitement grew massively.

But precisely because these 14 Democratic senators are elected officials, their move opened up a whole front of legalistic minutiae, opaque and inaccessible to the vast majority of the citizenry. At the same time, as a media storyline, the 14 drowned out the other risk-taking constituencies—rank-and-file union members, non-obedient law enforcement workers, unorganized private-sector workers, and high school, college, and graduate students. As movement voices, the Senate Democrats presented solutions in terms of legislative compromise and electoral strategy. While we credit them for their timely move, for all the above reasons, the flight of the 14—i.e., inserting themselves into the movement—in hindsight represents a structural *moderation* from within the movement.

This was confirmed when some of the returning 14 Democratic senators spoke to more than 150,000 people who gathered around the Capitol for a huge rally on Saturday, March 12. They spoke almost exclusively of the movement as an electoral effort, and neglected to credit the chain of escalations that made their own move possible. For us, the lesson of the day was that the grassroots would do well by refraining from over-valorizing the 14. And we would do better by reflecting on the actions of fellow workers and global citizens in Egypt who inspired us during the first week—the ones who peacefully toppled a 30-year autocrat partly thanks to an unwavering general strike. In times like this, when public unions are fighting for their very existence, and a wide range of constituencies face attacks that threaten to undo decades of hard-earned progress, all tactics are needed to win, including strikes and direct action. No action can be ruled out.

From the point of view of the raging non-unionized grassroots and many rank-and-file union members, a one-day strike should have been called on the day that Walker signed the anti-union bill. The hot potato then would have been thrown back into Walker's hands, confronting him with the queasiness of having to carry out his stated threats to fire public workers. But it did not happen. The union leadership responded with words, not actions, thereby severing the chain of escalations, and *accepting defeat*. By this time the movement had for all practical purposes become identified, including from within, as union-led, leaving the non-union grassroots with nowhere to channel their outrage, energy, and willingness to share risk. A precious historic opportunity was lost.

What we've been reminded of in Wisconsin over the last two months is that once started, following through on the chain of escalations gives us a better chance of winning specific battles and puts our opposition on the defensive—as long as we have the courage, vision, and creativity to increase the pressure when the opportunities present themselves. Strategically speaking, the events in the chain of escalation itself are what generate the spaces for new possibilities, new ways of relating to each other as citizens, the beginnings of the democracy we want, and the ground on which new leaders and new ideas emerge from the grassroots. Electoral politics alone do not accomplish this. Neither do the cautious tactics of labor leaders. Ask yourself, when has labor won a significant victory without calling a strike? And when has a social justice movement won significant demands without the one-two punch of electoral politics *combined* with civil disobedience and actions that led to mass arrests?

Now that the chain has been broken and the conservatives have prevailed for the moment, the question is how to restart a series of meaningfully oppositional actions. In other words, if this movement is to be sustained, it can no longer be exclusively or even primarily about unions, collective bargaining, or the GOP's greed and lies, as egregious as they are. In order to win, we need to imagine and articulate *the society that we want to live in*, not simply fight defensively against the latest round of GOP/corporate attacks. The Wisconsin uprising must evolve into a movement that speaks to the priorities of immigrants and the inner-city poor, the unorganized private-sector workers, the struggling farm communities, the unemployed, and the incarcerated—as loudly as it speaks to the concerns of the unionized. We need to ask what it would take to make this movement truly popular. *We have the power of numbers* but we remain separated by walls of division.

As we move forward we need to examine why overly cautious labor leaders and unimaginative Democrats took the reins of a movement that held such promise, and how we let them. We urge our fellow citizens and grassroots activists to reserve our power separately from the "leadership" and prepare for the next uprising, the one that will erupt in a day, a week, a month, or years down the road—the one in which we do not let the opportunity slip away.

Dan S. Wang is a writer and artist who lives in Madison and works at Columbia College in Chicago, where he is a member of the part-time faculty union (PFAC).

Nicolas Lampert is a Milwaukee-based activist-artist who teaches at the University of Wisconsin-Milwaukee and belongs to the TAUMP union (American Federation of Teachers-Wisconsin). He is a member of the Justseeds Artists' Cooperative (www.Justseeds.org).

@AndrewKroll Andy Kroll
T-minus fifteen mins until **#wiunion** protesters scheduled to be moved out... **#wearewi**
3:15pm Feb 27

@evale72 evale72
The voice you hear is the our advisers instructing the crowd on their legal options and non violent civil disobedience tactics.
3:16pm Feb 27

@LegalEagle Legal Eagle
Hello awesome tweeps: I'm not PLANNING to get arrested. Just prepared for all contingencies. Thanks for your concern. **#wiunion**
3:27pm Feb 27

@AndrewKroll Andy Kroll
RT @MikeElk: When arrests begin, in capitol we will play Dr King's final speech where he was in Memphis to support AFSCME sanitation workers
3:28pm Feb 27

@ddayen David Dayen
People planning on not leaving holding up their hands **#wiunion**
3:40pm Feb 27

@micahuetricht Micah Uetricht
All of a sudden press is everywhere. all it took was a few hundred people ready to get arrested. **#wiunion #wearewi**
3:49pm Feb 27

@ddayen David Dayen
Chant "stand our ground" **#wiunion**
3:51pm Feb 27

@evale72 evale72
RT @brandzel 3rd police officer in a row whose simply said, "thank you for being here". Something very unusual is happening..
3:56pm Feb 27

@ddayen David Dayen
Countdown to 4:00 **#wiunion**
3:59pm Feb 27

WISCONSIN AND BEYOND

Kim Moody

AGAINST THE CURRENT, MAY/JUNE, 2011

"I believe leaders of the business community, with few exceptions, have chosen to wage a one-sided class war in this country..."
– Doug Fraser, UAW President, 1978

"...20 years or so down the road we'll be talking about the 'before Wisconsin' and 'after Wisconsin' movements."
– Tom Juravich, labor organizer and researcher 2011

"...the organization does not supply the troops for the struggle, but the struggle, in an ever growing degree, supplies recruits for the organization."
– Rosa Luxemburg, *The Mass Strike,* 1906

As the last decade or more has demonstrated, unions don't grow incrementally as a result of their patient, even persistent efforts to recruit. Rather, unions grow more or less rapidly in periods of intense conflict and labor upheaval. Such was the clear experience of the 1930s. In a somewhat more uneven fashion, the period from the mid-1960s through the 1970s saw rising numbers of strikes, increased rank-and-file rebellion, and the addition of 4 million members to the ranks of organized labor.

While some level of organization is required to spark a rise in labor's side of the class struggle, Rosa Luxemburg was essentially right that it is "the struggle, in an ever growing degree, (that) supplies recruits." The

February–March events in Wisconsin, across the Midwest, and indeed around the country, have already ignited a spark that has drawn tens, perhaps hundreds of thousands into action.

It's not just that the demonstrations have been big and bold, which they certainly have been. Nor is it that fairly high-placed union leaders called for actions, refreshing as that is. Rather it is that these events, the occupations, the growing numbers, the rallying of non-union supporters, the national outpouring, are the consequence of countless grassroots initiatives—of worker self-activity—that carried these events beyond what those who might have initiated them had ever imagined possible, or perhaps desirable.

Like the beginnings of upsurge in earlier times, the rebellion that began with Wisconsin's public workers—against one of the most far-reaching attacks on workers' rights in some time—came as a result of anger building after years of pressure on public employees all across the nation.

Real wages of Wisconsin public employees, for example, grew by less than 1 percent from 1999 through 2009. Municipal employees in Madison hadn't had a wage increase for three years. But we are to imagine that they are to blame for the state's newly manufactured deficit, even though the research arm of the National Nurses United found that two-thirds of Wisconsin corporations paid no taxes. So, to injury was added insult.

Crisis and Pressure

These kinds of pressures, of course, are not unique to public-sector workers. Enormous pressures of work intensification have joined slumping income and attacks on benefits of all kinds. The Great Recession brought still more pressure on those with jobs, while continuing the shift of the workforce as a whole to lower-paid work. I'm suggesting here that these same attacks and erosions of power, which have brought about labor's retreats and stalemates, may also be what impels people to rebellion.

Not surprisingly, the recent Great Recession dealt another blow to a very weakened labor movement. In 2009 and 2010, after a couple of years of moderate growth, the unions lost 1.4 million members, with all the net loss in the private sector. Collective bargaining outcomes followed suit. In 2008, according to Bureau of National Affairs reports, the average negotiated first-year wage increase was 3.6 percent. By 2009 it had sunk to 2.3 percent, and by the first nine months of 2010 to 1.7 percent. State and local public-workers did even worse as first-year increases dropped from 3.2 percent in 2008 to 2.0 percent in 2009 and 1.3 percent in the first nine months of 2010. In this latter year 35 percent of all agreements contained no first-year wage increase.

Benefits had been eroding for some time, and by 2009 only 20 percent of all workers still had a defined benefit pension. The percentage of workers with employer-provided health insurance fell from over 68 percent in 2000 to just under 62 percent in 2008. Of course, union workers are more likely to have such coverage, but here too erosion has been at work as more workers pay more in deductibles, co-pays, or even premiums. The results among different groups of workers varied, of course, but what seemed to be the object of capital was a gradual redefinition of what "subsistence" would amount to in the Marxist sense, i.e., the historically and culturally acceptable living standard for the "average" worker.

Ongoing increases in the intensity of work had become a regular feature of the 2000s, after the recession of 2000–01. From 2002–2007 productivity grew by 2.2 percent a year, much higher than even the rate of the 1983–89 recovery. The Great Recession provided still another opportunity to increase this rate even more, as production grew faster than hiring. Not surprisingly, corporate profits hit an all-time high at $1.7 trillion in the third quarter of 2010, an increase of 28 percent over the year before. And it was not the financial sector that brought these new profits, but the domestic profits of the non-financial sector where profits soared 40 percent in that period.

With strikes at an all-time low, a little over 100 in 2009 according to the Federal Mediation and Conciliation Service, it might be concluded that Doug Fraser's "one-sided class war" was still the reality. But prolonged periods of massive pressure on work, particularly when joined by falling incomes, tend to build resentment and anger.

This may be expressed in both negative and positive ways. Disgusted union voters stay home or even vote for Republicans, as in 2010. A few may join the largely middle-class Tea Party movement. But sooner or later the anger is likely to find the real culprits and explode. This is what happened in the 1930s after five years of speed-up and wage cuts, and in the mid-1960s as the impact of what Mike Davis calls "the management offensive of 1958–63" took its toll. This may well be what has happened in Wisconsin and around the country in early 2011.

Create Crisis, Blame the Workers

The fiscal crisis that the states find themselves in today has to be understood in the context of the massive shift of income that occurred in the last 30 years or so, as labor income shrank from 73.9 percent in 1979 to 70.4 percent in 2006. Much of this was simply the huge rise in the rate of surplus value extracted from the working class over this period (see "Crisis and Potential in Labor's Wars," *Against the Current* No. 145, March/April 2010), but some of this shift unquestionably derives from the reduction of taxes on corporate America.

Thus the annual share of after-tax profit as a proportion of total profits rose from 54–55 percent in the 1960s and 1970s to two-thirds in the 1990s and 2000s. At the state level corporate taxes fell from 9.7 percent of total (non-federal) receipts in 1970s to 6.7 percent in 2006. This underlying source of state fiscal problems would be enhanced in Wisconsin by the actions of Governor Scott Walker.

As noted above, Wisconsin public workers have not seen any real increase in weekly wages for a decade. Indeed, as one study by the Economic Policy Institute shows, Wisconsin public employees make 14.2 percent less than comparable private-sector workers in annual wages and 10.7 percent less in hourly terms. They have better benefits, but they pay more for them: 26.7 percent of total public-sector compensation goes to non-wage benefits, compared to 19.4 to 22.8 percent in the private sector.

Health insurance accounts for 12.9 percent of compensation for public employees, compared to 7 percent to 9.7 percent for those in the private sector. The comparable figures for retirement benefits are 8 percent to between 2.5 and 4.9 percent. Yet Walker and his big business allies, including the billionaire Tea Party backers David and Charles Koch and the far-right business group Club for Growth Wisconsin, are saying in ads and elsewhere that public-sector workers aren't sacrificing like everyone else (everyone?).

Demonizing public employees has been a nationwide campaign for some time, and recently no group of public workers has been more systematically targeted than teachers. Campaign after campaign has claimed that "bad teachers" are to blame for America's slumping test results, as though these were the measure of everything. *Newsweek* ran a 2010 cover suggesting the solution to poor education was to fire poor teachers. Last August the *Los Angeles Times* rated thousands of teachers as bad, based on leaked test scores.

President Barack Obama's "Race to the Top" has also demonized teachers. The drive to deprive teachers of seniority and collective bargaining has gained momentum, despite the fact that states with strong teachers' unions and collective bargaining are among the highest scoring. Furthermore, nationally between 2000 and 2006 teachers' salaries have fallen behind inflation by 3 percent. Wisconsin teachers actually make $2,600 a year less than the national average. Teachers, of course, played a big role in the Wisconsin rebellion.

Nevertheless, Walker's entire case for his draconian anti-union legislation rests on the assertion that public workers are to blame for the state's deficits, their wages and benefits said to be "unsustainable." So it is necessary not only that these should be cut, but that the workers' ability to resist such cuts be removed entirely.

On top of anger about their own economic reality is the fact that Wisconsin's public-sector workers know they are not the source of the deficits. It was known that Walker has ballooned the deficit for the next fiscal year, mainly by handing out $140 million to various business and special-interest groups. Had he not done this, there would be no crisis with which to beat up the state's public employees.

Indeed the problem in Wisconsin, as in many states and within the federal government, goes back even farther. A study done by the research arm of the National Nurses United showed that two-thirds of Wisconsin corporations had paid no taxes for years. Public-worker anger not only had more fuel, it also had a culprit—in fact, a cluster of very well-off culprits.

Walker, along with other newly elected Republican governors and state lawmakers, are on a rampage to destroy public-sector unions and collective bargaining. As any number of commentators have argued, this is about power, class power, not budgets. His legislation not only limits collective bargaining to wages, which he has vowed to cut, but eliminates dues check-off and requires an annual decertification vote, a combination that would certainly destabilize most unions. This is, in short, an attack on the unions as institutions, a fact that in itself explains much about the origins of the fight in Wisconsin, above all the unusually militant responses of the state's top level union officials.

Dynamics of the Struggle

The call for escalating demonstrations beginning on Tuesday, Feb. 15 from the local American Federation of State, County, and Municipal Employees

(AFSCME), Wisconsin Education Association Council (WEAC) and American Federation of Teachers (AFT), was meant specifically to protest the bill that was to be introduced on that Thursday. The threat to the very institution of unionism was enough to stir the top leaders to action. AFSCME President Gerald McEntee came to Madison on the first day, John Nichols tells us in *The Nation* (Feb. 15, 2001), "not merely to protest but to lobby."

In other words, militant tactics were tied to conventional strategies— lobbying to stop the bill. As the crisis deepened, WEAC took a step further and urged its members to call in sick and rally in Madison. After two days they would call off the sickout. Furthermore, with the institutional defense foremost in mind, these leaders agreed in advance to grant Walker the cuts he was asking, including an 8 percent wage cut.

Whatever the narrow, if understandable, objectives and means the top officials had in mind, they had set something in motion that would go far beyond conventional lobbying or protest and even, for some, beyond the official union goals. The escalating numbers, rising to 30,000 on Friday the 18 and then 70,000 on Saturday, the occupation of the Capitol's rotunda night after night by workers and students, the growing out-of-state contingents, reaching a peak of perhaps 100,000 on Saturday the 26, all spoke of grassroots initiatives.

Observers called the growing demonstrations and occupations "spontaneous," and pointed to the roles of volunteers in organizing the overnight occupations of the Capitol. Local unions took turns volunteering for "sleepover" duty on different nights. Car pools from around the state and then from out-of-state were organized by local unions, groups of activists, and even individuals.

In short, the union officialdom had called into being a movement that exceeded its expectation or intentions. A lobby and demonstration became a major disruption that drew thousands from their jobs into the streets of Madison, the halls of the statehouse, and then cities around the country. The dynamics of class conflict had revealed themselves for all to see.

This truly mass movement has had unexpected and unconventional results. The 14 Democrats who left the Capitol for Illinois on Feb. 17 certainly did something out of character. The fact that they remained out-of-state for as long as they did was also a consequence of the mass movement—they had looked their electoral base in the eye and saw it demanding action. Indiana's Democratic legislators took the cue and did the same. If in the end, the movement could not stop the Republicans from ramming through their bill, it did disrupt politics-as-usual to an extent rarely seen in the United States.

The dynamics of the struggle also pushed past the expectations and intentions of most top union officials in at least three other ways. For one thing, the mass movement galvanized public opinion. "Which side are you on?" goes the old song and by almost two to one the public, both in Wisconsin and nationally, sided with the movement against the governor.

Perhaps less desired by some union officials was the anti-concessions wing of the movement that developed around the National Nurses United (NNU). This led to a demonstration explicitly opposing the state labor leaders' agreement to accept Walker's cuts, including the 8 percent wage reduction and the cut which would cost 70,000 people Medicaid coverage. On March 3 a no-concessions "funeral" march, led off by a New Orleans-style brass band, drew 7,000 people. The march was addressed by Jim Cavanaugh, president of the South Central Federation of Labor (SCFL), which played a central role throughout the movement.

Then there was the resolution passed by SCFL calling for education and preparation for a general strike if the legislation passed. The resolution passed with the votes of all but one of its 97 affiliates in both the public and private sectors. A committee was set up to consult with European union about how they organize such strikes. General strike or not, the idea came from an on-the-ground central labor council composed of local union delegates caught up in the spirit of rebellion.

The fight against the anti-union laws proposed in several states didn't actually begin in Wisconsin. To the 400 or so Minnesotans who stormed their state Legislature the week before belongs that honor. And of course workers and their unions in Ohio, Indiana, and elsewhere launched their own demonstrations and occupations of resistance. But it was the massive nature of events in Wisconsin that brought union members into the streets across the entire nation on Feb. 26 in support of their struggle.

The speculation on the impact of all of this ranges from "D-Day" to "Dunkirk," as labor analyst Harley Shaiken put it. Some union leaders seem genuinely inspired. The CWA, for example, intends to recruit veterans of the struggles in Wisconsin, Ohio and Indiana to help them organize 20,000 T-Mobile workers. Certainly the thousands who participated in one way or another have not only been inspired, but have learned much about the reality of class politics in America. There is an enormous opportunity here.

An "After Wisconsin" Movement?

If there is to be the sort of growth organized labor desperately needs, it will not be just a matter of more and better organizing tactics and strategies. It will have to come through an intensification of the level of struggle that, as Luxemburg put it, "supplies the recruits to the organization."

There are at least two ways in which the recent events, including the passage of the anti-union legislation in Wisconsin and soon across the Midwest, can aid this process. The first is the obvious possibility that thousands of people who participated and/or were inspired by the Wisconsin upsurge will become the volunteer army that U.S. labor has long needed to grow. The second flows from the fact that the Republicans have made labor rights a political issue in a way they have not been for a long time.

Like the "black box" of work itself, labor rights are seldom considered media-worthy despite the alarming state into which they have fallen or been pushed. The relative invisibility of labor rights in mainstream political discourse was one reason why it was so easy for Obama and the Congressional Democrats to bury the Employee Free Choice Act (EFCA). No one outside the unions themselves and a handful of academics saw this as a make or break political issue.

With public opinion now running two to one in favor of labor rights as a basic cornerstone of democracy, it is possible that this could become the national debate it needs to be—perhaps even to the point of reviving the EFCA as an issue in the 2012 elections. This must not, however, be just another election techno-mobilization a la 2008, but a grassroots movement in the streets, schools, and workplaces (union or not) of the nation. As with the labor movement of the 1930s and the social movements of the 1960s and 1970s, it is mass action that alters the political agenda in U.S. politics.

Both these possibilities depend to a dangerous degree on the ability of the labor officialdom to provide leadership, resources, and support to such a movement. I say "dangerous" because the track record is not good. The almost congenital proclivity of America's top labor leaders to turn progressive mood swings into a conventional, though no doubt well-funded and staffed, Democratic Party election campaign may well prove irresistible. If this is all that happens, a great opportunity will have been lost.

Among the many lessons of the Wisconsin events is that politicians develop backbone to the degree their base is in the streets and "out of control." Should the Democrats take back various statehouses, perhaps even Congress, and the mass movement subsides, they will fall back into their pattern of compromise and retreat. Post-Wisconsin politics need to be a politics of mobilization and direct action if the debate on workers' rights is to replace that of austerity and increasing empoverishment.

For the past two years, the right and their Tea Party shock troops dominated political discourse in the style of a semi-mass movement, sometimes attracting the angry and frustrated with their sharp rhetoric. This year in Wisconsin and across the Midwest, the Tea Party efforts to support these Republican governors were pathetic and that movement was reduced to its true proportion as a middle-class minority. This year, the working-class majority spoke in the loudest voice and clearest terms it has for decades, and attracted broad support in the process.

A growing labor movement can drown the sound of the right, but growth will not be orderly or commanded from some center. The events in Wisconsin did not reach the point of a mass strike movement. Nevertheless, once again the words of Rosa Luxemburg concerning the fears of union officials that their organizations will "fall in pieces in a revolutionary whirlwind like rare porcelain" remind us that, on the contrary, "from the whirlwind and the storm, out of the fire and glow of the mass strike and the street fighting rise again, like Venus from the foam, fresh, young, powerful, buoyant trade unions."

@MelissaRyan Melissa Ryan
Announcement: The Capital is now closed. **#wiunion**
4:01pm Feb 27

@DefendWisconsin Defend Wisconsin
If you are at the capitol and want to leave, you should do so now. If you choose to say, move peacefully to the first floor rotunda.
4:07pm Feb 27

@MelissaRyan Melissa Ryan
Everyone is quite calm.
4:09pm Feb 27

@AndrewKroll Andy Kroll
Have **#wiunion** protesters called @govwalker's bluff? Cops aren't moving, neither are protesters...Capitol looks about the same...
4:21pm Feb 27

@DefendWisconsin Defend Wisconsin
Chanting is loud as ever, protestors are determined not to leave **#wiunion** **#wearewi**
4:27pm Feb 27

@LegalEagle Legal Eagle
We're still here! We're still here! Fuck. Yes. (because if anything ever deserved the fbomb for awesomeness, it's this)
4:29pm Feb 27

@micahuetricht Micah Uetricht
No way cops are arresting anyone any time soon. Too many people. Incredible **#wiunion**
4:33pm Feb 27

@WEAC WEAC
RT @edcetera: Whether you are for or against **#wiunion** take note of how Twitter, uStream Qik, etc helping coordinate everything
4:52pm Feb 27

@micahuetricht Micah Uetricht
My take: protesters will be here all night. Can't confirm but it appears police won't make a move. **#Wiunion**
5:15pm Feb 27

THE WISCONSIN UPRISING IS A BOTTOM-UP MOVEMENT - SHOULD WE HOPE DC LEADERS DON'T GET IN THE WAY?

Mike Elk

ALTERNET, MARCH 5, 2011

Since the financial crisis and President Barack Obama's election in the fall of 2008, there have been two major actions taken by working people that commanded the attention of America's financial elite—the 2008 occupation of Republic Windows and Doors factory in Chicago and the current Wisconsin Capitol occupation. Both events won enormous public support.

However, these types of events not only threatened economic elites that run our economy, but posed a challenge to established progressive leaders in Washington; how to incorporate them. The mass, spontaneous civil disobedience and direct action allowed workers to take matters into their own hands and upset the normal function of the insider relationships the progressive elite tend to rely upon.

As the president came into office in December 2008, United Electrical Workers (UE) at Republic Windows and Doors in Chicago shook the world when they occupied their factory after its closure was announced. For eight days and nights, the factory occupation held the attention of state, national, and international media as unions around the world issued statements of solidarity. Even President-elect Obama—then in downtown Chicago, just miles away from the factory—announced his support for the workers. The workers were ultimately successful in winning their legally-owed severance from Bank of America. As a result of the attention drawn to the struggle, the workers were able to find an owner to reopen and run the factory.

Despite the success in Chicago, there was no follow-up in terms of factory occupations by unions, plants employing thousands continued to close under Obama with little resistance. The progressive movement has so far not responded to the economic crisis in the way that the activists during the Great Depression did. They did not engage in the mass campaign of factory occupations and strikes that led to the New Deal nor did they engage in the campaigns of nonviolent civil disobedience that won civil rights for African Americans in the 1960s. And little effort was made to incorporate the success of Republic Windows and Doors.

"There were these big expensive conferences where people talked about how to build a progressive movement, but never was I or anybody from our union invited to talk about how we could replicate the tension with the banks that led to victory at Republic Windows and Doors," said veteran UE Political Action Director Chris Townsend. "Instead, the progressive movement just went back to relying on the same overpaid media consultants, playbook, and insider relationships that had resulted in their betrayal during the Clinton administration and the Carter administration before that."

And talk of nonviolent direct action was virtually nonexistent until events forced state public workers to rise up in Wisconsin. It seemed as if Governor Scott Walker was on his way to crushing public-sector unions in Wisconsin—and then something unexpected happened. Protesters occupied the Wisconsin Capitol, inspiring 14 Democratic senators to flee and effectively shut down the Wisconsin state Legislature. The current Capitol occupation has shaken elites throughout the country, created a political stalemate in Wisconsin, and forced governors in states like Indiana, Michigan, Florida and Iowa to back down from assaulting workers' rights.

Through dozens of interviews I conducted on the ground in Wisconsin with people involved in the protests at all levels, it became abundantly clear to me the protests in the early stages were not driven by top-down organizations or even the leadership of the Wisconsin-based labor organizations, but by the activists and workers themselves. While the leadership of these organizations played somewhat of a role in promoting the protests, the size and intensity of the protests was not something their leaders had the capacity to organize.

"When Governor Walker announced his budget-repair bill the Friday before, we met and thought it would be difficult for us to get 5,000 people for a rally the following Tuesday," says Dave Poklinkoski, president of IBEW Local 2304 and a prominent member of the 45,000-member Madison-based Wisconsin South Central Federation of Labor (SCFL). "When nearly 20,000 people showed up I was amazed. People saw what was happening and just simply showed up in solidarity."

One of the major sparks for these actions occurred at a little high school in a conservative suburb of Madison known as Stoughton. On Monday, Feb. 14, about 100 students at Stoughton High School decided to walk out of classes in a sign of solidarity with their teacher. While this high school walkout occurred, thousands of college students were spontaneously walking out of classes at the University of Wisconsin-Madison to attend rallies at the Capitol and in front of Walker's house. These two actions inspired high school students the following day to walk out of schools throughout Madison in the thousands and attend a rally with 20,000 people, mainly students, at the Capitol.

Madison teachers, inspired by their high school students who had left class that day, decided Tuesday evening to go on a strike themselves on Wednesday. As news of the call of the Madison teachers' strike spread, members of the Teaching Assistants' Association decided to occupy the Capitol overnight, which helped escalate the intensity of the protests dramatically. On Wednesday, 30,000 people showed up at the Capitol, far exceeding the wildest expectations of local labor leaders.

At this point on Wednesday when a critical mass of support had been grown by individual activists without much top-down organizing, the Wisconsin Education Association began to call on teachers unions throughout the state to call in sick on Thursday and Friday. Dozens of protests began to appear in cities and towns throughout Wisconsin that had never in their history seen protest crowds of that size. Even the conservative bastion of Appleton, Wisconsin, hometown of Joseph McCarthy, saw an unheard-of protest with over 2,000 people.

By Thursday, Feb. 17, the day the vote was expected on the budget-repair bill in the Wisconsin state Senate, crowds had grown to nearly 50,000 at the Capitol. State senators watched the crowds from their windows as they caucused that day and decided to flee the state. Many would later claim the senators were inspired to flee after seeing the massive outpouring of support on the lawn of the Capitol. These protests were organic; they weren't orchestrated by the direction of some established leader, but they certainly inspired leaders.

Since the protests, many progressive leaders in Washington who were nearly invisible during the first two years of the Obama administration have been attempting to take the spotlight, positioning themselves as representing the masses gallantly occupying the Wisconsin Capitol. An article appeared in *The Washington Post* shortly after the protests, claiming, "the president's political machine worked in close coordination Thursday with state and national union officials to get thousands of protesters to gather in Madison." In the dozens of interviews I conducted in Wisconsin, I did not encounter a single person who said they showed up at the protests because of an email from Obama's Organizing for America or the Democratic National Committee.

The internet-driven advocacy group, Progressive Change Campaign Committee got attention this week from sources including *The Atlantic*, *Talking Points Memo*, and *AlterNet* when they announced they were paying for thousands of dollars of robocalls in an effort to jumpstart the recall efforts of eight Republican Wisconsin state senators. These articles did not mention that most people find automated robocalls annoying and intrusive. Nor did they note that actual activists in Wisconsin had already been blanketing voters with calls in these districts for two weeks gauging support for recall efforts.

Many D.C.-based groups have spoken on behalf of the Wisconsin events as though they had some real role in the events, using tactics that have little proven effectiveness: press releases, passive internet-based activism, and expensive TV ads and robocalls. But how serious are these groups? Would they push to go as far as needed to actually win the fight in Wisconsin? On the ground, you can hear workers and local activists calling for a general strike.

The governor and the Republicans clearly intend to follow through on their assault," says Dave Poklinkoski, a forklift driver at a local utility company and president of IBEW Local 2304. "As history in America has shown, and most recently in Egypt has shown, it is when the working class begins to strike and shut things down that the capitalists start thinking seriously about backing off."

Poklinkoski played a key role in getting the 45,000-member SCFL, the local chapter of the AFL-CIO for the Madison and Southern Central Wisconsin area, to vote last week to make preparations for a general strike.

The motion passed the 97-member body nearly unanimously, with only one dissenting vote.

One person who worries about the role of D.C.-based organizations hampering the spreading of mass direction action is Stephen Lerner. One of the labor movement's brightest stars, Lerner led SEIU's famous Justice for Janitors and Wall Street/Bank Campaign.

"Labor, civil rights, and other groups that are involved in building a progressive majority and infrastructure are important to the movement but can't lead or control such a campaign. They are essential to funding, to creating capacity, credibility and scale," says Lerner.

"But the reality is that there is just enough political access, financial assets, and institutional interests to hinder and ultimately strangle a campaign, whose strategy must be built around tactics designed to create the level of disruption and uncertainty needed to force fundamental changes in how the economy is organized," says Lerner. "That's why the campaign needs to be independent, and not controlled by institutions with too much to lose."

The progressive movement is at a turning point. Will we embrace the same passive messaging and online activism tactics that led to progressive defeat in the last two years? Or will progressives adopt the tactics of civil disobedience and direct action used during the 1930s and 1960s that led to massive progressive gains?

Under the Taft-Hartley Act, a general strike in support of other workers is illegal; the key words of the SCFL resolution were the calls for the federation—not individual unions—to "begin educating affiliates and members on the organization and function of a general strike."

Many private-sector unions would not formally endorse the idea of a general strike out of fear of being of sued by their employer, but workers without formal endorsement of their unions could engage in wildcat strikes by simply deciding to walk out individually.

"If the unions do not make a formal call for a general strike, it probably avoids a Taft-Hartley issue," says Don Taylor, an assistant professor at the University of Wisconsin School for Workers.

In order to create conditions in which workers might walk out of work on a type of general strike, there has to be a great deal of discussion in the progressive and labor movement by organizations encouraging them to do that. If most of these online-based D.C. advocacy organizations wanted to show true solidarity with the protesters in Wisconsin, they would send out emails to their millions of members educating them about the possibility of a general strike in order to save collective bargaining in Wisconsin. Unlike unions, these organizations could legally do this under Taft-Hartley because of their non-union status.

If the large progressive advocacy organizations were willing to educate workers and activists about how to organize a general strike, it could spur on a dramatic people-powered political act not seen since the 1930s. Does Wisconsin represent the birth of a new, powerful progressive movement or is it simply the last violent, desperate gasps of air of a dying movement?

@ddayen David Dayen
Basically we all suck compared to these amazing kids and activists holding the Capitol in Madison **#wiunion #onedaylonger**
5:22pm Feb 27

@micahuetricht Micah Uetricht
Firefighters, teachers and students literally hand in hand right now. Like Seattle. Totally incredible **#wiunion**
5:32pm Feb 27

@brandzel Ben Brandzel
Just got a message on qik from someone singing we shall overcome with us from switzerland. **#SwissForSolidarity** :)
5:36pm Feb 27

@micahuetricht Micah Uetricht
Only the most jaded souls or the most hardcore Friedmanites could not be moved by what I am witnessing right now **#wiunion**
5:45pm Feb 27

@WEAC WEAC
RT @mikeelk: Women sit in a knitting circle to stop arrests - classic midwest union move **#wiunion**
5:49pm Feb 27

@LegalEagle Legal Eagle
If you can help spread the word that we're still here & we did not go quietly into the night, I'd appreciate it. News has it wrong. **#wiunion**
6:02pm Feb 27

@AndrewKroll Andy Kroll
Well, folks, we seem to be at a stalemate right now. Cops not moving, protesters just doing their thing, drumming and chanting.
6:11pm Feb 27

@micahuetricht Micah Uetricht
@AndrewKroll Don't think this is a stalemate. Looks more like the protesters are winning. **#Wiunion**
6:18pm Feb 27

WHAT NEXT: MOBILIZING OR ORGANIZING?

Monica Adams

MARCH 20, 2011

The following is adapted from a talk given by Monica Adams at the 2011 Left Forum.

It's clear that most everyone in Wisconsin is opposed to Governor Scott Walker's bill. What is not clear is what exactly are we for? I mean this in a larger scale, outside the context of the specific bill. What exactly will bring hundreds of thousands of people together again? Will it be to protect free lunch, or will it be to protect reduced lunch? Will it be to save food share, or will it be to save BadgerCare, health insurance to low-income families with children under age 19? In this sense, there's a lack of unity.

It's very clear that we are collectively shouting, "Kill the Bill." But what is not clear is what is the alternative. Is the vision to simply go back to the way things were a year ago? Or is the vision something greater?

Kwame Ture, also known as Stokely Carmichael, brings up an interesting point in thinking about building movements. He says there's a significant difference between mobilizing and organizing. Mobilizing is when a group of people are against the same things. Organizing is when a group of people are for the same things. While we've been proud of the work we've been doing in Madison, in fact, it's a huge mobilization effort and not so much a big organization effort. I think we need to spend more time figuring this out. If we're all trying to build a vision or to figure out what it is we're for, we know our work has to go beyond the sectors in which we participate. What's happening in Wisconsin can no longer be talked about as just what's affecting public-sector workers. It can no longer be talked about as just a movement of unions. It can no longer be talked about as groups of people—firefighters or cops or teachers. Instead, we have to understand the response to what is happening in Wisconsin as part of a larger movement that strives for racial and gender justice, queer liberation, as well as dismantling ableism and other larger forms of oppression.

My experience doing the work in Wisconsin is that it has been incredibly inspiring to be part of a large group of people who are out mobilizing to achieve something. But, at the same time, it has also been troubling. The harsh truth of the matter is that a lot of the workers who are out there mobilizing against Walker are the people who put him in office to begin with. It's important to understand this because it's going to determine how to build a solid base in order to build a movement. A lot of people who voted for Walker initially did so because they believed the all-too-common narrative of "lazy workers"—thinking it was just a targeted attack on people of color and immigrants, when, in actuality, he was talking about all of us. Surprise.

While we are supporting workers' rights, people of color, immigrants, and fighting in solidarity, we have to ask the critical question: "Will the same group of people be with us on our issues?" For example, in the bill there is a piece of legislation that says health-care providers will no longer be required to pay for contraceptives for women, but they would still pay for Viagra. Instead of thinking of this as just some small piece of legislation or something peripheral to the larger fight around collective bargaining, we must view this as a fundamental attack on women's reproductive health rights.

What's central in movements is that people have an identity around something and it cannot just be a mobilization. It cannot be that we all just agree on this—that's a coalition. If we're talking about a movement, we all have to collectively strive for something and be able to identify with each other on some sort of level. So the question is, "Who is the "we" of Wisconsin?" Is the "we" just the workers or just the middle-class public sector, or is it also the undocumented workers who make up a significant part of the dairy industry? Is it the chronically unemployed, underemployed, and those who never get the chance at a meaningful job due to structural racism, classism, and genderism?

Also, is the playing field leveled for all to participate in this movement? For example, what does the leadership and decision making look like? Frankly, I've been in too many places where all the people look the same. If we are building a movement of people and for the people, where the hell are all the people?

I think what's unique about this opportunity is now we are forging an alliance of folks who are not traditional allies. This could be something incredibly good, but we have to be able to do the hard work to ensure that it's something incredibly good and not give Walker, Republicans, and Tea Partiers the opportunity to play divide and conquer antics.

Also, in that spirit, we've been doing a lot of assuming about us having a common enemy, therefore necessitating that we are friends. I think we see on many different levels that's not necessarily true. So, how deep is the alliance? Is there really solidarity? For instance, what happens if we win collective bargaining? What happens if Walker says, "Damn it, I'm tired, you've won?" What if he says he'll leave the rights of collective bargaining alone? Do we all go home? Or do we say, "No, we're going to knock this Capitol down if you don't give back BadgerCare?"

In thinking about identities of folks, we also have to translate that into what kind of strategies we take up to further the movement. As I mentioned, not all of us have the same identities, so all of us can't equally participate in the same strategies. For example, do you honestly think that 150,000 black people can occupy the Capitol for 16 days? We have the ability to mobilize that many, but will we be there in solidarity with the police? Absolutely not. So this means we have to think about building inclusive strategies. I also think it took an incredible amount of privilege to be there. I was there for a few days, but I also had the privilege to be able to be there because I didn't have children. Folks I knew who had children who wanted to be there were not able to do so. Like all these other things, if we're talking about building a movement for the people, we have to create entry points so that all people can participate in all of the work that we are doing.

In that same spirit, we have to do the hard work of base building, but coming from a place of solidarity, which means we need ongoing political education around not just what it means to be a Republican, or what it means to be a Democrat, or how the mayor's office runs, but around what have been the struggles of folks of color in this country. How is 100 years of oppression tied to current policies?

In addition to political education, we need to get back to grassroots training. I think it's very attractive and easy to engage in some of this academic and high policy work, but what about the everyday ability to knock on doors and get people out who have no idea that this is going on?

We need to begin to escalate strategies, which we are beginning to see more of. So we need to be training folks around direct action organizing. Not only are we going to be peacefully protesting—we're still going to be nonviolent—but we're going to turn up the fire. We're going to shut down M&I Bank, but we're going to do more things. It's very clear that the right—Walker and others—has a very escalating strategy. Not only do we need to match it, we need to be able to defeat it, which requires us to develop our own escalating strategy.

We also need to be able to develop strategies that are relevant for people in their lives. Marches and protests feel very attractive, but we need to use people's skills and put them in more relevant areas. For example, if teachers want to strike, by all means strike. But I also think teachers are in a unique position to be able to mobilize an entire youth body by using their teaching skills to educate and politicize the youth. We know all social movements need young folks, and there are more schools than just UW-Madison. We also need to think about the way that people live their daily lives and how that can be politicized and connected to a larger movement. There's a lot of wisdom in the resistance that people carry every day, so I really want to connect that to a larger struggle.

Lastly, we need to start to build alternatives. I question any structure, any government that is able to take away so many rights so quickly. How does that happen? We cannot support such a structure. My rights should not be determined by whether or not this person in office is hopefully a good person. We should begin to invest in grassroots structures, in folks building alternative societies who have been doing it all along. As is written on the BadgerCare card, as the state motto goes, as the movement demands it: "Forward."

Monica Adams is a community organizer from Milwaukee, working in Wisconsin's black, Southeast Asian, and queer people of color communities to build an alternative society as the means to ending oppression.

@MelissaRyan
I will never stop loving the sound of the drums.

ON WISCONSIN!

THE WISCONSIN UPRISING WAS SO HUGE, so unexpected, and so unlikely, that there are no clear answers to the question of "What comes next?" Will we as progressives be able to turn the Wisconsin moment of transformation into a lasting movement? Will we be able to avoid returning to timid and defensive ways of the past, and instead continue to fight with a reawakened sense of boldness and possibility?

Many of the contributors to this collection have some pretty great ideas that, while by no means easy, speak to what is needed to create a larger movement of Wisconsin-like breakthroughs:

Emphasize progressive identity and history wherever you are, building today's fights atop legacies of the past whenever possible. Connect different progressive fights under a common banner to strengthen each and build a larger movement as a result. Create a strong progressive infrastructure everywhere—it was Madison's many cooperatively run institutions, left-leaning university departments, and strong local alternative media that helped raise the profile of the Wisconsin uprising early on and provided support networks for the protesters once it was underway. Develop good relationships with local police, so that they're on our side when it matters. Embrace a wide spectrum of people and organizations on the left—from anarchists and socialists to Democrats in the center, not dismissing each other but figuring out what each can contribute toward common goals. Tell our own stories through social media, and highlight the work of writers, photographers, and videographers—both amateur and professional—who are showing what's really happening. Think about ways to involve first-time activists. Make sure that anyone who wants to take part can plug in to real leadership positions, rather than being forced into low-level roles within a top-down organization. Recognize that people want to be connected, not divided, and they want to be part of a meaningful experience and community. Capitalize on moments of transformation. Force elected officials to take bold action. Keep asking the question of how we'll do this—to everyone you know—because the answer is contained in that continued questioning. Don't count us—progressives, the labor movement, radicals—out. Many like to speak about a movement taking its dying breaths, but if Wisconsin proved anything, it's that we're just getting started.

– Erica Sagrans

@AndrewKroll Andy Kroll
Every time I pass a big groups of police officers, at least one is using iPhone to take video of protests **#wiunion #wishyouwerehere**
6:44pm Feb 27

@MikeElk Mike Elk
POLICE said Protestors can stay the night in Wisconsin Capitol **#wiunion**
6:53pm Feb 27

@cabell Cabell Gathman
RT @kimberlycreates: RT @sickjew I can't believe the only way I can watch US history is from some dude's iPhone: http://qik.com/video/38
7:22pm Feb 27

@MelissaRyan Melissa Ryan
And on day 14 we kept our house. **#wiunion**
7:30pm Feb 27

RETURN TO WISCONSIN: THE BEGINNING OR THE END?

Andy Kroll

TomDispatch, March 31, 2011

It is easy to see the beginnings of things, and harder to see the ends.

– Joan Didion

In the February weeks I spent in snowy Madison, Wisconsin, that line of Didion's, the opening of her 1967 essay "Goodbye to All That," ricocheted through my mind as I tried to make sense of the massive protests unfolding around me. What was I witnessing? The beginning of a new movement in this country—or the end of an existing one, the last stand of organized labor? Or could it have been both?

None of us on the ground could really say. We were too close to the action, too absorbed by what was directly in front of us.

Of course, the battle between unions, progressive groups, and Wisconsin Republican Governor Scott Walker is not over. Not by a long shot. A county judge recently blocked "publication" of Walker's anti-union legislation, saying it was possible Senate Republicans violated Wisconsin's rigorous open-records law when they rammed through a vote on his bill to do away with the collective bargaining rights of state workers. The case could end up before the state Supreme Court. But that didn't stop the state's Legislative Reference Bureau from publishing Walker's bill anyway, touching off another round of arguing about the tactics used to make the bill into law. As of this writing, its actual status remains unclear. If a judge does force a new vote, it's unlikely the outcome will change, though even that's not certain.

Either way, the meaning of Madison, and also of what similar governors are doing amid similar turmoil in Columbus, Indianapolis, and other Midwestern cities, remains to be seen. Without the ability to bargain collectively, unions may indeed be fatally weakened. So, you could argue that the wave of attacks by conservative governors will gut public-sector unions in those states, if not wipe them out entirely.

On the other hand, those same efforts have mobilized startling numbers of ordinary citizens, young and old, educated and not, in a way none of us have seen since perhaps the 1930s. I know this for a fact. I was there in Madison and watched hundreds of thousands of protesters brave the numbing cold while jamming the streets to demand that Walker back down. The events in Madison radicalized many young people who kept the flame of protest burning with their live-ins inside the Wisconsin Capitol.

What remains to be seen is whether the new spark lit by the Republican Party's latest crusade against unions can in some way fill the space left by those unions which, nationwide, stare down their own demise.

"Take the Unions Out at the Knees"

Madison was the beginning. When Walker threatened to use the Wisconsin National Guard to quell a backlash in response to his draconian "budget-repair" bill, it set off a month of protests. Almost as soon as Madison erupted, Ohio Republican Governor John Kasich, a former executive at Lehman Brothers, unveiled a union-crushing bill of his own, known as Senate Bill 5. Kasich sought even more power to curb unions than Walker, proposing to curb bargaining rights for all public-sector unions—Walker's exempts firefighters and cops—and even outlaw strikes by public workers.

As in Madison, thousands of protesters poured into the Ohio Capitol in Columbus—that is, those who got inside before state troopers locked and blocked the doors. They brought megaphones and signs saying "Protect Workers Rights" and "Daughters of Teachers Against SB 5." And in response, like Walker, Kasich has shown not the slightest willingness to negotiate; earlier this month, he promised to sign the bill into law as soon as the legislature approves it.

Meanwhile, the union-busting movement continues to spread. Iowa's

House of Representatives, controlled by Republicans, passed its own law in March gutting collective bargaining rights for public-sector unions. The measure, nearly identical to Wisconsin's, would have made it to the desk of Republican Governor Terry Branstad, who backed the bill, and into law had the state's Democrat-controlled Senate not killed it on the spot.

In early March, Idaho's Legislature voted to eliminate most bargaining rights for public school teachers, not to mention tossing out tenure and seniority. Two separate anti-union bills are wending their way through the Tennessee Legislature—one in the House that resembles Idaho's, and another in the Senate that aims to outlaw collective bargaining for teachers altogether.

And now comes Alaska, one of the latest states to join the fight. There, on March 21, a Republican state legislator introduced a measure nearly identical to Wisconsin's that would strip most public-sector unions of the right to collectively bargain on health-care and retirement benefits. By one estimate, more than 20 state legislatures are considering bills to limit collective bargaining for unions.

Not to be forgotten is Indiana, where Democrats in the Legislature's lower chamber camped out beyond state lines for more than a month (as had Wisconsin Senate Democrats before them) to protest multiple pieces of legislation that would hurt unions and public-education funding. They returned to Indianapolis on Monday to cheers from supporters, their protest having killed a bill that would have made Indiana a "right-to-work" state while undermining support for other anti-union measures.

Even if, in the end, its lawmakers don't pass any anti-union legislation, Indiana is already illustrative of what happens when collective bargaining is wiped out. With a flick of his pen, Republican Governor Mitch Daniels banned it for state employees in 2005 by executive order. The result, as *The New York Times* reported, was significant savings for the state, but skyrocketing health-insurance payments and a pay freeze for state workers. Management fired more experienced employees who would have had seniority under old union rules. And union membership among state workers dwindled by 90 percent, with one former labor activist claiming workers, fearing repercussions from their bosses, were afraid to pay union dues.

Not that unions can't exist in states without collective bargaining rights. In Arizona and Texas, for instance, unions still operate, even though both are heavily conservative "right-to-work" states, which means employees can opt out of union membership but still enjoy the wage increases and benefits negotiated by unions. Still, in those states, organized labor's influence pales when compared to that of unions in Michigan or Wisconsin.

Then there are the political ramifications. Elected officials in each of these embattled states denied that any political motives lay behind their bills, but that's obviously not true. Public-sector unions like the American Federation of State, County, and Municipal Employees are a pillar of support for the left wing of the Democratic Party. Knock out the unions, and you effectively "defund" that party, as my colleague Kevin Drum put it recently.

Despite their pleas of ignorance, Republicans in Wisconsin, Iowa, Tennessee, Ohio, and every other state where legislation of this type is being considered understand perfectly well the damage their bills will inflict on their political opponents. As the top Republican in the Wisconsin Senate said, "If we win this battle, and the money is not there under the auspices of the unions, certainly what you're going to find is President Obama is going to have a ... much more difficult time getting elected and winning the state of Wisconsin."

Indeed. So, in one sense, the intensifying assault on unions across much of the nation may represent an ending for a labor movement long on the wane and at least 30-years under siege by various Republican administrations, national and state. It is visibly now in danger of becoming a force of little significance in much of the country.

This is exactly what conservatives and the GOP want. As a director for the Koch brothers-backed advocacy group Americans for Prosperity recently admitted, "We fight these battles on taxes and regulation, but really what we would like to see is to take the unions out at the knees so they don't have the resources to fight these battles." If the bills mentioned here make it into law, the power wielded by public-sector unions—to fight for better wages and benefits, to demand a safer workplace, to elect progressive candidates—will wither. And with history as a guide, if union clout fades away, so, too, does the spirit of democracy in this country.

If you look at the last 150 years of history across all nations with a working class of some sort, the maintenance of democracy and the maintenance of a union movement are joined at the hip," Nelson Lichtenstein, a professor and labor historian at the University of California, Santa Barbara, said recently. "If democracy has a future, then so, too, must trade unionism."

The Radicalization of Tom Bird

If the events in Wisconsin and elsewhere do signal an end, they may also mark a beginning. I saw it in the outpouring of protesters in Madison, the young and old who defied convention and expectation by showing up day after day, weekend after weekend, signs in hand, in snow or sun, to voice their disgust with Walker and his agenda. For me, the inspiration in that crowd came in the form of a tall, string-bean-thin 22-year-old with a sheepish smile named Tom Bird.

Bird's radicalization, if you will, began innocently enough. As he told me one evening, when the news leaked out about the explosive contents of Walker's bill, his reaction was typical: angry but resigned to the fact that, in a GOP-controlled legislature, it would pass. "What was I going to do about it?" was, he said, the way he then felt.

Bird was no labor activist. Far from it. A master's student in nuclear engineering at the University of Wisconsin-Madison, he felt at home in the world of plasma physics. He'd opposed the Iraq war, but collective bargaining, walkouts, picket lines… well, not so much. He joined his first student-organized march from the university campus to the Capitol downtown in the days after Walker announced his bill more out of curiosity than indignation. He was, he told me, just tagging along with a friend.

Yet something kept pulling him back to the growing protests. He'd drop in on the demonstrators on his way to and from campus, wading through the throngs of people, admiring the signs taped to the walls of the Capitol rotunda, taking in the exhortations of the speakers at its center. The first night he spent in the Capitol, Bird testified in the all-night hearings taking place by reading a statement once given by Clarence Darrow, the famous civil liberties lawyer, in defense of a man named Thomas I. Kidd charged with treason for inciting workers to unionize in Bird's hometown of Oshkosh. And in doing so, Bird felt something new: an urge to be part of a movement.

Day after day he gravitated closer to the drum circle and the speaker's pulpit, the beating heart of those Capitol protests. And then, one day, someone handed him the megaphone. It was his turn to speak. He hadn't necessarily planned this, so feeling the energy of the moment he simply stepped up and said what he thought. Before long, he was an activist whose impassioned cries rang out in the rotunda as loud as anyone's. Any time I ventured into the Capitol I looked for Bird, with his Wisconsin baseball cap, lining up new speakers and keeping the drums beating. Someone even dubbed him "Speaker of the Rotunda."

Bird and his newfound activist friends even organized the disparate groups inside the Capitol—the medic team, university teaching assistants, protest marshals, and more—into the Capitol City Leadership Committee. The CCLC, while short-lived, was created to ensure that the protests remained safe, peaceful, and forceful. It had its own leadership structure and governing bylaws. Once the police squeezed the protesters out of the Capitol for good, instead of dissolving and disappearing, the group evolved into the Autonomous Solidarity Organization, an outfit now determined to continue the fight for workers' rights and social justice.

I've thought a lot of about Bird since then. If a 22-year-old plasma physics geek can be transformed into an activist in mere weeks, then maybe the crushing effects of Walker's and Kasich's bills and all the others can be channeled into new energy, into a new movement. It may not look like organized labor as we've known it, but it could begin to fill a void left in states where governors and legislatures are gutting the unions.

In Wisconsin, the upcoming weeks will put this new energy to a test. Right now, campaigns are under way to recall eight Republican state senators for their support of Walker's "repair" bill; in the case of GOP Sen. Randy Hopper, opponents have already collected enough signatures, including that of Hopper's estranged wife, to demand a recall vote. And on April 5, Wisconsinites will go to the polls to choose between a liberal candidate and a corporate-backed Republican for a seat on the state Supreme Court. That race is the first since the protests, and so could be the first true test of whether the crowds that stormed the Capitol can translate their anger into pressure at the polls.

No one can say for certain what Wisconsin, or Ohio, or Iowa will look like if organized labor is whacked at the knees. Will public-sector unions find a way to reinvent themselves, or will they slide into irrelevance like so many unions in the private sector?

As grim as the bills may be, I can't help but feel hopeful, thinking about the massive protests I witnessed in Madison. I particularly remember one frigid night, when a group of protesters and reporters adjourned to a local bar for beers. At some point, Tom Bird bounded in, so full of energy, moving restlessly between our table and another with friends.

At one point, he rolled up his sleeve to reveal a scrawny bicep. Some of his fellow activists, he told me, wanted to get tattoos of one of the most enduring images from the protests, a solidarity fist in the shape of Wisconsin. "Except on mine," he told us, "I want the Polish version: *Solidarnosc.*"

That, of course, was the labor movement that, after a decade-long struggle, helped bring down the Soviet Union. Who knows what could happen here if Bird and his compatriots, awakened by the spark that was Madison, were to keep at it for 10 years or more? Who knows if Wisconsin wasn't the beginning of the end, but the beginning of something new?

@AndrewKroll Andy Kroll
Protester standing next to me: "we *did* it. we kept this thing open."
#wiunion #wearewi
7:36pm Feb 27

@MikeElk Mike Elk
More tweets from journos about Andrew Sullivan leaving the Atlantic
than **#wiunion** not leaving Wisc state Capitol **#SHAME**
8:09pm Feb 27

@brandzel Ben Brandzel
So, apparently that feed had over 100k people on it. Um, wow. Your
support means so much to folks here. We really are all in this together.
10:14pm Feb 27

@AndrewKroll Andy Kroll
Tweeps, it pains me to say this but time to go for me. flight's at 6am tom,
need to pack, eat, say my goodbyes. it's been amazing!! **#wiunion**
10:22pm Feb 27

FIFTY DAYS OF WISCONSIN LABOR SOLIDARITY HAVE CHANGED MY LIFE

Jenni Dye

ISTHMUS, APRIL 5, 2011

Monday, April 4, marked the 50th day since protests started at the Wisconsin Capitol in Madison over a bill that would gut public employees' collective bargaining rights. Fifty days of Wisconsinites standing up and making their voices heard—through hearing testimony, through meetings with their elected officials, through letters and emails to the governor's office, through protests, through where they chose to sleep, through signs, through chants, through showing up and taking part, through recall canvassing, and through adding their signatures to recall petitions. Fifty days.

When the protests started, I didn't know enough about the bill to know what its impact would be. I just knew that I was opposed to the idea of a "budget-repair" bill that substantially changed workers' rights being rammed through the Legislature in a week, which was the reported Republican plan. I thought that, at the very least, it was an issue that deserved more time for the public to gather information and participate in the debate. So I showed up at the Capitol to make sure my voice was heard. My dad showed up. My friends showed up. People who I never even knew were interested in politics showed up. And it became something a lot bigger than any of us.

On Feb. 16, when I stood in the stairwell leading to the room in which the Joint Finance Committee was about to vote, I yelled with the crowd,

"The people united will never be defeated," and I knew that this was different than anything I'd seen before and, possibly, anything I'll ever see again. As that first week unfolded, I educated myself about the contents of the bill and found I didn't at all like what it contained. My motivations changed from merely procedural to substantive—I wanted to stop that proposal in its tracks. I wanted compromise. I wanted our elected officials to sit at a table and talk.

During that first week, which I mostly spent protesting with my dad, my former teachers, and a few close friends, I felt a sort of hope that had been dormant for years. Hope that people joining forces really can make a difference. On Day 50, I stood on the State Street steps to the Capitol and listened as Rev. Jesse Jackson spoke about Dr. Martin Luther King, Jr.'s legacy on the anniversary of his assassination.

Jackson told the crowd that it was our responsibility to ensure that Dr. King lived on through us, that his dream was not ended with a single bullet. As Jackson spoke, I stood next to a fellow protester whom I had never met 50 days ago, but now consider a friend. Behind me, two protesters held a sign bearing the Martin Luther King quote: "Our lives begin to end the day we become silent about things that matter."

Our voices have been largely ignored by Governor Scott Walker, brothers Sen. Scott Fitzgerald and Rep. Jeff Fitzgerald, and their allies. They tried to trample our hope by locking us out of the Capitol, but we brought our sleeping bags and blankets and showed them that it didn't matter if we slept inside or out, our opposition remained steady.

They held public meetings with minimal notice, trying to cut us out of the process. But we showed up in force anyway, and we refused to allow violations of Wisconsin's open-meetings law to go unchallenged. They tried to make us go away by "passing" the legislation, but that night, we filled the streets surrounding the Capitol and continued our protest. And now, seven weeks after we started, we are still standing up and making our voices heard, letting them know we don't like their budget-repair bill, their infringement of our constitutional rights, or their way of "opening" Wisconsin for business by closing our open government.

We may not have gotten through to Walker or the Fitzgeralds or their friends yet, but those of you who have also devoted your time and your energy to this movement have gotten through to me in a way that is permanent and life-changing. For every moment in my past where I have questioned whether there are good people out there, the compassion and commitment of those raising their voices at our Capitol have proved 10 times over that there are people who care about each other, care about perfect strangers, care about Wisconsin, care about democracy and open government, and care that things are done the right way, even when the proposal itself is abhorrent.

There have been days when my voice is not strong, but I've found that I can rely on others to carry the load. There have been days when I literally might have collapsed into a sobbing heap on the Capitol floor were it not for the kindness of friends and perfect strangers. There are days when a hug is an absolute lifeline to maintaining any sanity at all. Sometimes relief and renewal have come in the form of inspiration from the words of speakers at a rally and sometimes from perfect strangers who are also dedicating their time to the cause. I'll never be able to thank you all individually. I'll never be able to thank you all enough.

It's not enough, but I will forever be grateful for what the individuals involved in this movement have given me. And I plan to keep giving it my all until we take Wisconsin back.

@YoProWI Young Progressives
Access to the capitol is reportedly restricted to those who have official business, or those who are attending a hearing!
11:08am Feb 28

@TAA_Madison TAA Madison
Medical supplies running low in Capitol. They need: handwarmers, rubber gloves, children's Tylenol, ibuprofen, toothbrushes, soap **#wiunion**
2:07pm Feb 28

@DefendWisconsin Defend Wisconsin
Latest: Ppl not being let into Capitol right now. Protestors mtg w police to determine how many will be let in **#wiunion**
2:23pm Feb 28

@TAA_Madison TAA Madison
Dems are starting a public hearing. You will be escorted inside & out. Info we have now is that you will not be allowed to stay. **#wiunion**
4:31pm Feb 28

@DefendWisconsin Defend Wisconsin
If we can't take the building we'll take the whole square. Bring tents, heaters, and warm sleeping bags @ king! **#wiunion** even when its cold!
7:52pm Feb 28

@LegalEagle Legal Eagle
I can't stop smiling. As much as Walker's actions are abhorrent, the people here sticking it out in the cold are amazing. **#wiunion**
10:26pm Feb 28

@LegalEagle Legal Eagle
There's a lot of people settling in here at **#walkerville**. Thanks to @TAA_Madison and everyone else who brought extra blankets! **#wiunion**
1:42am Mar 1

POSTCARD FROM A NEW AMERICAN PROGRESSIVE MOVEMENT: THE WISCONSIN STRATEGY

David Dayen

FIREDOGLAKE, MARCH 1, 2011

Thomas M. Bird was a mild-mannered graduate student from Oshkosh, voting Democratic but paying only slight attention to politics, before Governor Scott Walker announced his "budget-repair" bill. He didn't make it over to the Capitol in Madison until Feb. 17, four days into the protests. Within a couple weeks, he was a ranking member of the Capitol City Leadership Committee, an umbrella organization made up of the different groups performing tasks in the building—the megaphone people, the Teaching Assistants' Association, the volunteer marshals, the information station coalition, the medical station volunteers, and the Wisconsin Workers Solidarity Sit-In. Bird participated in meetings coordinated under their own democratic rules. "The group meets regularly and we ensure that each meeting has an even number of people. Any business is put to a democratic vote. If there is a tie, there are three rounds of debate and then the motion is tabled. The Wisconsin Republicans could probably learn a thing or two from us." This is a protest, Wisconsin-style.

As Walker cracks down on the activists inside the Capitol rotunda on the day he releases his 2011–2013 budget, he will be unable to quash the spirit of people like Thomas M. Bird, whose life will never be the same.

What may not be clear from outside of Wisconsin is the level to which the grassroots protesters and the Democratic members of the Wisconsin

Legislature have become one throughout this struggle. Not just the "Fab 14" group of senators who still reside in Illinois, denying the Republicans a quorum and stalling the budget-repair bill that would strip most collective bargaining rights from public employees. But the Democrats in the state Assembly have become activists themselves. They are readily identifiable in the orange "Assembly Democrats: Fighting for Working Families" shirts they've been wearing for two weeks. They help negotiate access to the building and use their resources to get in people and supplies. They hold public hearings through the night to force the Capitol to stay open. They spent 63 hours on the Assembly floor stretching out debate on the bill, forcing the local media to report on what it contained. One Assembly Democrat had reconstructive surgery for skin cancer last Tuesday, and was back on the floor Wednesday for debate. She was in the Capitol Sunday night, with a bandage on her face, as the protesters readied themselves to be arrested. "This is civil disobedience at its finest," she told me.

"Our Democrats, often disappointing, have delinked from the compromises of the Democratic party, and linked in to the opinions of the progressive grassroots," said John Nichols, writer for Madison's *The Capital Times* and *The Nation* and unofficial mayor of Madison. He was speaking to "The People's Legislature," at a Crowne Plaza conference room on the east side of the city. A group called Fighting Bob, named after the legendary progressive leader Robert La Follette and organized by the popular reformer and former U.S. Senate candidate Ed Garvey, was meeting to discuss their next move to respond to the assault on public workers taken up by Walker. Nichols said proudly, "We have in a sense retaken the Democratic Party in this state," and the People's Legislature wanted to make good on that. Over the course of a day-long meeting, they plotted out a multi-pronged strategy that also has echoes of the kind of medium-term and long-term fights that the grassroots in the Capitol rotunda will wage.

Everyone is focused on the short-term goal of stopping the budget-repair bill, and that may happen. The *Milwaukee Journal Sentinel*, which endorsed Walker on its editorial pages, now routinely criticizes him and today came out against the bill. Walker's ramping up of out-of-state-funded TV ads shows his nervousness over whether his allies, the Senate Republicans, will waver and eventually lack the numbers to pass the bill. Charles Koch himself, and not a Buffalo-based blogger, actually placed an op-ed in *The Wall Street Journal* to announce support, which only extends the focus

258 | ON WISCONSIN!

on that prank call, one which may have led to a host of legal trouble for Walker. So the possibility exists that this gets stopped. But even if it doesn't, Wisconsin's grassroots, growing by the day, and buttressed by a completely responsive Democratic Party which protesters and activists will now crawl across glass for, have a plan. It goes like this:

• **Legal Claims Against the Bill.** Milwaukee's city attorney came out today and declared that the budget-repair bill is unconstitutional:

Walker's budget-repair bill would be unconstitutional because it would violate the constitutional "home rule" that protects cities and villages from interference in local pensions by the state, according to a legal opinion issued today by Milwaukee City Attorney Grant Langley.

In a letter to Milwaukee Alderman Joseph Dudzik, Langley stated, "In our judgment, the courts would find the statue unconstitutional on three grounds: First, that it unconstitutionally interferes with and intrudes upon the city's home-rule authority over its pension plan; second, that given certain vested rights or benefits that have accrued to employees currently in the plan, the statute would constitute an unconstitutional impairment of contract rights under the state and federal constitutions; and third, given these same vested rights or benefits, the proposed statute would violate the due process clauses of the state and federal constitutions because it would abrogate the terms and conditions of the Global Pension Settlement ..."

Milwaukee Mayor Tom Barrett (who lost to Walker in the gubernatorial race) has already asked Walker to seek a legal opinion from the state attorney general on the topic. These aren't the only legal questions about the bill. AFSCME has filed an unfair labor practice claim against Walker for refusing to negotiate while under a collective bargaining agreement. There is still a lingering sense that the Assembly vote was illegal. Democrats are still looking at all footage of the vote, to see if their suspicions are correct that Republicans leaned over and voted by electronic device in place of their missing colleagues. "The most important thing over the next two weeks," Nichols told the People's Legislature, "Is to maintain the rule of law and the rules of the Senate. We can't let them roll over process." The point is that lawyers plan to sue the state the moment Walker signs any budget-repair bill that includes the stripping of collective bargaining rights. "I believe there are enough good judges left in this state to get injunctions and slow this down."

• **Legal Claims Against Walker.** The phone call from "David Koch" features a number of statements from the governor that could violate ethics, labor, and election laws, according to Peg Lautenschlager, the state's former Democratic attorney general. There are campaign finance questions regarding Walker's acceptance of an offer to come to California after he "crushes the bastards." There's the infamous answer "we thought about that" to the question of why Walker isn't using planted thugs to disrupt the protests. There's the admission that Walker is trying to break public-employee unions like Reagan broke PATCO, and how layoffs in particular would be used in that fight. All of these things have questionable legality, and I believe the claims will be filed.

• **General Strike.** The *Capital Times* picks up on the fact that the Wisconsin South Central Federation of Labor (SCFL) has endorsed the notion of a general strike. That's basically all they can do; the federation has no authority to call a strike. But after March 13, state public-employee unions will be operating without a contract. At that point, all bets are off. And workers throughout Madison, though barred by Taft-Hartley requirements from joining strikes, may do so anyway. If the bill passes, chances are there will be at least some portion of Wisconsin that will go on a general strike for some amount of time. There's a very large piece of construction paper in the Capitol with thousands of names of people who signed their support for a strike.

• **State Supreme Court.** On April 5, there's a race for a state Supreme Court seat between an incumbent Republican, David Prosser, and the Democrat, JoAnne Kloppenburg. Supreme Court races in Wisconsin are actual elections. They feature TV commercials and debates and retail politics. And the Democrats are both energized and ready. "This will be a national-level battle, a proxy Presidential race," said Nichols, who thinks that $10 million will be spent on it between both sides. Prosser has said publicly that he would coordinate his rulings in alliance with Republican ideology. He's part of a 4-3 Republican advantage on the state Supreme Court. This would shift the balance of power there and provide a major setback for Walker and the Republicans. Organizing has begun and is intense inside the Capitol and throughout the state.

• **Legislative Seats.** The same day as that April 5 special election, there are primaries for three state Assembly races, vacated by three Republicans who joined Walker's cabinet. While at least two of the three are seen as strong Republican seats, progressives in Wisconsin plan to contest all three. "If this (protest) means anything, it means that the rules of where we compete have to be thrown out," Nichols insisted. "We fight for every inch of Wisconsin!"

• **Recalls.** There will absolutely be recall elections for many of the "Republican 8" state senators who can be recalled immediately. The organizing for this has already begun; a Democratic strategist in the state found the Republican 8 vulnerable to recall because of the heightened passions around the issue. This will also happen on the Democratic side; a group from Utah has already begun that process. You will see many recall elections in the coming year, putting the closely divided state Senate up for grabs in Wisconsin. Recall elections are basically do-over elections in the state, with primaries and general ballots. "The recall is the progressive gift to the citizens of this state," Nichols said to the People's Legislature. "It was established for this moment. ... We have a duty to recall those legislators who failed us, and defend those who stood with us."

One particular recall battle stands out, and progressives may take it on first. Sen. Alberta Darling is the co-chair of the Joint Finance Committee, which reported out the budget-repair bill. She represents a North Shore suburban Milwaukee district, which is heavily Jewish and fairly Democratic. It's the kind of seat many Democrats lost in 2010. In 2011 in Wisconsin, there's already a candidate lined up for the recall, former Assemblyman Sheldon Wasserman. "This will be a critical contest," said Nichols. "There's our referendum."

And then there's the possible recall of Walker, which could not begin until January 2012. Whether progressives take it up could depend on whether they win these fights prior to it. They have a very deliberate strategy to build momentum at every step of the way. They are fighting for workers' rights on a host of fronts. And they have the Democratic Party behind them. This is a new synchronicity between the party apparatus and the grassroots, and it's starting to spread. Perhaps more remarkable than the Wisconsin battle is the one happening in Indiana. State House Democrats walked out there in protest of a bill that would have crushed private-employee unions. The

Republicans pulled back on that. But Democrats REMAINED out of the district, and vowed to stay put until an education bill that would set up a voucher system was scotched. Indiana Democrats are not exactly known as fighting progressives; in some cases they may be to the right of Wisconsin Republicans. But they have responded to their grassroots and are standing by them.

Ultimately, that's how this new American progressive movement will move forward. The activists and the politicians, the protesters and the reformers, the signature-gatherers and the people fighting in the streets, the unions and the college students, all must unite on a series of goals dedicated to the rights of the worker to have a good job and a house and a reasonable way of life for themselves. People power, basic fundamental rights, and justice. These are the tenets of the movement. "The question shall arise in your day: Which shall rule, wealth or man?" said Edward Ryan, the Chief Justice of Wisconsin's Supreme Court, in an address to the law school in Madison in 1873. "Which shall lead, money or intellect; who shall fill public stations—educated and patriotic free men or the feudal serfs of corporate capital?"

The spirit of that has not yet been extinguished in America.

@DefendWisconsin Defend Wisconsin
Restraining order has been granted, so start heading to the Capitol!
Doors are opening soon. **#wiunion**
11:26am Mar 1

@DefendWisconsin Defend Wisconsin
We have confirmed that there will be a hearing at 2:15PM on public
access to the Capitol in room 4A of the Dane County Courthouse.
11:59am Mar 1

@millbot Emily Mills
RT @LegalEagle: Why in God's name are the doors still locked? When
a court order means nothing, our system has failed. **#wiunion**
3:09pm Mar 1

@millbot Emily Mills
Only 20 members of the public allowed in to watch budget address.
Assuming Walker scuttled into Capitol via tunnel. Pretty lame. **#wiunion**
4:09pm Mar 1

@millbot Emily Mills
I don't think Walker has more than one facial expression. **#wiunion**
4:32pm Mar 1

@MelissaRyan Melissa Ryan
Apparently if I take $200 from you, what I'm actually doing is giving you
the tools you need to succeed. **#Walkernomics #Wlunion**
4:41pm Mar 1

@WEAC WEAC
Dedicated supporters are sleeping outside the Capitol again. Follow
#wiunion and **#walkerville** for their coverage. Thank you!
9:38pm Mar 1

@millbot Emily Mills
RT @LegalEagle: Access to the Capitol is more restricted right now than it
was in the days and weeks following 9/11, when I worked there ...
11:18am Mar 2

THERE WILL ALWAYS BE A TOMORROW

Daniel Schultz

A PASTOR'S NOTEBOOK, MARCH 11, 2011

I attended an ecumenical conference on rural ministry this past weekend, held annually in the city of Dubuque, Iowa. That I would take up such an opportunity for professional development ought to tell you something about just how exciting my life has become these days.

The opening speaker was a professor of rural sociology with a thick Missouri accent who was met by an impatient room of pastors fiddling with empty coffee cups and wondering when dessert would arrive. The professor cheerfully attempted to help us understand the people in our pews with the help of corny jokes and stories and cultural insights so old they might have had grandchildren. I don't want to harp on the man, because he was sincere and intelligent and genuinely committed to the well-being of the church. But if anyone has not heard by now the idea that different generations see the world differently, they should check into the validity of their college diploma. My guess is it will turn out to have been printed on high-quality cardboard that could have been put to better use as a cereal box.

After almost an hour of talking about such tidbits as the formative effect the Challenger disaster had on my generation, the professor got around to what I thought was the obvious point, which was how economics shape cultural perspective. Though traumas stick out in our minds, the stagnation of real income for most of the past 40 years has done more to shape people my age than the loss of 10 space shuttles could ever achieve. When asked why Gen-Xers are so cynical, I used to reply that our first memories of watching television often ran to seeing President Richard Nixon resign or helicopters being pushed off the side of aircraft carriers as Saigon fell. Now I believe that it has more to do with seeing our economic opportunities chipped away, year by year. We've never thought there was much future in being us.

You might think that recent events in Wisconsin would confirm this bias. Indeed, some people have claimed that no matter what the legislative outcome, conservatives have scored a big win in this battle. I suppose, if you can claim running down teachers as winning something worth having.

About that legislative outcome, though: It will no doubt face legal challenges, and the state senators who voted for it will come up against well-organized and well-funded recall campaigns later this year. But for now it is done. We will have to wait to see its final disposition.

There is a lot left undecided in Wisconsin these days. If I can impress upon my out-of-state friends any single point, it is the terrible uncertainty Cheddarheads live with these days. Our school district, like many others, has no idea what its budget might look like next year because state aid has not passed the Legislature. The projected shortfall runs into the millions. It's possible that teachers may be laid off. It's also possible that our son's school may be shut. We have no way of telling. I say nothing about cuts to social services that may or may not affect our daughter's treatment.

Again and again I am asked, how does this end? I don't know.

Come what may, I discern a light, for myself and my children. It may seem today that the battle is lost. Republicans had the votes to shove through legislation canceling collective bargaining. In short order, they will have enough bodies in the Senate and Assembly to authorize the meanest of budgets. But the cost to them has been delay and thousands—possibly hundreds of thousands—of ordinary people pouring into the streets in opposition. Governor Scott Walker has poked a hornet's nest of immense proportions, and seems determined to keep poking it to suit his ideological bent.

Tyrants fear tomorrow, because where there is a future, there is hope that things could be different. It is no accident that Walker continually pleads that crisis forces his hand. Nor is it accidental that the most controversial measures are the ones that move the quickest. If it doesn't have to be done right now, it opens the possibility that it doesn't have to be done at all. Or perhaps things don't have to be the way they are arranged presently. Tomorrow is the greatest threat there is to an unjust today.

The protesters in the streets of Madison and anyone who watches them with any astuteness have learned this lesson well. The protesters have learned that their voices can be heard, that they can change outcomes, that when they stand together, they can have a future that is meaningfully different than the present. There is no political structure, however imbalanced, however stacked against ordinary people, that can withstand this mix of hope and social solidarity. On Feb. 17, it seemed certain that the story had run its course and any opposition to the original bill would come to nothing. Since then, the people have forced one tomorrow after another, evading every opportunity to end the situation today. Even now, after the legislation has passed, the end is nowhere near manifest. Tomorrow, tractors and 200,000 protesters are expected on the Capitol square. By March 2012, it is possible that we may have replaced every senator eligible for recall and be preparing to vote on Walker's future. I don't envy him next year.

I am perhaps fanciful enough to see in this chaos the hand of the trickster God Yahweh. He has a track record of being a singularly ill-behaved deity, refusing to bow to conventional expectations of the divine, such as endorsing the rule of whoever happens to be on top of the social heap at the moment. God is no respecter of wealth and privilege, but he does seem inordinately fond of creating new possibilities and disrupting "the seemingly self-evident way things must be." When the Israelites cried out under the oppression of Pharaoh, the Lord heard them, and began to move them toward freedom, new and unheard-of possibilities. No one ever thought that the most powerful ruler in the world could lose his slave labor force! This was simply not the way things were done.

But it did happen, or so the Bible tells us. It took a very long time: Moses was 80 years old when he appeared before the king of Egypt, and after dickering with him, it took another 40 years before Israel had enough of its stuff together to enter into the promised land.[1] In all that time, God remained patient, tugging his children into a new future gently but insistently, creating a way forward where there was none. I will teach my son that in the streets of Madison, God did it again, and that with a little faith

---

[1]They promptly slaughtered the previous residents. I hope this is one piece of the story that will not repeat itself.

and a little grace, the people who have been weighed down for so long with legal and economic injustice can once again be free. I hope and I trust that years in the future, when some sociologist shorthands the character of his generation, he will note their sunny optimism formed by the knowledge that pharaohs come and pharaohs go, the economic tides for working-class families rise and the tides fall, but through it all, there is always a tomorrow.

@analieseeicher Analiese Eicher
Yesssssssssss!!!!! MT @sandycullenWSJ: 4 Dem Reps. moved desks outside the Capitol to meet with constituents who can't get inside. **#wiunion**
2:37pm Mar 2

@WEAC WEAC
RT @finnryan Assembly dems have moved their desks OUTSIDE Capitol & are meeting w/ constituents. Go talk to them! North wing **#wiunion**
2:47pm Mar 2

@abeckettwrn Andrew Beckett
Hearing on Capitol access lawsuit will go to a third day. Testimony expected to resume at 1pm Thursday. **#wiunion #wibudget**
6:29pm Mar 2

@analieseeicher Analiese Eicher
No order from judge kicking ppl out of the cap tonight. Stay strong rotunda community! **#y'allrock! #wiunion**
6:36pm Mar 2

@edcetera Ed Cetera
Everyone hang in there. The light is making its way through the cracks. We're so close to victory. **#wiunion**
7:48pm Mar 2

@DefendWisconsin Defend Wisconsin
News: WI Senate passed a resolution ordering arrest of Senate Dems if they don't return by 4 p.m. today. Constitutionality unclear. **#wiunion**
12:38pm Mar 3

@millbot Emily Mills
Walking around downtown the city feels decidedly changed. Hope for that state, too. Officially not just protest but a movement. **#wiunion**
1:09pm Mar 3

@DefendWisconsin Defend Wisconsin
3 PM rally outside of the Capitol to demand that the public be allowed to enter their house!
3:02pm Mar 3

@YoProWI Young Progressives
The State is now seeking a court order to remove the people from the capitol.
3:12pm Feb 28

@analieseeicher Analiese Eicher
Hulsey said getting into bldg was easier for himself today, but not for constituents. **#wiunion**
3:20pm Mar 3

@abeckettwrn Andrew Beckett
Closing arguments done. Judge taking a few minutes, but expected to rule soon. Hints decision may include restraint on sleeping at capitol
5:19pm Mar 3

@DefendWisconsin Defend Wisconsin
Judge drafts letter asking Rotunda to be vacated after the closing of business hours tonight. **#wiunion**
5:41pm Mar 3

@DefendWisconsin Defend Wisconsin
Let's give the exiting demonstrators a heros' welcome when they leave the building! Meet at the Capitol @ 6pm. Pizza will be there. **#wiunion**
5:53pm Mar 3

@millbot Emily Mills
RT @benmasel: March out proud tonight, march in proud in the morning. **#wiunion**
6:37pm Mar 3

EPILOGUE:

THE SPIRIT OF WISCONSIN

John Nichols

The Nation, March 3, 2011

LATE ON A FRIGID WISCONSIN AFTERNOON, an hour before another of the evening demonstrations that brought thousands, then tens of thousands, then more than 100,000 public employees, teachers, students, and their allies to the great square that surrounds the Capitol in Madison, Sarah Roberts was sitting in the Ancora coffee shop warming up. With her blunt-cut blond hair and hip retro glasses, the library sciences grad student looked the picture of urban cool, except perhaps for the decades-old factory ID badge bearing the image of a young man. "A few weeks ago I asked my mom, 'What made my grandfather such a civic-minded man? Why was he always there to help someone who had lost their job? Take food to someone who couldn't make ends meet? Serve on the City Council? What made him so incredibly engaged with his community and his state?' Mom looked at me and she said, 'Labor.'"

So it was that the granddaughter of Willard Roberts—a 45-year employee and proud union man at the Monarch Range plant in the factory town of Beaver Dam—pulled out her grandpa's ID and pinned it to her jacket when she learned that Wisconsin Governor Scott Walker was proposing to strip state, county, and municipal employees and teachers of their collective bargaining rights. "This state was built by people like him; this country was built by people like him. I think we all kind of forgot that until the governor woke us up," she said. "Walker thought he could bust the unions, privatize everything, give it all away to the corporations. But that was a great misfire. Because when he attacked the unions, he reminded us where we came from. We're the children and grandchildren of union workers and farmers and shopkeepers. That goes deeper, way deeper, than politics. This legislation is an affront to my whole family history."

After three decades of attacks on public-sector unions, dating back at least to President Ronald Reagan's breaking of the air traffic controllers in 1981, the mass uprising against Walker's attack has revealed a popular understanding of the necessity of the labor movement that is far richer than even the most optimistic organizer imagined. The bonds are not just economic or political; they are emotional and personal. And when the determination of corporate interests and their political pawns to destroy unions—not by slow cuts, as is so often the case, but all at once—is revealed, all that talk of building coalitions, of creating movements linking union members with those who have never joined, suddenly moves from theory to practice. Thousands of students show up for an impromptu show by rocker Tom Morello and pump their fists in the air as they shout the lyrics of union songs they are only just learning. Tens of thousands of citizens—not just public workers fearing for their livelihood but students fearing for their future and small-business owners fearing for their community—chant in unison as they rally in cities across the state, "An injury to one is an injury to all." After we finished talking, Roberts told me she couldn't go to the demo just yet: "I'm meeting my mom here. She's driving in. She wanted to be here to honor her father and to stand on the side of the workers."

The remarkable events that have transpired in Wisconsin since Feb. 11, when Walker announced he would attach proposals to a minor budget-repair bill to strip away the rights of public employees and teachers to organize in the workplace and to engage in meaningful collective bargaining, have made Wisconsin, in the words of AFSCME President Gerald McEntee, "ground zero in the fight for labor rights in the United States." They have also created what the Rev. Jesse Jackson, who rallied more than 50,000 demonstrators on a freezing Friday night, describes as "a Martin Luther King moment" for supporters of economic and social justice. The size of the demonstrations, which have filled the central square of this capital in much the way that demonstrators filled Tahrir Square in Cairo just weeks earlier, has focused more attention on an American labor struggle than has been seen in decades. This struggle—all but certain to see legislative disappointments, legal challenges, and dramatic electoral twists and turns before it is done—raises key questions about whether mass movements can forge not only a new and better economy but a new and better politics. Walker will get his way on some issues—too many issues. But that's not the most important story out of Wisconsin. The most vital story is the one that people on both sides of this struggle least expected: After years of efforts by unions to rebrand and reposition themselves as "partners" and "constructive collaborators" with employers, many Americans still recognize that perhaps the most important role of the labor movement is as a countervailing force not just in the workplace, but in politics. And this at a time when public services and education are under constant assault from corporate privatizers and billionaire political donors who are more than ready to "invest" in election results that will lower their taxes and serve their interests.

Joel Greeno, a dairy farmer from western Wisconsin, finished his chores on a Saturday morning one week after mass demonstrations prompted Democratic state senators to flee the state in order to deny Walker's legislative allies a quorum to pass the bill. Greeno then drove his truck to Madison to join what would turn out to be probably the largest demonstration in Wisconsin history and one of the largest pro-labor demonstrations in American history. "The big corporations are organized. They're in this fight with all the money in the world," he shouted above chants of "What's disgusting? Union-busting!" "The big-money guys, they know what it's all about: If they can take away the collective bargaining rights of unions, if they can shut them up politically, we're all finished. How are farmers going to organize and be heard? If this goes through, none of us stand a chance."

Walker actually agrees with Greeno. It was clear from the beginning that Walker's initiative, backed by big-money TV ad campaigns and by such national conservative groups as the Club for Growth, had more to do with politics than balancing budgets. His bill, like similarly motivated if not quite-so-draconian measures proposed by GOP governors in other states, uses a fiscal challenge as an excuse to achieve a political end. The governor says he must eliminate most collective bargaining rights to deal with shortfalls in revenues. But state Rep. Mark Pocan, a Madison Democrat who is former co-chair of the powerful legislative Joint Finance Committee, says, "Wisconsin can balance its budget. We've actually dealt with more serious shortfalls. This isn't about revenue and spending. This is about finding an excuse to take away collective bargaining rights and to destroy unions as a political force." The governor disputes Pocan's argument, and there is great debate over whether this "budget-repair" bill is needed. Pocan points to a review by the nonpartisan Fiscal Bureau that suggested the state might be able to end the year with a slight surplus if a tax dispute with Minnesota and issues regarding Medicaid payments are resolved. While Wisconsin faces a genuine shortfall, it is much smaller than the one former Governor Jim Doyle and Democratic legislators sorted out two years ago in cooperation with state employee unions.

Walker's real goal has always been clear. Let's consider some context. A year before the governor took office in January—after winning a relatively low-turnout fall election that also saw Republicans take charge of this traditionally blue state's Assembly and Senate—the U.S. Supreme Court's *Citizens United v. FEC* decision removed barriers to corporate spending in election campaigns. GOP candidates reaped tremendous benefits from that ruling, which cleared the way for former White House political czar Karl Rove and fellow operatives to spend hundreds of millions on federal and state races. The Republican Governors Association, having collected a $1 million check from billionaire right-wingers Charles and David Koch and smaller contributions from other corporate interests, invested at least $3.4 million in electing Walker. As Lisa Graves, who heads the Madison-based Center for Media and Democracy, noted, "Big money funneled by one of the richest men in America [David Koch] and one of the richest corporations in the world [Koch Industries] ... put controversial Wisconsin Governor Scott Walker in office." Walker's debt to the Koch brothers, whose PAC donated $43,000 to his campaign, was highlighted in the governor's budget-repair bill—which in addition to attacking unions outlined a plan to restructure state government so Walker could sell off power plants in no-bid deals to firms like Koch Industries, while restructuring state health-insurance programs so that tens of thousands of Wisconsinites could be stranded with no access to care.

The Koch-Walker connection became a central issue of the Wisconsin uprising when the tape of a prank phone call—in which the governor can be heard talking over strategy with a blogger impersonating David Koch— was released to the public. On it, Walker talked about coordinating spending campaigns to shore up GOP legislators who back the bill. But even more telling is the governor's repetition of the phrase "This is our moment." At one point, Walker recalled a dinner with cabinet members on the eve of his announcement of the anti-union push. "I said, you know, this may seem a little melodramatic, but thirty years ago, Ronald Reagan ... had one of the most defining moments of his political career, not just his presidency, when he fired the air traffic controllers," said Walker. "And, uh, I said, to me that moment was more important than just for labor relations or even the federal budget; that was the first crack in the Berlin Wall and the fall of Communism. ... And, uh, I said, this may not have as broad of world implications, but in Wisconsin's history—little did I know how big it would be nationally—in Wisconsin's history, I said this is our moment, this is our time to change the course of history."

Walker certainly understands the stakes. Across the United States, but particularly in the swing states of the Great Lakes region and the upper Midwest, public-employee unions like AFSCME, the American Federation of Teachers, and affiliates of the National Education Association are more than labor organizations. They are the best-funded and most aggressive challengers to attempts by corporate interests and their political allies to promote privatization, to underfund schools, and to win elections. If unions in Northern states are disempowered—as they are already in much of the South, where "right-to-work" laws are common—a debate already warped by the overwhelming influence of corporate cash will become dramatically narrower and even more deferential to wealthy donors and big business.

Progressives have been talking about these concerns for a long time. They have tried to create movements to push back, sometimes with success, sometimes not. The same goes for organized labor. So what is different about Wisconsin? And, more significant, what potential is there to build a movement that extends far beyond one state?

Trade unionism has deep roots in Wisconsin. It was here that the forerunner to AFSCME was founded in 1932 and that pioneering labor laws were enacted, including the first state law allowing local government workers and teachers to engage in collective bargaining, signed by Governor Gaylord Nelson in 1959.

Wisconsin has often been a political outlier. More than a century ago Robert La Follette forged the progressive movement in the state. It grew so strong that when the former Wisconsin governor ran for president in 1924 as an independent radical backed by the Socialist Party and the labor movement, he beat the Democratic and Republican presidential nominees in Wisconsin. The maverick strain was maintained through the 20th century by liberals and radicals who briefly governed the state under the banner of the Progressive Party, by Milwaukee voters who kept electing Socialist mayors well into the 1950s (even as a right-wing populist, Joe McCarthy, was winning statewide and stirring a red scare nationally), and most recently by former Sen. Russ Feingold. Pride in the progressive tradition runs so strong that as many as 10,000 people gather each September for an annual "Fighting Bob Fest" in rural Sauk County, where invariably there is a reading of the words of the man who inspired La Follette, former state Supreme Court Justice Edward Ryan, who said in 1873: "There is looming up a new and dark power. ... The enterprises of the country are aggregating vast corporate combinations of unexampled capital, boldly marching, not for economical conquests only, but for political power."

When students affiliated with the Teaching Assistants' Association marched from the University of Wisconsin to the Capitol in one of the initial protests against Walker's bill, they decorated the area around the bust of La Follette. And as protesters slept-in at the Capitol while Democratic legislators kept hearings going 24 hours a day in the early stages of the struggle, union activists like AFSCME's Ed Sadlowski kept a vigil at the La Follette bust. But it's not just nostalgia or tradition that distinguishes Wisconsin in general and Madison in particular. Madison was a hotbed of 1960s protests and has remained a center of activism and independent media. There are strong community stations like WORT-FM, and even commercial radio hosts like John "Sly" Sylvester have given daily coverage to the protests. Progressive TV and radio hosts like MSNBC's Ed Schultz, *Democracy Now!*'s Amy Goodman and radio's Thom Hartmann have broadcast from Madison in the past, and Schultz and Goodman returned for live broadcasts as the current dispute developed. Local elected officials tend to be progressive and pro-union; Dane County Sheriff Dave Mahoney played a critical role in easing tensions at the Capitol, making it possible for demonstrators to maintain a sleep-in after the governor and GOP legislators tried to force them out. That infuriated Walker so much that he and legislative allies initiated a clampdown limiting access to the Capitol before a judge ordered its reopening. Mahoney responded that his deputies weren't "palace guards."

Wisconsin's history and progressive infrastructure created a sense, expressed by many in the state, that was perhaps best summed up by an instructor at Madison Area Technical College, Mary Bartholomew, who declared, "I'm so glad it came here first. But I know it's going to have to go everywhere." Bartholomew is right; it does have to go everywhere. But that will not happen easily. While Walker is not backing down, other Republican governors will be smarter than Walker, as will Democrats who seek to make cuts in public-employee pay, benefits, pensions, and workplace protections. Noting the news from Wisconsin, Michigan Governor Rick Snyder announced, "We're going to go negotiate with our unions in a collective bargaining fashion to achieve goals. It's not picking fights."

But even if other governors avoid Walker's divisive rhetoric and extreme tactics, that does not mean the labor movement and progressives can't learn powerful lessons from this fight. The first is that even after years of right-wing messaging, Americans—at least in key swing states—don't have much taste for union-busting, even in the public sector. A Public Policy Polling survey of likely Wisconsin voters, released Feb. 28, found that if they were electing a governor today, Democrat Tom Barrett would defeat Walker by a 52–45 margin. And other surveys have found solid support for collective bargaining rights. Recent national polls suggest that Americans favor protecting collective bargaining rights by a 2–1 margin. That's important when public employees and teachers are under assault from conservative think tanks and their media echo chamber.

The second lesson is that when the assault comes, it is vital to be bold and flexible. Members of the Teaching Assistants' Association were among the first to start sleeping at the Capitol, and that inspired others. So did a decision by members of Madison Teachers, Inc. (MTI), the city's education union, to take four days off to march and lobby against the bill. When Walker tried to set police and firefighter unions against the broader movement by exempting them from the worst assaults, MTI's John Matthews immediately went to firefighters and got them to join the protest in solidarity; the initiative was so successful that firefighter and police union members became key players. When the teachers went back to school, parents and private-sector union members stepped into their places on the picket line. When Walker tried to portray the unions and their members as greedy, union leaders made the not wholly popular choice to concede on a host of economic issues so the focus would remain squarely on the fight to keep collective bargaining rights. When Walker claimed that the demonstrators were being bused in from out of state, marchers began carrying signs naming the towns, villages, and counties they came from; many state and local employees showed up in their work uniforms. The international unions certainly provided tactical and economic support, but they did so with an awareness of the need to be open to new ideas and approaches learned from the 1999 WTO protests in Seattle; indeed, the Seattle influence was so deep that some of its slogans were adopted, particularly "This is what democracy looks like."

The third lesson is that Democratic politicians can act in smart and courageous ways, especially when they see tens of thousands of their constituents through their office windows. The decision by state Senate Democrats to leave the Capitol to deny a quorum for the governor's bill was essential in giving its opponents time to build their numbers and rally communities. The marathon resistance by state Assembly Democrats, who forced a 60-plus-hour debate led by younger legislators like Mark Pocan, Racine's Cory Mason, and Milwaukee's Tamara Grigsby, strengthened opposition and further expanded the movement. This outside/inside strategy was critical for protesters and legislators. Ultimately, some Democrats still disappointed, and communication between the unions and the Democratic senators was stilted and at times dysfunctional. The Democrats are not a labor party in any classic sense, but the best of the Democrats championed labor's cause at critical junctures.

The final lesson is that the influence of corporate money in our politics must be highlighted, in order to show how fiscal crises are often manufactured or twisted for political gain. Even when the problems are real, the answers offered by Republican governors like Walker are not. One of the most popular signs on the streets, distributed by National Nurses United, said, "Blame Wall Street." Instead of concessions, the nurses argued, it's time to focus on the corporate CEOs and speculators; as they point out: "In U.S. states facing a budget shortfall, revenues from corporate taxes have declined $2.5 billion in the last year. In Wisconsin, two-thirds of corporations pay no taxes, and the share of state revenue from corporate taxes has fallen by half since 1981." The same is true in other states. These facts must be stressed, repeatedly and aggressively, if the debate is going to shift from cuts in public services and education to demands for fair taxes and the revenues necessary for services and schools.

For all the excitement of Wisconsin, for all the hope the protests have generated, we are still only at a point where we can talk about changing the terms of the debate. But that's a big deal. After the policy compromises of 2009 and the electoral setbacks of 2010, which were so disappointing to progressives, the upsurge in Wisconsin has inspired people so powerfully that national labor leaders like United Steelworkers International President Leo Gerard were ecstatic as they addressed the crowds of students, young teachers, and state employees at the Capitol. "You have inspired this fat old white guy!" Gerard said.

But it's not just the labor leaders who are inspired, and that's the most important lesson. "Something about this has struck a chord of fairness and humanity that runs deep in all of us," Sarah Roberts told me as she waited for her mom. "We've been pushed around for so long, told we didn't have any power for so long. But I think our grandparents and our parents, they planted something in us, some values. And if we get pushed too far, we are going to push back. I think it started here, and I am so excited to see where we take it."

APPENDIX:

What Happened in Wisconsin: A Timeline

During the extraordinary protests that took place this winter in Wisconsin, events developed at a breakneck speed. What follows is an overview of what happened over the first few months of Wisconsin's struggle for workers' rights, presented as a timeline of the major developments in what was often a complex and rapidly changing situation.

What set these unprecedented demonstrations in motion was this: On **FRIDAY, FEBRUARY 11**, Scott Walker, Wisconsin's newly elected Republican governor, launched an attack on state workers in the form of his now-infamous "budget-repair" bill. Walker had come into office as part of the 2010 conservative wave that ushered in Republican control of the U.S. House of Representatives; in Wisconsin, the governorship flipped from blue to red and a Tea Party-supported billionaire ousted progressive champion Senator Russ Feingold.

Walker's bill proposed severely limiting state employees' right to collectively bargain on wages, and would take away unions' ability to negotiate on sick leave, workplace conditions, grievance procedures, and benefits. The bill would force unions to undergo annual elections to maintain their existence, allow employers to fire or discipline workers without cause, and would require public employees to contribute a much higher percentage of their pay into pensions and health care costs, reducing their paychecks by eight percent. While the governor claimed the bill was necessary to address the state's budget shortfall, many saw his move as a blatant assault that used the state's budget crisis as pretext for weakening public unions in Wisconsin—the first state to allow their existence. Adding insult to the blow, Walker announced that he was willing to mobilize the state's National Guard to suppress dissent or prevent a potential workers' strike.

The first day of large demonstrations took place on **MONDAY, FEBRUARY 14**, when a thousand University of Wisconsin students marched to the Capitol. They carried Valentine's Day cards that read "I Heart UW," and they urged Walker to not cut university funding. Though the rally had been planned weeks before Walker announced his bill, the new attack on workers and unions energized many more to come out and join in.

On **TUESDAY, FEBRUARY 15**, more than 10,000 outraged Wisconsinites filled the Capitol to express their opposition to the bill that they saw as a direct attack on their state's identity and its deeply-rooted values. The crowds included 700 students from Madison's East High School, who walked out of classes to march to the Capitol. People filled the Legislature's Joint Finance Committee hearing on the bill, signing up to testify by the hundreds, and crowding into overflow rooms around the Capitol. Organizers from the University of Wisconsin graduate assistants union, the Teaching Assistants' Association (TAA), and other groups saw an opportunity: In Wisconsin, the Capitol is required to stay open as long as a hearing is taking place. So they encouraged people to continue signing up to testify in order to keep the momentum of the packed Capitol going strong. Hundreds watched and waited for their turn to speak, and as afternoon became evening, protesters continued streaming in, bringing food, drinks, and sleeping bags. As Alexander Hanna from the TAA said, "If you go home and come back you're going to have a lower turnout the next day. ... We were staying." Yet Republican members of the Joint Finance Committee repeatedly tried to end the marathon hearing, and eventually succeeded in cutting off the official session at around 3 a.m. that night. But with hundreds of people still waiting to speak, Democratic members kept an informal hearing going throughout the night, and the Capitol remained open as people testified—one after another in two-minute time slots—until dawn. In this way, as a sleep-in started by those waiting to testify against Walker's bill, the Capitol occupation was born.

On **WEDNESDAY, FEBRUARY 16**, more than half of Madison's teachers called in sick to protest Walker's bill, completely shutting down the city's schools until February 22. They too joined the Capitol protests, and their act of defiance—and the fact that they risked their jobs by leaving work and effectively going on strike—energized many others. Firefighters and police officers, two groups that Walker had specifically exempted from the bill's reach, came to show solidarity with protesters, and were greeted with raucous cheers by the crowds in the rotunda. But after hours of testimony, Walker's bill passed out of the Joint Finance Committee. For the second night, protesters slept inside the Capitol.

The bill then moved to the state Senate—but before a vote could be held, on **THURSDAY, FEBRUARY 17**, Wisconsin's 14 Democratic senators fled the state. By doing so, they stood with the thousands of protesters in the Capitol that day, including hundreds of people who had been holding a sit-in in front of the Senate chambers to block senators from going inside. With no Democrats present, Republicans were left one senator short of the quorum required to hold a vote, and unable to move forward with the bill. State troopers were sent to Democratic senators' houses to track them down, but they remained on the run, moving from hotel to hotel across state lines in Illinois, where Wisconsin police had no jurisdiction. Their dramatic move energized the crowds of protesters, who swelled to an estimated 25,000 that day, with hundreds continuing to sleep inside the Capitol.

On **SATURDAY, FEBRUARY 19**, 68,000 people took part in rallies outside the Capitol. A smaller group of between 3,000 and 5,000 turned out for a counter-protest, where they heard from Tea Party favorites Joe the Plumber, Andrew Breitbart, and Herman Cain. Despite the close proximity of the two opposing groups, the gathering remained peaceful.

On **WEDNESDAY, FEBRUARY 23**, news broke that Walker had been punked. *Buffalo Beast* editor Ian Murphy recorded a call to Walker, in which Murphy pretended to be billionaire Tea Party and Walker campaign-donor David Koch. Murphy talked to Walker for 20 minutes, during which time Walker admitted that he had considered attempting to lure Democratic senators back to the state under false promises of negotiation and had thought about planting rabble-rousers amongst demonstrators to create a violent image of the protesters.

In the early hours of **FRIDAY, FEBRUARY 25**, with the legislation still blocked in the Senate by the 14 Democrats' absence, the Republican leadership in the State Assembly suddenly called for a vote on Walker's bill. There had been 60 hours of debate, but representatives had only seconds to cast their vote, and many Democrats who attempted to vote didn't even have time for their choice to be registered. Crowds of protesters shouted, "Shame!" from the rotunda at the Republicans as the legislators hurried out of the building after the vote. Later that day, police announced that on Sunday the Capitol would close at 4 p.m. for cleaning, and would return to "normal business hours" on Monday.

SATURDAY, FEBRUARY 26 saw between 70,000 and 100,000 protesters gathered in Madison amid freezing temperatures and heavy snow. Across the country that day, MoveOn.org held solidarity rallies in all 50 state capitals, where more than 50,000 people gathered to show their support for the Wisconsin fight.

The next day, police tried to put a stop to the Capitol occupation that had gone on for more than a week. As they had announced on Friday, on **SUNDAY, FEBRUARY 27** police continued to announce their plans to close the Capitol to protesters at 4 p.m., saying that protesters would have to leave so that the building could be cleaned for public health reasons. Tension built throughout the day, and many protesters made preparations to engage in civil disobedience and be arrested rather than voluntarily leave the Capitol. Yet as the announced deadline approached and then passed, the police did not take action to arrest the protesters. Hundreds remained inside the Capitol; by having held their ground they achieved a powerful victory. Yet while police refrained from making arrests, they began tightening security, with entry to the Capitol severely limited from that day forward.

On **TUESDAY, MARCH 1**, Walker unveiled his full proposed budget, a separate piece of legislation from the budget-repair bill, with an address at the Capitol, where he was rushed in and out through an underground tunnel to avoid the protesters. The number of demonstrators inside the building dwindled—with only one protester being let inside for each one who left— as the courts heard legal challenges to the governor's attempts to force and keep protesters out of the building.

On **WEDNESDAY, MARCH 2**, Democratic state representatives moved their desks outside, into the freezing cold temperatures, where they met with constituents in protest of how restricted access to the Capitol had become.

The Capitol occupation came to an end on **THURSDAY, MARCH 3**, 16 days after it had begun. Protesters were exhausted—many had been in the Capitol continuously since access had become tightened several days before—but they promised to continue the fight and return once the building was reopened after the weekend.

Without warning, on **WEDNESDAY, MARCH 9**, Republican legislators decided to quickly separate out the fiscal provisions from Walker's bill and vote on only the union-busting measures, making it clearer than ever that Walker's push was not a response to the state's budget crisis, but a targeted political attack. Since a quorum of 20 senators is only needed for a fiscal bill, Republicans went ahead with a vote with no Democrats present—passing the bill through the Senate on **MARCH 9**, and through the Assembly on **THURSDAY, MARCH 10**. Amid a massive outpouring of opposition, Walker signed the bill into law on **FRIDAY, MARCH 11**.

On **SATURDAY, MARCH 12**, the Democratic state senators returned home. They were greeted with a hero's welcome in Madison as they marched into town and through the streets outside of the Capitol. With estimates of more than 100,000 protesters out that day, March 12 was the biggest of the Madison rallies—the largest Wisconsin had seen since the Vietnam War, and one of the largest labor protests in American history.

On **MARCH 18**, Dane County Circuit Court Judge Maryann Sumi blocked Walker's bill from being implemented, ruling that the way in which it was passed may have violated Wisconsin's law requiring 24-hours notice before a vote.

On **MARCH 25**, the Legislative Reference Bureau published the bill anyway, circumventing the Secretary of State and following the instructions of Republicans who said they would enforce the new law.

On **TUESDAY, APRIL 5**, Wisconsinites went to the polls to vote in the first election to be held after the protests. The race was for the Wisconsin Supreme Court, between upstart challenger JoAnne Kloppenburg and David Prosser, the Walker-backed incumbent judge. Were Kloppenburg to win, her victory would shift the balance of the Wisconsin Supreme Court—the body who would ultimately decide whether Walker's budget-repair bill had been passed legally. On Election Day the race was unexpectedly close, and the challenger that people hadn't heard of just a few weeks before ended the night with a lead of fewer than a thousand votes, though the race remained too close to call. Days later, a Republican county clerk found 7,000 uncounted votes that had been stored on her home computer. Many were outraged, accusing Republicans of Florida-style election shenanigans. Kloppenburg challenged the findings—but after a lengthy recount process, Prosser was determined to be the legal winner.

On **MAY 26**, Judge Maryann Sumi voided Walker's bill, saying that it was passed illegally in violation of Wisconsin's open-meetings law.

But on **JUNE 14**, the Wisconsin Supreme Court reversed Judge Sumi's ruling, arguing that the closing of the Capitol doors did not violate the constitutional mandate that the building stay open while the Legislature is in session.

On **JUNE 29**, following months of protests, Walker's budget-repair bill became law in Wisconsin.

At the time of this writing, many of the protesters in the Wisconsin struggle are immersed in the efforts to recall six Republican state senators from office. In all of Wisconsin history, only four previous recall efforts have been attempted. In 2012, Walker himself will be eligible for recall, and many groups have already pledged that this will be a major focus.

While the tale of the Wisconsin struggle evolves each day, this collection captures a moment in time that is part of a much longer story that has only begun.

A Statement from Thomas M Bird
MARCH 1, 2011

At several points in this collection we meet Tom Bird: a Wisconsite whose story, for a number of authors, came to represent many first-time activists who were involved in the Wisconsin fight. A 22-year-old engineering gradu-ate student from Oshkosh, Wisconsin, Bird decided to check out the protests several days after they had begun. Once there, he quickly became part of a tight-knit group of protesters, none of whom knew each other previously, who lived in the Capitol for days on end and played an important role in keeping the occupation going strong.

What follows is Bird' story, in his own words—the original and unedited text of a statement Bird wrote in early March, reflecting on what for him had been a life-changing few weeks in February.

On Thursday, February 17th I entered the Capitol building for the first time during these protests. I write this early in the morning on March 1st. 12 days have passed since this began for me but I cannot even comprehend those 12 days through my usual perception of time. It feels like a month. My life has been irreparably changed in ways that I am only starting to come to terms with. I began by simply trying to write a brief timeline of what happened on each day... and there are entire days that I cannot place any specific events into. As I write this I am gripped with a sense of purpose that

I have never felt before in my life. All I can do now is try to describe what I have experienced in the hope that I do not forget more.

First, a brief history of my life as is relevant to these events. I grew up in Oshkosh, Wisconsin. I became politically aware around the time of the first Iraq war in 2003, when I was only 14 years old. A friend of mine was a first generation American from Lebanon. He was very politically involved and active in the local peace and justice movement. I can't remember what exactly galvanized me to oppose the Iraq war so strongly at such a young age, but the day the war started I walked out of school, following my friend's lead, and spent the day protesting. It was a great experience but did not change my life in any significant way.

From that point on I was aware of the broader political movements in the country. However I did not begin to follow politics rabidly until the financial crisis and presidential election in 2008. At this point I began to self educate myself on macroeconomics and began to tune myself in to the national political scene. As this happened it became clear to me that I agreed very strongly with the major tenets of the Progressive movement, which of course happened to be born here in Wisconsin. While I have mostly voted Democrat, I have always felt disappointed in the national Democratic party due to their tendency to let the radical Republican party frame the debate and control "the center", which the Democrats would promptly claim as their new territory and the process repeats. The progressive members of the Democratic party have been the only thing holding me back from complete cynicism. I could not be prouder to say that I was able to cast a vote for Tammy Baldwin and Russ Feingold.

The 2010 midterm elections deeply saddened me. Russ Feingold was defeated by a man who is significantly less qualified than myself to be a United States Senator, and that is not to say that I am particularly qualified, but rather that Ron Johnson's only real qualification was the number of digits in his bank statement. The Republicans took complete control of the state government of Wisconsin. Prior to the past few weeks I had not followed the state government all that closely, but I knew it would be nothing but bad news for Wisconsin and our proud, Progressive tradition. We have one of the better public education systems in the country (which I benefited from immensely), one of the finest state universities in the country or world (which I have also benefited from to an even greater degree), and a strong social safety net (growing up as the son of a paraplegic I also benefited from this.) Wisconsin had a proud history of being a union stronghold, pioneer-ing many of the rights that workers across the country enjoy. I knew we would begin to see much of this dismantled, and I felt rather hopeless and cynical. But there was little I could do and my life went on.

I believe it was Friday, February 11th that the details of the "Budget Repair Bill", (SB 11 in the state senate) began to be released. I saw that col-lective bargaining rights were being stripped from nearly every public em-ployee union in the state, with a few exceptions (firefighters, some police). I couldn't believe it, but I also did not believe anything could be done. Pro-tests began on Monday the 14th. My life continued as normal, going to classes and attending to my research. On Thursday the 17th I did not have any classes, so I decided to join the University of Wisconsin student walk-out which met on campus and marched to the capitol square. I entered the building for the first time during these protests and my life has never been the same.

I quickly met my first "protest friend" after chatting briefly while stand-ing on the 1st floor overlooking the rotunda floor. At this point rumors began circulating that the 14 Senate Democrats had fled the state. I couldn't believe it, but my spirits were immediately raised. We took part in a sit-in outside of the senate chamber, blocking anyone from entering (the 19 Republicans were inside but needed 20 members for a quorum to pass any financial legislation.) We complied with the police to allow anyone to leave. For the first time it crossed my mind that I might be arrested, which was exciting but I was still nervous about it. Eventually the Republican senators left and I wandered around outside the capitol, still not understanding what was about to happen. I decided I would join those sleeping in the Capitol building for at least a night, perhaps just as a novelty. My new protest friend and I spent most of the night awake, discussing politics and everything else under the sun. I signed up to testify in the public hearing the Assembly Democrats were running around 1 am. My friend found a wonderful state-ment for me to read from Clarence Darrow, a famous ACLU lawyer, in de-fense of Thomas I. Kidd who incited workers to unionize in my hometown of Oshkosh and was charged with treason.

At around 4am I entered the room where the hearings were taking place. Unfortunately I didn't get to testify until 7am but it was a powerful three hours. I saw, for the first time, several brave young men who I now view as my family. I heard incredibly articulate high school students give impassioned statements out of love for their teachers. I heard passionate teachers describe how collective bargaining allowed them to keep class sizes smaller. Not one word about pension contributions, not one word about salary. I heard downtrodden union workers describe how they would gladly see their salary go down (many of them already had) but merely wanted to protect their basic right to collectively bargain. It was emotional and incredible. The Assembly Democrats running the hearing listened intently and provided thoughtful, intelligent commentary. I began to fall in love with them. That sounds a bit cliché but it is the only language I know of to describe what I felt.

At 7am on the morning of Friday, February 18th I left the Capitol building and was greeted by the now risen sun. It felt strange... and yet I still did not understand what was to come. I went home and showered, and then returned to campus for the next UW student walkout. It wasn't until 11am but I ended up helping organize the march. I found myself in the front row of the student march, locking arms with new friends I had just met. We slowly marched up State Street from campus to the Capitol square, in contact with the police who were escorting us. It was my first taste of being an organizer. It was a wonderful day, but I don't remember too much at this point. I decided to spend the night and testify again, but this time I had no other friends in the Capitol. Some students from Milwaukee had a megaphone and drum circle set up on the ground floor in the center of the rotunda. Emboldened by others who stepped up and talked into the megaphone, I did it for the first time. I testified again and thankfully ran into a friend whose group I slept next to that night.

Saturday the 19th saw even bigger protests. An estimated 70,000 protested, including a Tea Party counter-protest. I cannot verify the statement because I spent the entire day inside the Capitol building, staying close to the center of the rotunda. I spoke on the megaphone again, this time to a massive crowd. I merely decided to thank the 14 Senate Democrats, starting a "Fab 14" chant. At some point I joined the drum circle and started pounding on a plastic bucket with a drumstick. I began to meet the others drumming or running the megaphone who would become my family. There was still no organization at all amongst the protestors... just a beautiful open microphone for anyone to speak and all to listen.

That night I joined some of my new drum circle friends to sleep in our little encampment on the 1st floor overlooking the rotunda floor. Eventually we would come to be called "the cuddle puddle", though the name came from a random passerby. I left valuables unattended several floors up the entire day as thousands poured through the building. Food orders were pouring in from across the country by this point. Some people had set up an information station, some people had set up a makeshift medic station, but there was no overall organization. The UW Teaching Assistant Association had access to a room where they were distributing food and had an army of laptops set up. Volunteers donned marshall vests to help the police maintain order. It was a beautiful, organic thing. Everyone pitched in to keep the building clean.

Sunday the 19th saw smaller rallies inside the rotunda where I continued drumming and built a stronger relationship with my new friends. We let a young child join us on our drum and ended up spending hours having a lot of fun. The child's mother eventually became such a good friend that she left her child with us for 30 minutes at a time, knowing that we would keep an eye on him. That night we drummed our hearts out and had a lot of fun. A group of ballroom dancers joined us to help entertain. I started to get a feeling that something special was happening. I had never been more well fed in my life.

Monday the 21st through Wednesday 23rd were a bit of a blur. At some point, Tom Morello of Rage Against the Machine spent a night with us in the capitol. I stood next to him as he spoke into the megaphone to a packed building, reading a statement from one of the leaders of the Egyptian revolution offering complete support to our movement. I couldn't even fathom how that could happen at the time. I had spent the past few weeks following the situation in Egypt very intensely and was inspired by the incredible, brave struggle of the Egyptian people. The United States had long supported the oppressive dictator whom they overthrew, and within days they were standing in solidarity with us. I am still in awe of that. I met Medea Benjamin of Code Pink, a wonderful person, just back from Egypt. She shared with us the lessons of Tahrir square, but there was still no formal organization so it merely planted ideas into our collective conscience.

Union workers from across the country had come to the Capitol in massive numbers, offering their support. I began to hear about similar political battles beginning to erupt across the country. The infamous prank call happened at some point. It became very clear that we were at the focal point of a decade long assault on unions in the United States. It became clear that Wisconsin was targeted due to its proud union history and history of pioneering new workers rights. I began to feel a true sense of purpose.

On Thursday the 24th, the Senate Republicans tried to pass a Voter ID bill to bait the Democrats into returning. In principle, the bill was not financial and did not require the 3/5ths quorum of financial legislation. I had followed this issue in the past and knew it was a naked, political attack on the poor designed to discourage voters who tend to vote Democrat. I left the rotunda and sat upstairs listening to the Republican Senators speak, feeling sick to my stomach. Fortunately, prior law in Indiana required that free identification cards must be provided for this bill to be legal, which required funding thus making the legislation financial. I read this online on my iPad and literally ran down to the rotunda to announce it on the megaphone. The crowd erupted into a massive cheer. Perhaps years of spending my free time reading about politics were beginning to pay off.

That night, the Assembly voted. My understanding was that the Capitol building could only stay open outside of its normal hours if the legislature was in session. The Assembly Democrats had kept the building open by running public hearings on the bill throughout each night. After that vote, we thought we would be asked to leave. I was preparing to be arrested. There had been numerous information sessions on civil disobedience so I understood that I would not face any significant charges. I was a bit excited. I believed in the cause and wanted to peacefully be arrested in defense of it. I was nervous and excited. I listened intently as the Assembly Democrats poured their hearts out in front of the cameras. The representative from Oshkosh, my hometown, described the wonderful physics teacher he learned from at his high school. It was the same teacher I learned from, who inspired me to take up the career path I have embarked on. That was a powerful moment and only strengthened my resolve. The bill was supposed to come up to a vote at around 4am. At 1am, the Republicans broke their own legislative rules and forced a vote. Only roughly a third of the Democrats even had a chance to vote.

The Republicans filed out of the chamber as the Democrats shouted "Shame! Shame!". The mood in the rotunda was incredibly tense. Many were angry, justifiably so. We knew this was an important moment to maintain peace. It was difficult but many of us quieted the crowd and kept it peaceful. Some of us gathered in the center of the rotunda on the ground floor for a group hug, preparing to be arrested. It was incredibly emotional.

Several Assembly Democrats came down and spoke. A friend of mine gave a powerful, moving speech. I even gave a speech, but I forget what I even said now. We embraced each other and prepared to be asked to leave. It never happened, and eventually we went back to sleep.

That night, the different groups running various aspects of the new "Capitol City" began to organize. I was asked to stay in the center of the rotunda by the microphone and ensure that we kept a peaceful, open microphone for all to have their voices heard. We knew the coming weekend was important. I don't remember Friday the 25th all that well sadly. I believe it was when 160 union workers from Los Angeles chartered a plane and showed up all at once, marching into the rotunda. That was quite a moment. I had already met so many wonderful union workers from across the country, but Los Angeles really surprised me being so far away. We were building momentum and I began to feel a confidence which has yet to leave me. The Polish Trade Union "Solidarity", who helped bring down the Communist government there, had come out in support of us. Our victory was their victory, they said. Another incomprehensible honor which I will forever feel unworthy of.

Saturday the 26th was another massive protest day. A large snowstorm passed through yet the crowds likely surpassed 100,000. They began to limit what food we could bring into the building. The first half of the day I was reminded what caffeine depravation felt like, which wasn't pleasant. It was very stressful to watch over the megaphone and try to get as many people's voices heard while still making administrative announcements. I knew the most important thing we could do was initiate recall elections for the 8 Republican senators who could be immediately recalled. I started to announce their names over the megaphone as frequently as I could without overriding the peoples voices. It was a delicate balance and very stressful. We began to hear that on Sunday they would ask us to leave at 4pm and the building would return to normal hours. The Capitol City Leadership Committee, an umbrella organization of the 6 different groups which had been performing various tasks in the building, had been meeting by this point. I was technically in their command but I didn't need to know much to do my part. The meetings are a paragon of the democratic process. Each meeting has an even number of representatives. All business is put to a democratic vote. In the event of a tie, there are 3 rounds of debate and then the motion is tabled. Eventually we will release videos of this process. The Wisconsin

Republicans could probably learn a thing or two from us.

Sunday the 27th was an intense, emotional day. I finally told my own story on the megaphone, to a massive crowd and many many cameras. A video of this will be released soon... but I was able to channel years of frustration with the Republican Party into a coherent, emotional message. It felt amazing. A group of musicians and actors spontaneously broke out into a song from Les Miserables in the rotunda at some point. One of my new friends, whose ancestors were Polish, brought a Polish flag with "Solidarity 1980" written on it. I stood next to him holding this flag as we sang a song written about the French revolution, in Madison Wisconsin. It was really just designed to be a fun event, obviously we weren't seeking to evoke the French revolution as our inspiration, but it was still powerful. Once again a brave woman with colon cancer whom I had become good friends with came to the megaphone and spoke. This bill, if it passes, will almost certainly result in her losing her chemotherapy as it gives the governor direct control over funding to our healthcare programs. I had been able to avoid tears up to this point, some how, but I broke down and cried. I doubt I will ever be more motivated by a single story than I have been by her brave struggle.

As 4pm approached it became a bit chaotic. Rumors were constantly being spread that the police had dogs and were targeting the leaders. The police had protected us for nearly two weeks at this point and had been nothing short of incredible, so I did not believe those rumors. We were expecting to be asked to leave, and those of us who would refuse would be arrested. We constantly were imploring the crowd to cooperate (that is to say, those who wished to be arrested would at least go peacefully and not force the police to drag them out) over the megaphone while also continuing to let everyone who wished to speak do so. Representative Brett Hulsey asked the crowd to peacefully follow him out of the building when asked. They announced over the speakers that we were being asked to leave, and for those who wished to refuse and be arrested to go up to the first floor. I made one last speech imploring people to cooperate and headed up to the first floor. It was starting to become apparent that maybe we wouldn't actually be arrested, so I jubilantly walked around the 1st floor with someone collecting signatures for recall petitions for the 8 Republican senators.

Those of us who stayed were not arrested. Later that night I eventually left, exhausted, as my sleeping supplies were no longer in the building. As

I write this the Capitol building has still been not reopened to the public since 4pm on Sunday the 27th. The longer they keep the building locked down, the more they lower their profile and raise ours. This was an unprecedented, beautiful, peaceful event. I believe that there are no rational, honest reasons for continuing to lock us out of the building. Some of my friends who I cherish as family are still inside and I do fear for them, but I can only hope that decency will prevail.

I believe that the progressive movement and the labor unions are the only political force left in this country capable of standing up for the brave, hard working Americans who have seen their voice drowned out by the influence of corporate campaign donations. These Americans are not partisan ideologues, many do not have the leisure of intensely following the political developments in this country, nor would they want to waste their time on such things. And this is bigger than just America. Although our stature has been lessened recently, the United States still sets an important example for the rest of the world. Whether we win or lose, it will echo across the country and the world.

The Democratic representatives of the state of Wisconsin have converted me from being a cynic into being an activist. It is the greatest honor of my life that I have been a part of this fight, and I will do everything that I possibly can do continue it. I should proof read and edit this statement, as I'm sure I've constantly reused the same language, but it came directly from my heart, and I will leave it as it is.

Wisconsin Progressive Blogroll

BLOGGING BLUE
www.bloggingblue.com

BLUE CHEDDAR
www.bluecheddar.net

COGNITIVE DISSIDENCE
www.cognidissidence.blogspot.com

DAN CODY: LEFT ON THE LAKE
www.dancody.org

DANE 101
www.dane101.com

FIRST DRAFT
www.first-draft.com

FORWARD LOOKOUT
www.forwardlookout.com

FOLKBUM
www.folkbum.blogspot.com

ILLUSORY TENANT
www.illusorytenant.blogspot.com

THE POLITICAL ENVIRONMENT
www.thepoliticalenvironment.blogspot.com

UPPITY WISCONSIN
www.uppitywis.org

THANK YOU

Christopher Hass, my designer, editor, and partner at every step of this process.

Mike Elk for being a shit-kicking labor journalist and for supporting this book from the beginning.

John Nichols for your encouragement, stories, and Wisconsin history lessons.

Kristian Knutsen and the other editors of Madison's *Isthmus* newspaper, whose online protest coverage helped me find the majority of the tweets in this collection.

Thank you to Alex Hanna, Jill Hopke, Magda Konieczna, Ben Stein, and the rest of the Teaching Assistants' Association.

Tom Bird, Matt Wisniewski, Bill Fetty, and the whole Autonomous Solidarity Organization.

Melissa Ryan, Andy Kroll, Paul Adler, Ben Manski, John Peck, Natalie Foster, Joel Handley, and the Justseeds artists.

Thanks and #solidarity to the London crew behind *Fight Back! A Reader on the Winter of Protest,* the book that helped inspire this one. Let's keep it going.

Thank you to all of the contributors to this collection, to the tweeters and bloggers and others who told this story, and most importantly, the people of Wisconsin who made it happen.

SOLIDARITY  FOREVER